W9-BFG-353

LOVE

and the

FACTS

of

LIFE

LOVE and

Designer: Si Frankel/Illustrations: Andre Ecuyer

the FACTS

of

LIFE

by Evelyn Millis Duvall

replacing her Facts of Life and Love for Teen-Agers

Association Press, New York

LOVE AND THE FACTS OF LIFE

Paperback Edition

Published, 1967
First and Second Printings, 1967
Third Printing, 1969
Fourth Printing, 1970
COPYRIGHT © 1963 BY

National Board of

Young Men's Christian Associations

Cloth Bound Edition
First Printing, 1963
Second Printing, 1965
Third Printing, 1966
Fourth Printing, 1968
Fifth Printing, 1969
Association Press

291 Broadway, New York, N. Y. 10007

All rights reserved, including the right
of reproduction in whole or in part in any
form, under the International, Pan-American,
and Universal Copyright Conventions.

SBN 8096-1630-0

Library of Congress catalog card number: 63-8880

Printed in the United States of America

Introduction

BECAUSE YOU ARE CONSIDERABLY more mature than young people your age were when *Facts of Life and Love for Teen-Agers* first came out, this new book has been especially prepared to meet your present-day concerns.

Your questions — more than 25,000 of them — are the basis for this book. Most of your questions now are about how to understand your feelings, and how to know where you are going in the midst of current confusions and contradictions. You ask—what is normal? What is healthy? What is right, in all sorts of situations that you find yourself in today? So this new book, LOVE AND THE FACTS OF LIFE, focuses on these questions. The answers have come from many sources—research and clinical evidence from medicine, sociology, psychology, human development, and social work, and any valid facts that would be possibly helpful. Where facts are clear and definite, they are presented in ways that may provide you with a personal sense of direction. In the many cases where the only good answer to a particular question is, "It depends"—upon the person, the situation, the goals and possibilities involved—then the discussion is in terms of alternatives.

Young people have always been interested in growing up. Teen-agers naturally wonder about changes in their bodies and emotions, about the differences between boys and girls, and what it is like to become a full-fledged man or woman. Adulthood is just ahead, and there are endless questions to be asked about it. Perhaps you already understand many things about growing up but would like to fill in some details. Maybe you know the "facts of life" pretty well but want to be sure you've got them all straight. Possibly you are one of those people who are just getting really interested in the subject and have not yet found out much about it.

You often ask for assistance in pronouncing the correct technical terms, so that you may substitute them for the vulgar vernacular in speaking about sex and other bodily processes. So in this book you will find phonetic spelling in parentheses immediately following the words or terms you may want to learn.

Many young people have the kind of parents with whom they can talk easily about intimate things as they come along. Such fortunate ones among you will read this book with easy enjoyment and reassurance, discussing new questions as they come up along the way. Other young people may have fathers and mothers who for some reason are not able to discuss the process of growing up in a helpful way. To them, as well as to their parents, LOVE AND THE FACTS OF LIFE may be welcome.

Maturing, dating, and being in love are not things that just naturally turn out well. They can be pretty complicated, even painful, at times. Learning to get along with the other sex can make you miserable and all mixed up inside at first. Learning how to handle the romantic situations that will be coming up between now and adulthood is a big job, and one that has to start with your understanding what to expect and knowing where you stand.

LOVE AND THE FACTS OF LIFE was written to help you do this job. You will not find pat answers to *all* your questions in any book like this. There is much about the way people feel and behave that is still not understood. Human behavior is only just beginning to be seriously studied. What is known that may be helpful to you is what this book offers you, to help you get off to a good start in life. What is not yet known may be a challenge for your generation to discover.

Much of the information you find here has been carefully checked by generous friends and associates who are experts in special areas of human development and behavior—to them I express sincere thanks. I am grateful too to the Museum of Science and Industry, in Chicago, for graciously permitting Vories Fisher of the museum staff to photograph its exhibit *The Miracle of Growth* especially for this book.

But the deepest gratitude that I have to express is for the privilege that has been mine of working so closely through the years with you young people in local, county, state, national, and international programs. This book was inspired by you and is dedicated to you, with the hope that in it you will find adequate answers to the questions that most concern you just now.

Evelyn Millis Duvall, Ph.D.

Contents

part ONE | YOUR LOVE FEELINGS

part FOUR | **YOUR LIFE AND LOVES**

List of plates

11

part ONE

YOUR

LOVE

FEELINGS

CHAPTER 1

How do you feel?

YOU OFTEN ARE ASKED, "How do you feel?" You probably reply without thinking or elaboration, "Fine, thank you." And that's that—or is it?

How DO you feel? Way down deep what are your feelings—about other people? about your family? your neighbors? your casual acquaintances? your closest friends? your boy friend or girl friend? yourself? Ask the question that way and it is not easy to answer at all. Partly because your feelings are so mixed up, uncertain. Partly because your feelings about yourself and others, about life itself, change from time to time. Chances are you are not sure yourself how you do feel—about anything.

Right now while you are in your teen years, your feelings about many things are changing more rapidly than they ever have before. This is because you are no longer a child,

but are rapidly becoming a person in your own right. These are the times when you are struggling to find your place in life, to get used to the new YOU that you are becoming, and to find out what you are going to do about yourself. These are the years when your relationships with the members of your family are under strain as you try to assert yourself as no longer a little youngster to be told what to do all the time by others.

These are the days and nights when you are exploring the new depths of friendships with members of the other sex, who now are so much more excitingly provocative than they used to be when you were younger.

These are the years when you dream night and day of what you are going to be and do when you grow up into full adulthood. You picture yourself in a variety of settings, doing wonderful things that will make your friends and family sit up and take notice of what a fine person you are. You want to succeed, and you are afraid to fail. You want terribly to grow up, but you hesitate to stride too fast, too far away from the security you have always known. So you are mixed up at times. Anyone in his right mind would be. There is nothing wrong with having all sorts of feelings about all sorts of things. That is part of what it means to grow up and come to terms with life and with yourself.

CHANGING
feelings about your parents

Sure, you love your parents. But if you are honest with yourself, you have to admit that sometimes you don't feel very loving toward them. Sometimes you get so mad that you can hardly hold in your anger. So you burst forth with some resentful remark that takes you by surprise quite as much as it does your mother or father. You find yourself doing and saying things that do not seem like you, for reasons that appear to be completely irrational.

Lois has tears in her eyes as she asks, "Why am I so mean to my own mother, who would do anything in the world for me? She's the best friend a girl ever had, and yet I treat her like dirt. What's the matter with me?" Lois is putting into words the baffling situation that many fellows and girls her age find themselves in through the early and middle teens. Lois does love her mother, but she can't take all her mother is doing for her that keeps her from being as grown up as she wants to be. Right now, Lois is urgently trying to become a young woman and no longer a little daughter with a doting mother who cares for her. She must grow up and become a woman on her own, no longer dependent upon her mother's loving care. So her emotions flare up, just when her mother has been most thoughtful, as a way of pushing off from too much "smothering." This is baffling to both Lois and her mother. It is painful, too. And yet it has to be done during the teen years if Lois is to grow up without her mother's cord of love too tightly tied.

Watch yourself closely around home and you'll notice that usually when you have been particularly disagreeable, you bend over backwards in being sweet and thoughtful again.

This makes sense, too. You make an unpleasant scene in declaring your independence. Then you get to thinking over what you have done, and realize how mean you have been. So the next thing you know you are doing something to prove how fond you really are of that family of yours.

Take David as an illustration. He had an awful row with his parents one morning at breakfast time. He got so mad he slammed out the back door with an angry, "You just don't understand," as his parting rejoinder. He seethed inside all the way to school. By the time his first-period class was over he was starved, not just because he hadn't finished his breakfast, but mostly because the thought of food was comforting just then. So he gobbled down two candy bars, and then he did feel awful. His digestive tract had stopped functioning when he got mad, and those candy bars lay in his stomach like a leaden lump. He got through the rest of the day somehow, and by afternoon he felt thoroughly ashamed of the way he had behaved. He remembered that his father had been after him to wash and wax the car. He stopped on his way home from school to pick up some automobile wax and hurried home to get the job done before his father returned from work. By evening the car looked fine, and Dave came into the house feeling better about his folks, himself, and the whole situation.

In time, you begin to come to terms with your family, so you don't have to fight them so much. You establish your independence and take responsibility for yourself in ways that earn the respect of your parents. By the late teens, young people get along fairly well with their parents. Studies show that the middle teens are the hardest for both teenagers and their parents to weather with each other. Some do better than others, partly because they are willing to learn from their experience and to understand their own changing feelings about themselves and the others in the family.

There are times when your feelings about one situation spill over into another. Have a bad time with your folks, and you are apt to take out your miserable mood on anyone else who happens to cross your path. If you feel unloved and unappreciated at home, you are quite likely to overrespond to any loving you can get from others outside. This is one reason why your feelings for your special friends can be both so intense and so unstable.

MIXED-UP
feelings about others

It is during the teen years that you discover members of the other sex in new and exciting ways. You possibly have had little sweethearts before. You quite probably had a special girl friend way back in first grade. Or as a girl you may have been kissed by a boy before you were five. But not like this. Now you daydream of being kissed long before your lips ever touch. When you close your eyes as you are kissing now, what strange wonderful feelings are sometimes yours!

Kiss a girl and what does she feel? It is likely that her first reaction is something like, "He's kissing me; he must love me, for his very own!" It takes no time at all for a girl's feelings to shift into second gear and to explore all the wonderful possibilities of what others will say when they learn that she has found a boy who loves her most of all. It is a simple thing now for her to slip into high and see herself in white gown and veil as a bride. She goes into overdrive and pictures herself as a happy wife and mother, with children at her knee and an adoring husband beaming at her in their split-level home in the nicest surroundings. She comes to with a start along about now and opens her eyes to see HIM with something like surprise in her heart. She pushes him off and is more baffled by her own feelings than by his in their encounter.

The boy—what does he feel when he kisses a girl? The chances are that he responds first to the response itself. "She lets me kiss her. She likes me for myself," is quite possibly his first reaction. The contact may be made with a sense of awe and tenderness. But the boy quickly senses a confusion of feelings as his lips meet hers. His mood changes rapidly to one that he hardly recognizes himself. A new sense of urgency wells up within him. He cannot get close enough. He feels smothered by her fragrance. His blood pounds in his veins and he feels all man now. He wants to crush her to him with a roughness that frightens him. He drops back impressed with his power, yet confused about what it is that he feels for this particular girl.

It is too easy to explain these new feelings that each

sex is beginning to have for the other as just physical "sex." There is a mystery in the attraction between man and woman that involves deep psychological and spiritual feelings as well. With time and maturation, both a girl and a boy can learn to recognize and deal with the many feelings of which they both are capable.

LEARNING
to appraise your feelings

Right now you are building your emotional repertoire. You started out as tiny baby who felt either comfortable or uncomfortable. Then you let the world know how you felt by cooing and gurgling happily or by howling until you were made comfortable once more. As you grew up, you added new ways of feeling as you responded heartily to your father, more gently to your mother, competitively to your brothers and sisters, like a pal with your closest buddy, and in quite different ways with every other person you have ever known intimately.

Through your teen years your ability to respond to others with a wide variety of feelings increases at a rapid rate. By the time you become fully adult, you will have learned to recognize many emotions of which you are capable, tell one from another, and keep them under control responsibly. This is not always easy, as young Sam found.

Sam had a problem. He had to ask a girl to the sophomore party Friday night. But he couldn't decide which of three girls he should take. He knew that if he took one, the other two would feel hurt. The trouble was not that he was indifferent about these girls. Just the opposite, he knew he loved them all.

But he loved them each in such a different way that it was hard to decide which he really loved the most. Ann he loved as a pal, and indeed she was the nicest companion a fellow ever had. He could talk over anything with Ann, and often did. They would go off on their bikes on Saturday afternoon, and he'd squeeze her cold little hand with warm appreciation for all they had shared of their dreams and hopes and plans for the future. But he had never kissed Ann. He had never even felt like it. It just was not that kind of love feeling he had for her.

How differently he felt about Rosie! He couldn't talk over anything with Rosie. But somehow he didn't feel like talking when he was with her. She brought out all the man in him. When she was close he could hardly keep his hands off her. Feelings rushed through him that no other girl had ever aroused. He wondered whether this was what real love was, and if so, why was he so tongue-tied with her?

The third girl was Mary. She went to his church, and they always sat together at young people's meetings on Sunday nights. With her at her end of the hymn book and him at his, a feeling went through Sam that made him want to achieve important things, to become a great man, to be worthy of Mary and their feelings for each other. She inspired him as no other girl ever had. He felt uplifted, just being near her.

With which of these girls was young Sam really in love? Fortunately he did not have to decide before Friday! His uncle took him off for a fishing trip and gave him time to appraise how he felt about all three girls. Eventually when he got married, it was not to Ann, nor to Rosie, nor to Mary, but to Jacqueline, who was something of all the other three and a great deal more besides. For what young Sam was going through was the ABC's of loving a woman —as a companion, as a sex partner, and as an inspiration. Surely a man needs all three in a wife, as well as the rest of the emotional alphabet that young Sam had yet to discover in himself.

Young men and women spend the second decade of life growing away from childhood and into adulthood. It is during these important years that they must learn to appraise their feelings and to develop the rich emotional repertoire upon which they can build the rest of their lives.

DEVELOPING
an emotional repertoire

You never feel exactly the same way about any two people. Every individual whom you get to know brings out another facet of your response. With one person you are gay and silly. Another makes you feel the very depths of your being. One friend gives you self-confidence and assurance. With another you become humble and apologetic. Each relationship you share with someone else is unique unto itself. Every friend you have or ever will have highlights a part of your potential that you can either discard as unworthy or develop as an aspect of the you that you want to become.

As you become acquainted with more and more persons of both sexes, in many different types of situations, you learn to respond in a wide variety of ways that become your emotional repertoire. You develop your personality in interaction with others throughout your lifetime, but especially now when you are settling upon the kind of person you are in the process of becoming.

This is one reason why your social participation in a wide variety of settings is so important right now. It is the basis for the policy of interaction with many, rather than settling too soon upon one other person or one small group of pals as your only associates. You build your emotional responses not only through deeply meaningful associations but also within many more contacts with different individuals.

Pity Mary Lou, who "fell in love" at fifteen, married at sixteen, and by eighteen described herself as "an old married woman before my time. Here I am with two babies, a tired husband, and nothing to live for but more work than I can manage. I've been nowhere, seen nothing, and am nothing but a drudge. Other girls my age have dates and good times, get to graduate from high school, go on to college, and make something of themselves. But not me. I had to marry the first man who came along—even before I knew what I was doing or even who I was."

The tragedy of Mary Lou is not only that she has to work so hard and is getting so little fun out of life. Quite as pathetic is the fact that she did not give herself a chance to grow up, to develop the many sides of her own personality that were latent within her, and to get a sense of who she was as a person before getting married.

UNCERTAINTIES
about yourself

Like Mary Lou, you too might try to escape the problems of growing up by lunging into a premature marriage, or some other involvement that appears to "settle things" for you. This is understandable. It is hard to remain free and flexible when you so want to have something definite to tie to. It is sometimes difficult to keep yourself growing and learning long enough to develop your talents and potentials when others appear to "have it made" so much sooner. It is because you feel unsure of yourself that you are tempted to tie to something or someone who promises you security and certainty.

It is normal to feel unsure about yourself while you are a teen-ager. These are the years when your life is open to so many possibilities that you are bound to be uncertain of just who you are and what you are to become. Indeed, discovering yourself is the main task you must accomplish in order to emerge a full-fledged adult.

It takes time to develop a mature human personality. Time to discover who you are and what you are to do with your life. Time to find out what life is and where you best fit into it. Time to get the education that will help you establish a place for yourself in today's world. Time to feel the sensitive awareness that makes living worthwhile. Time to develop appreciation for the beauty and the grandeur of the universe and all it contains. Time to cultivate within yourself a basic respect for others and a reverence for their potentials as human beings. Time to become a loving and lovable person wherever you are—that is, to overcome self-centeredness and become normally outgoing. Time in which to develop all the feelings and values and ambitions and attitudes that make you uniquely and meaningfully YOU in whatever you do.

In the meantime, you can feel mighty uncertain through your teen years. You are not yet sure what life is all about, or where you will find your place in it. You probably are not sure what kind of work or how much education you can manage. You are uncertain about what and whom you like and how long the feelings you now have will last. You are unsure of yourself and probably are anxious about how you look to others, or even of how you appear to yourself. Such uncertainties are part of the price you pay for the flexibility that is yours right now in the second decade of life. For now life stretches ahead of you in innumerable pathways, any one of which could possibly be yours.

Erik Erikson sees the teen years as those in which each person struggles toward a clear sense of identity. Out of the confusions that each of us has as we leave childhood, gradually emerges a sense of self that is needed for a satisfying life. This process cannot be forced, but rather must be experienced in full as a solid basis for the many years that lie ahead.

So if you are uncertain about yourself, relax and know that to be otherwise as a teen-ager is an even greater threat. As you keep yourself open to life, to love, to grow and to become, you build inner security based upon the full maturation of the human spirit. You risk far more in hasty, premature efforts to get things settled for yourself too soon than you do in developing over a period of time the talents and feelings that potentially are yours.

Right now it may help you to get straight some of the facets of your own growth: what it means to love and be loved; what is involved in growing into adulthood; what others expect of you as a friend, a date, a sweetheart, and as a family member. As you understand such things more clearly, you may find answers to some of your present questions, and you can clear the way for your ongoing search for the YOU you want to become.

Why do love

feelings differ so?

BY THE TIME YOU ARE OLD enough to read a book like this, you have already learned that there are many kinds of love feelings. You may have wondered why your emotions differ so greatly from time to time and from person to person. You may think that it is not quite normal to have feelings of attraction that appear to be so fickle. Now you can be assured that there are many ways of loving. The important thing is to recognize each for what it is. You cannot deny real feelings, but rather must learn to accept your own honest emotions and keep their expressions within bounds.

THE
language of love

Love is a language that expresses everything from poetry to profanity. It speaks in a whisper, in a sob, in a shout. We babble it as infants, and we speak it well only after years of learning to use it fluently. Love speaks with many accents so different as to be foreign one to another. Here are a few of the variations on the theme of love:

Jealous love is a possessive love, clinging to its own. The jealous lover is a child hugging his toy so closely that no one else can see it. Jealousy is almost always a mark of immaturity and insecurity. As we grow confident of love and of our loved ones, we are not jealous. We have faith in our ability to hold the love of other lovable persons as we mature, and so we need not cling in desperation to them.

When we are very young, we may look at jealousy as a badge of love. The girl says in delighted surprise, "Why, you're jealous! You must care for me after all." She may even provoke that jealousy in order to reassure herself that he cares. But as she grows more sure of her lover and of her capacity to hold his affection, she no longer enjoys his jealousy. Now she wants him to have faith in her as she has in him. They both promote each other's happiness. They are tied together not by possessive bonds but rather by their loving confidence in each other.

Jealousy is common during the teen years. When you are not quite secure within yourself, or sure of your ability to hold the other's devotion, the tendency is to demand the loyalty you fear you have not won.

Those who are more mature realize that a person never fully "belongs" to any other individual, and that imprisoned spirits either wither and die or rebel and revolt. Only when you trust each other, and encourage one another to have a full life, does love have a chance to thrive. But these things are learned through the years. Until they become part of you, you will be hurt from time to time by the demandingness of jealousy.

Passionate love is vigorous, rough, insistent, and urgent. It enters into the sexually focused relations of boys and girls and of men and women. It is driven by nature's desire to be fulfilled biologically, and operates often without rhyme or reason as far as the two personalities are concerned. Just being male and female is all that nature requires. Passion alone can be painful. It usually has an element of hurting in it. Lovers may want to bite and crush each other when speaking in these accents of love. By itself this kind of love is tempestuous and exhausting. Blended with other love forms it can be exhilarating and fulfilling.

Hostile love is love that raises its voice in anger against the beloved. Love and hate are closely related in our emotions. When we love someone, there may from time to time be real feelings of hostility against him, too. This tendency to hate those whom we love is called *ambivalence*. It can be rather simply explained by recognizing that although some characteristics of a person are lovable, others may be actually irritating. If we love somebody too ambitiously or possessively to accept his or her limitations, we become annoyed when he or she does anything that frustrates or displeases us, and our love takes on a hostile quality.

In capital letters on the screen of a girls' dormitory are written in lipstick the words, I HATE LOVE. We do not know who wrote them there. We have no knowledge of the circumstances that led the writer to block out such a sentiment. But all of us recognize the feelings. There are times when loving is so confused and bewildering that we are willing to wash our hands of it all. Then it is that we are hostile not only toward the persons whom we have been loving but, indeed, toward love itself.

Anguished love is the aching love of frustration. Our love is not returned, and we lash about in the agony of unfulfilled, unrequited love. This is the love that seems to have no future, that leads only to despair. Our first reaction is usually one of hopeless pain, sorrow, and a loss of interest in life. As we begin to work through the feeling, we mobilize ourselves with a burst of energy that may vent itself against the source of our trouble. This is the emotion that has given rise to the statement, "Hell hath no fury like that of a woman scorned." Or we may come out of the feeling with energy focused on attaining success in some other way. Some students who throw themselves into academic life with a wholehearted zeal are motivated partly by their desire to escape the pain of unfulfilled love feelings. Anguished love can go on indefinitely. Then we say, "He still carries a torch for her." More often it gives way to more satisfying love forms.

Tender love is happily satisfying. It is not only beautiful in itself, but it increases the loveliness of the lover. When we love another tenderly we feel warm and outgoing, we have the other's interest foremost, our faces glow with affection, and we look as well as feel lovely. This is the radiance that a mother's face takes on when she loves her baby. It is the miracle that transforms a plain face into one of beauty when it belongs to the beloved. Tender love is protecting, kind, solicitous, and sympathetic. It plays a part in many of our love relationships. As we grow more mature it becomes an increasingly familiar and satisfying accent in love.

Loyal, friendly love feelings are sturdy faithful embers

that glow through many years. They are neither the flaming fires that consume nor the hostile urges that hurt. They often have elements of the tender love feelings in them but are of a somewhat more relaxed, comfortable quality. We are held to our friends with feelings of mutual response and understanding. They understand us, and we understand them. Our friends know us and love us for what we are. Little we do really shocks a true friend, for in his loyal friendship he understands. We share many things with each other in the realm of friendship. Life has new meaning as it is shared between friends. Friends take on special importance when life's meanings are plumbed together.

Friendships come early in life as preparation for the vigor of mate love, and they remain long afterward to warm the later years. Loyal friendship can thus be seen to be the most permanent and durable of all the love feelings. It is possible in childhood, and it becomes increasingly fluent as life continues through the years. Blessed indeed is the person with real friends, for he will love and be loved through the years.

Brotherly love is a mature love that only a few achieve. It comes with a sense of true relatedness to all mankind. It sweeps over a person with a recurrent and overwhelming realization of being at one with others. It is the essence of "belonging." It is what the Bible means when it says, "Love your neighbor as yourself." It is a humble love, aware of one's debt to others. It is an outgoing love, seeking to pour back into the pool of humanity the fullness of life that one has so richly received. It is the love of thanksgiving and of gratitude that seeks to repay a part of the debt each person owes to all men.

Love of life is a song always ready to bubble forth in praise of living. It is heard in the baby's merry gurgling, in children's happy play, in youth's moments of exuberance, and in the slow, sweet smile that lights the older face.

Walt Whitman has been an able spokesman for the love of life. In his incomparable way, he sees life as the very signature of God when he says in "Song of Myself":

I see something of God each hour of the twenty-four, and
each moment then,
In the faces of men and women I see God, and in my own
face in the glass,

I find letters from God dropt in the street, and every one is
    signed by God's name,
And I leave them where they are, for I know that wheresoe'er
    I go,
Others will punctually come for ever and ever.[1]

STEP
by step in love development

There is a process of love development that reaches from
the cradle to the grave. You started to love soon after you
were born. You have made your way through several stages
of love development as you have learned more and more
about loving and being loved through the years thus far.
Now you find that you feel attracted to all sorts of persons
in many kinds of situations. Your emotional development
is unique for you, and proceeds at the pace that is right for
you. Your capacity for love may be ahead of, behind, or
similar to that of others of about your age. But each person
takes one step after another in about the same order as
that outlined below.

SELF-LOVE

The first person you loved was yourself. Little babies are
capable of loving no one else at first. They have not had
enough experience even to be aware that there are other
persons to love. So you started on the first rung of the ladder of love with yourself.

You loved yourself in a very simple sense at first. You
loved your fingers and sucked them with pleasure. You
loved to handle your toes, and quite possibly you liked
them so much that you put them in your mouth too. You
enjoyed your body in a vigorous, lusty way as you kicked
and jabbered and laughed with yourself as a baby.

You loved yourself so much then that you insisted that
you come first. You were hungry and you yelled for food. If
it was not forthcoming at once, you became angry and red
in the face. It did not occur to you that there might be a
reason that your dinner was delayed. You were all that
mattered, because you were all you knew or cared about.
You were pleased when your demands were met. You were

[1]Reprinted by permission of Doubleday and Company, Inc., from *Leaves
of Grass.* Copyright, 1940.

mad when your needs had to wait. It was as simple as that.

It is quite possible that from time to time you still feel and act as you did at that first stage. You spend time just admiring yourself in front of a mirror—that crew haircut, that dimple! You get so self-centered that you are all that matters. You want something and you demand it impatiently and insistently, just as you did when you were an infant. When people give you what you want, you are pleased; when you do not get what you want, you make a scene. Recognize yourself at the self-love stage? All of us slip back there at times.

This stage is so apt to recur all through life that we have a word for it: *narcissism,* love of self. The word comes from the old Greek story of Narcissus who fell in love with his own image in a quiet pool of water. He so adored his reflection that he pined away and died, whereupon the flower that bears his name sprang up to mark his resting place. Today when a person loves and admires himself, we call him narcissistic.

At certain times this self-love interest is normally to be expected. When a little child first begins to be aware of himself as a separate individual, some self-love is natural. Again, at adolescence when the changes occurring in the developing body center attention for a time upon one's own maturation, a certain amount of preoccupation with one's self is usual. It is only when this love of self continues over a long period of time, and is so preoccupying that others do not enter in, that it may be a cause for alarm. In the meantime, a wholesome amount of interest in grooming and self-development is a part of growing up.

LOVE for Mother

There came a time when, as a baby, you began to associate your mother with your feelings of satisfaction. You were hungry and cried. She came bearing food and comfort for you. You learned to respond to her with affection. You smiled when she approached. You gurgled when she spoke to you. As she nursed you, you fondled her and held tight to her finger. Your love feelings grew out beyond yourself to include your mother as well.

True, your love was still demanding. If mother did not

come at once, you scolded her. Sometimes when she did come, you were still so mad at her for not jumping when you first called that you turned from her and would have nothing to do with her. Then you forgave her and took your dinner with a you-might-have-come-sooner look on your face. At this stage of affairs you repaid your mother for her services with your affection. When she came, you smiled. When she did not come at once, you scolded and acted as though you did not love her any more. People beyond their baby years still act that way at times. Ever see one? Ever act that way yourself, sometimes, still?

Your love for your mother was so strong that it may have tended to make you dependent on her in later years. Some mothers keep on loving their children *as if they were still babies*. Being tied to mother's apron-strings, being "mama's little girl" or a "mama's boy," is not uncommon. You may still be finding it hard to break away from this first childish love for your mother.

LOVE for Father

Quite probably your father was an important part of your early life. Frequently, a modern father helps to bathe and feed and care for his baby. He comes in from outside, usually bringing a hearty welcome and a sturdy hand that both mother and baby early learn to anticipate with eagerness. You soon learned to go to his arms for comfort, to run to him with toys to be fixed, to enjoy rough play with him, and to go with him on important jaunts outside the house. You loved his deep voice, his heavy step, his broad shoulders, and rough, mannish clothes—partly because they were different from your mother's. In fact, the first strain on your love for her may have come when you learned to take your father into account too.

Very early in your infancy you probably became aware that someone else loved your mother beside yourself. One widely accepted theory of love development says that you were then face to face with the eternal triangle in family life. You loved your mother. Your father loved her too. And so you were jealous of him. That green-eyed monster, jealousy, first came into your life when you realized your father's rivalry for your mother's attention.

Girls outgrow this jealousy by pretending to be their mothers and acting out being married to their fathers. When girls imitate their mothers this way, we say they *identify* with their mothers. When they imitate them so closely, they *are* mother in their minds. One little girl was delighted when her mother had to leave home for a few days. She said quite openly, "Goody, now I can take care of Daddy and he will love just me." All little girls put themselves in their mother's shoes when they are small. They play house, cuddle their dolls, cook make-believe meals, and welcome their daddies home very much as they have seen their mothers do. When you ask a little girl what she is going to be when she grows up, she quite likely will tell you, "I'm going to be a lady like Mommy and marry Daddy and have babies." When these little girls grow up, they may fall in love with somebody very much like their fathers.

Boys love their fathers in a different way. Even a little boy is aware of the fact that he is a boy and will become a man. He loves his mother. Then he senses that his father loves her too, and so he is jealous and feels like doing away with his rival. This is a widely recognized phenomenon called the *Oedipus complex,* after Oedipus, king of Thebes, who unwittingly slew his father and married his mother. The early hostility the boy feels for his father is normally outgrown as soon as he begins to try to be just like his father.

You probably have seen some little boy pretending to be like his father. He puts on his father's hat and rubbers. He carries his father's briefcase or lunch pail just as he has seen his father do. He "reads" the paper in the same chair with the same posture that he has seen his father use. Asked what he is going to be when he grows up, he more than likely replies, "I'm going to be just like my daddy." Here again is *identification*—the boy with the father, as we saw the girl with her mother. This love for his father is still operating years later when a boy can see no other vocation but "following in father's footsteps." He may even look for the same kind of girl that his father married: "I Want a Girl Just Like the Girl That Married Dear Old Dad." No question about it, your father has been quite an influence in your love life.

Of course you love your brother(s) and sister(s). At least sometimes you do. You learned this back in your childhood as another rung in the ladder of love development. Children in the same family often have lots of fun together, depend on each other, and stand up for one another when it is necessary. The very beginnings of feelings of brotherhood go back to the early childhood enjoyment of being members of a family together; but there are times in the best of families when the children do not enjoy each other at all. A brother or a sister can be a pest, and often is. *Siblings* (the word for brothers and sisters) are not only nuisances to each other but also rivals in the keenest sense. They are rivals for the attention and affection of their parents, for the equipment of the home, and in the never-ending struggle of competition in achievement.

Sibling rivalry is so common that it is expected as a normal part of growing up. Most of us outgrow a great deal of it by the time we mature. Remnants of it come back now and then in annoyance and irritation and sometimes open hostility. The farther up the ladder we go, the less these childish jealousies come back to haunt us. The more we grow up in our love life, the more we are able to genuinely enjoy and appreciate the others who shared our early family with us. But while we are in the process of maturing emotionally, there may be quarrels with brothers and sisters that had their beginnings back in our first feelings of rivalry and jealousy about each other.

LOVE of other relatives

A grandfather we know reports that his two-year-old grandson is his constant companion. He says, "He eats with me, he is with me in the yard and will leave anyone, even his mother, to come to or with me." Such an attachment of a little child for a particularly lovable grandparent or other relative fortunately is not too rare. It is a very precious and important part of the love life of many of us.

Children have a great deal to gain from association with grandparents, aunts, and uncles. Older relatives often bring a special sense of security, of quiet understanding and perspective that young parents have not so fully achieved. You may have found joy in hearing stories and songs as, only fond relatives can share them. You may have loved to hear them tell about "the old days" when your parents were children. You may have enjoyed just being close to some fine older person who seemed to belong to you in a very special way.

Cousins sometimes develop a special kind of attachment for each other, not only because they are together but also because they feel related.

FIRST loves outside the family

The day came when you had grown big enough to go exploring outside your home. You went out and played with other children of your own age. Soon you had favorites among them. Sometimes these first loves outside the family are of the same sex; sometimes they are of different sexes. If your first special friend was of the other sex, you may have been teased by your parents, but it did not matter; you adored each other. You sat with your arms around each other. Perhaps you kissed each other fondly. You quite probably insisted that the other get some of the special treats that came your way.

Childhood sweethearts are important in our love development. They help to wean us from the close attachments within the family that can become very binding. When we are young they give us the faith that people outside our own families are lovable and to be trusted. Later in life we can turn to outsiders with full confidence that it is safe to love them.

SAME sex, same age

Sometime when you were about halfway through elementary school, you quite possibly had a very close buddy or pal of your own sex to whom you were devoted. There was little that you would not do for each other. You were inseparable. You had an intense loyalty for each other, which flared up in active defense whenever there was threat of attack. You did everything together. You may have worn the same kind of clothes and sent for the same gadgets advertised on cereal boxes and over the radio. No treat was finer than having a meal together or being able to spend the night in the other's home. You shared your most precious confidences, told the darkest secrets, and planned your days in minutest detail with each other.

These early friendships between persons of the same sex give a special sense of security at a time when one is hungry for companionship, yet not quite ready to take on friends of the opposite sex. They often carry over to the more mature friendships of later years and are, indeed, a precious heritage.

Hidden fears of the other sex may halt one's love development at this point. An attachment to members of one's own sex in preference to persons of the opposite sex is called *homosexual* (same sex). This is normal during certain periods of childhood, and even for a while in early adolescence. Later it may become a cause for concern, for it may indicate that one has stopped in his love development. Normally persons of the other sex soon claim one's attention and interest. A boy or girl who does not seem to arouse the interest of the opposite sex, or to be interested in the opposite sex, has no reason to fear that he or she is a homosexual by nature. Time and growth are on his side.

SAME sex, older age

During your later childhood or early teens you quite possibly adored some older person of your own sex. Boys (and some girls too) worship cowboys, G-men, heroes of sport, and public figures of various kinds. Many girls copy the hair-do's and clothes styles of favorite movie actresses. Both sexes have epidemics of hero worship that are normal at this stage of development, as we shall see in detail in the chapter "Love—Embarrassment or Blessing?"

This is the stage when you may have dreamed about growing up and doing just what your hero or heroine of the moment was doing. You may have dreamed of becoming a movie queen, or a schoolteacher, or a nurse, or perhaps an airline hostess like your adored Aunt Betty. Similarly, a boy may develop a set toward one career or another just because the man he worshiped as a young lad was in that work.

Ned had an emergency operation when he was eleven that set him then and there to dreaming of being a surgeon. The doctor who was so kind to Ned during his operation and convalescence never knew how much Ned thought of him or how greatly he had influenced Ned's life. Years later when Ned became a doctor, he acknowledged that it was this meaningful contact years before that had set his feet into the path of medicine, as a profession.

These attachments help to wean us from our too close dependence on our parents and to love and emulate others outside the family circle. Such feelings are often intense. They may last so long that they become a cause of concern to the folks who care about us. But most of us grow normally enough into the next levels of development.

OTHER sex, older age

Did you ever have a crush on an older person? Do you remember how it feels to be so fond of some older man or woman that you can hardly stand it? It is quite possible that you do, for this, too, is a common stage in the process of development. It may not have lasted very long. But while it did, it gave you quite a time.

Girls at this age are often attracted to men old enough to be their fathers. They say that the boys of their own age are "childish" and "dumb," while older men seem to be men of the world, experienced, romantic. It is interesting to note that the romantic stars in the movies are often men in their fifties and sixties. Surprisingly enough, middle-aged women movie stars hold their box-office ratings quite as well. This would seem to suggest that many younger people, who are the regular movie-goers, find these older figures exceedingly attractive.

Girls who do not outgrow this stage in their love development become particularly susceptible to the love of men twice their age. They may be girls who were somewhat father-hungry in their early childhood, and so find special satisfaction in the attention they receive from older men later on. "May and September" marriages are sometimes made up of such combinations. Even more frequently, girls get themselves entangled in affairs with older men that lead nowhere. Normally, this phase is soon over.

This level of love development is, of course, the most interesting of all. It starts with general interest in the other sex and continues through dating, going steady, becoming engaged, and getting married. Love between members of opposite sexes of about the same age normally begins sometime in the teens and continues through all the rest of life. It forms the basis of mature love relationships between men and women. It provides the setting for home and family life. Upon the success of this stage of love development depends a great deal of the future of the individual.

All the other stages in the development of love feelings lead up to this one. Into your love for members of the other sex go many of the feelings and habits of loving that you have already experienced in your earlier love development. Even the kind of girl friend or boy friend that most appeals to you is influenced by your previous loves. When a boy is having difficulty breaking away from the intimate attachments he has with his mother, he may quite likely fall in love with some girl who closely resembles her. On the other hand, a girl who has not completely gotten over an early hostility to her father may pick out boy friends who are as different from her father as possible.

During the teen years young people of both sexes nowadays have a great deal of contact with each other. They attend coeducational schools. They participate in mixed recreational activities and enjoy many types of sports together. They meet and enjoy each other in the young people's activities sponsored by churches and many other community agencies. Sooner or later these casual contacts begin to focus on dating. Having a date with a person of the other sex just for the fun of it provides a very special opportunity for getting acquainted. It offers the chance to share many common interests and to participate in a wide variety of activities. Knowing how to take full advantage of the potentialities of dating adds greatly to the success of this phase of one's development.

This love of the other sex usually begins with a generalized admiration for almost any and all members of the opposite sex. For several years there may be a general excitement about many members of the other sex, punctuated by a series of rather intense infatuations. There may be a tendency to focus more specifically on just one person. This leads to "going steady," then to getting "pinned," with its "understanding" of "being engaged to be engaged." The next step is the engagement, and then, of course, marriage. This process, taking place over a number of years, leads into being settled as a full-fledged member of the young married set.

LOVE for children

With marriage and the feeling of being in a permanent love relationship comes a nurturing, protecting kind of love such as parents normally feel for their children. When the couple are fortunate in starting a family of their own right away, this love for children finds a ready outlet in caring for their baby. When for some reason the coming of the first child is delayed, this maturing parental type of love is often funneled into a love for pets, or a protective kind of devotion to each other. The tendency for young couples to "baby each other," as well as to take a great deal of delight in a beloved household pet, is illustrative of this stage of love development.

Young, happily married people sometimes take an active part in community programs, channeling their parentlike love feelings into interest in children generally. From this type of outlet, the next level of growth comes almost inevitably.

MATURE love for others

The adult who has successfully come up the ladder of love development eventually reaches a kind of love that affects not only his own dear ones with whom he is in closest contact but in addition many people whom he has never met. He is concerned with his responsibility to mankind. He does things to promote human welfare. He feels warmly toward the men and women and children whom he meets. He has faith in the power of love that can operate through the life of a really mature person in many ways. While inevitably leading one into hard work and some difficult trials, this kind of love builds character. Its strength comes from an inner peace that enables one to weather life's storms. It can be attained not in a single step but only through the mastery of the other steps of love development that lead to it.

PAST
loves that remain

Growth in love development does not come inevitably. Some people get stuck, or become *fixated,* on some one rung of the ladder and stay there. There are those who never quite outgrow their love of themselves. Others remain tied emotionally to their mothers. Some get so attached to members of their own sex that they are said to have homosexual tendencies. Love for members of the other sex can become fixated on a permanent playing-of-the-field basis in which the person is never completely happily married. Mothers sometimes become so devoted to their children that they find it hard to let them grow up, and are themselves unable to take the next step into wider love relationships.

Even the person who continues to grow up emotionally may find that from time to time he slips back to an earlier stage of love feelings. When we are tired or frightened, or feel unloved or unwanted, we all long to go back to a place in our growing up where we felt loved and wanted. This is quite understandable. In fact, all our lives most of us move up and down that ladder of love development, being quite mature at one time and rather immature at another. Growing up in our ability to love is a lifelong process. We may never attain complete maturity. We can continue in our efforts to learn to love more widely, however, and find the process deeply rewarding.

DEPENDENCE—
independence—interdependence

As we grow in our ability to relate ourselves lovingly to others, we shift the nature of our relationship to them. We all start by being completely dependent upon those we love. As helpless infants we have no other choice. Through childhood we gradually learn to take more and more responsibility for ourselves. By the time we reach our teens, most of us are ready for an independent existence. As young people, we do not like to be dependent upon our families.

Gaining independence from parents whom we have loved and whose love we have received for so long is not usually easy. It may be so difficult that young people feel they must cut the apron-strings in a mighty lunge of rebellion. Something like a declaration of independence is necessary, especially when parents themselves are finding it hard to let their children grow up.

Once a person has achieved a degree of independence in his relationships to those he loves, he is ready for the next stage—that of *interdependence*. This comes when he realizes that he cannot live his own life all on his own, for what he does is all tied in with the lives of many other people. He finds that other persons are important to him and that he matters to them.

Thus, as we grow, we mature to the stage where we join forces with the persons who matter most to us in a continuing we-feeling. Now we realize that all we are is dependent upon others, and that we can be helpful to them too. We come to feel deeply that our lives are intertwined with those of other people, that we are indeed One World. This growth into interdependence is a long process that can be interrupted at any point, and it goes on only with the personal dedication of the individual with the will to grow.

LOVE
can hurt

Breaking your heart is a phrase that has nothing to do with a cardiac condition. It refers to being hurt by someone you love. Falling in love may seem awfully simple, but getting over a broken love affair can be simply awful. Loving and being loved frequently hurts. As soon as you become involved with another person, you open yourself up to the pain that love can bring.

DID someone steal your sweetheart?

When you feel that someone has stolen your sweetheart, you are filled with mixed emotions. A sense of loss in no longer being sure of the one on whom you have been relying; anger at the one who has taken your place in your loved one's affection—these and other feelings torment you.

Yet, wait a moment. If your sweetheart has been "stolen" it is not like having someone steal your watch. This is an inanimate thing with no will of its own. But a lover is a person, with feelings and wishes and inclinations that make him or her a party to the alienation of affection. The completely satisfied sweetheart is rarely "stolen," for he or she is perfectly happy with things as they are. So, when the one you have been considering your own wanders off with someone else, it is usually a pretty good sign that your affair was about washed up anyway.

Of course, there are unscrupulous persons of both sexes who make a game of love. If your beloved has fallen into such a trap in spite of warnings that you may have tried to give, your only recourse is one of waiting until the awakening comes and the errant one sees the light.

UNREQUITED love

One of the saddest facts about love is that it is not always mutual. When you are terribly fond of another person who doesn't even seem to be aware of your existence, you can go through torture. When, in spite of all your efforts, the one you adore does not return your affection, there is nothing sensible that you can do except get over the stormy love that wracks you.

If someone loves you in a way that you cannot reciprocate, it may make you feel embarrassed and uneasy. You may not want to hurt the other person who so obviously adores you. Yet you are not wise to encourage a relationship in which you are not comfortable. So you carefully try to keep your distance and avoid situations in which you would be under pressure to express feelings that you honestly do not have. It is never *really* kind to go along with something outwardly when you are inwardly rejecting it. Frankly and kindly telling the other person that you cannot return his or her affection may become necessary. But even then, the strain between you may continue. Such things are sometimes a part of living and loving.

SHARING—
the measure of love

Caught in the middle of a love tangle, you may cry out in bewilderment, "Just how miserable can you get?" You see now that love has many faces and speaks in varied tongues. It is often confusing. It can surprise you with its changes of tempo and mood. But love is good, and you can have faith in it as long as you live.

You can dare to love, and know that it becomes increasingly fine and rewarding with experience. It is not a matter of being willing to lay down your life and die for love. Rather, the depth of your love can be measured in how much you can share, in how much you are willing to live for.

As you become increasingly mature, you will find yourself opening up to others in warmer, fuller ways. Although once you clung to your belongings with possessive pride, you reach the stage where you enjoy sharing what you have with others. Although once you enjoyed collecting all sorts of things, there will come a time when your pleasure will be more often in giving yourself to others and collecting friends wherever you go.

Sharing your thoughts and feelings, your values and interests, with other special persons is a measure of love in a mature sense. When you are still immature, you wait for others to give you the cues as to what to do and say, and even how to feel about certain things. Then as you become more sure of yourself, you share something of yourself with those with whom you have contact. You tell them how you really feel. You put your deepest values into words that communicate your philosophy of life to others. When you become truly fond of another person, you want to share much that is most meaningful to you.

When you really love another person, you not only care for him or her in an emotional sense; you care about what happens to him. You want things to turn out well for him. You wish him well, and you are personally sorry when things turn out badly for him. Your compassion is one kind of sharing your concern for other persons.

Just as you love a musical instrument the more you improve your ability to play it, so you learn to love by practicing caring for others through the years. There is a world of difference between the beginner's screeching dissonances and the experienced violinist's polished performance. Similarly, the expressions of love vary all the way from the first fumbling feelings to the loveliness of full-blown affection between two mature persons.

The important thing to remember during the teen years is that you do not have to DO anything about the way you feel toward someone else. You can acknowledge the feeling, and accept it for what it seems to mean as a part of your personality. Beyond that, you are wise to postpone any serious decisions that involve your love for another until you are ready to assume full responsibility for your life, your behavior, and your future. Right now you are learning to tell the difference between infatuation or "sex attraction" or "puppy love" and the mature love that lasts long enough to build your future upon without question.

Can you tell when you are really in love?

CHAPTER 3

HOW CAN YOU TELL WHETHER you are really in love? Are the love songs right? Do your knees go knockety-knock, and your heart, bumpety-bump? Do you lose your appetite? If people can't agree on things like these as signs of love, then what will work as a test?

It is important to know about your own love feelings. The more understanding you can get about yourself in and out of love, the better off you will be. Love is powerful and strong. It can hurt as well as help. We need real insights about the love part of our lives.

Love comes along in so many disguises that we may not realize we have already made its acquaintance. So many feelings look like love and aren't, and so many others do not feel like love and yet may be, that the facts of love are important to know.

In this country we marry for love. There are places where persons may marry for money or position or because their families have chosen to unite, but we pride ourselves on marrying for love. Unless we know what love is, and what to expect of it, we find ourselves in trouble when we base our futures so completely on it. This is especially true because many of the things we hear about love are just not so.

THE
great romantic fairy tale

All our lives we have heard the fairy tale of love. It has been our bedtime story through the years. It reaches us through songs, the advertisements for soap and cosmetics, television and radio, the movies, and the books and magazines we read. It is so much a part of our folklore that we sometimes do not realize all its elements and how they affect us. The story goes something like this:

Step 1. Nothing much had ever happened to her. She had been living a life of innocent waiting, doing her school work, being nice to her mother, helping with the dishes, and washing her hair on Saturday night. She was sweet and winsome and entirely undiscovered until—

Step 2. Suddenly HE appeared. He knew at once that SHE was for HIM. He saw her across the room and said to himself, "I'm going to marry that girl." He was all that she had ever dreamed of, tall, dark, handsome, and with a shy grin that lit up his face, and so—

Step 3. They FELL in love. Completely, utterly, suddenly in love. One minute she was alone in the world, an unclaimed treasure; the next, she was madly in love. Before he entered that room he was adrift, no one to tie to, no good woman to keep him from going to the dogs; the next, there she was. So naturally—

Step 4. They met and kissed and knew they were made for each other. What they did those first few minutes, those first days and weeks, did not matter except that they were together. Even if there had been any question about their love before, when at last he kissed her, all doubts flew and she sighed, "Oh, darling!" with all her heart. Then, of course, there is no alternative but that—

Step 5. They marry as soon as they can, for this is the real thing. Love is all that matters. Out of all the world there is one man for one woman, and when they are brought together by the hand of Fate, they must obey and marry before it is too late. The ending of the story is always the same—

Step 6. And they lived happily ever after. Their marriage was built on real love, so of course they will live happily ever after. If they run into trouble, then it could not have been real love after all. The real thing ends only in permanent bliss, a lifetime of sweethearts together, with never a cross word, never a dull moment, only the never-ending thrill of belonging to each other.

This is the story that has been told us through the years in many forms, with countless variations, and in many settings. But in all its tellings it remains essentially the same. We love it because it is so familiar. And, of course, it is a sweet story, the sweetest story ever told. But unfortunately, it is not entirely true. It is a fairy tale, a lovely, frothy, delightful fairy tale that comes true in real life about as often as the Prince finds his Cinderella or the pumpkin turns into a coach-and-four. We like fairy tales. We wouldn't want to lose them for the world. Yet when we grow up enough to begin to know what love really is like, it is time for us to know what to expect. Now we must learn the difference between the fiction and the facts of love.

WHAT
is known about love

During the years that storytellers have been spinning beautiful stories of love and lovers, another group of men and women have earnestly been trying to find out what the true facts are about falling in love and being in love and staying in love. These social scientists have been studying what actually happens as people grow up and become interested in each other. They have conducted studies on what makes for success and failure in marriage. They have observed enough of how real people act and feel in real situations to teach us a great many facts about love and life.

We do not know all the answers yet by any means. A great deal more research needs to be done before we shall have all the pieces of the jigsaw puzzle of loving each other. But we know enough today to be pretty sure of some of the things that are *not* so, as well as many other things that tend to be true.

YOU learn to love

Love does not simply spring forth some moonlight night without warning. You do not *fall* in love. You *learn* to love through a lifetime of experience in loving. By the time boy meets girl, a great deal has happened to both of them to make them ready for their interest in each other. In fact, by that time they both are old hands at loving, in many ways. Each has grown up through the phases of emotional maturity to the place where he and she are capable of loving and being loved. In a real sense you *grow* into love, both individually and as couples.

There may be some sudden feeling of attraction when two people of the opposite sex first meet. This is often called "love at first sight." It is a very moving experience. But in itself it is not love. It is more in the nature of infatuation.

Sudden, intense attraction between two persons usually is based upon one of two powerful forces. The first is sex attraction. Something about a girl, often some insignificant characteristic—the turn of an ankle, the look in the eyes, the modulation of the voice—trips off the boy's sex interest, and he may find himself head over heels in love with someone that he scarcely knows as a person. This can happen to girls, too. They report that sometimes the way a man walks, or talks, or looks at a girl may suddenly cause her to "fall for" him. Even smells may be a factor in this kind of attraction. Touch is a powerful stimulus, as many persons find to their surprise.

Edith had to sit on Chris's lap in the car in which they both were driving home with several others from a school party. She had never paid any attention to Chris before. Nor had he seemed to notice her. But by the time the car stopped at Edith's house that night, Chris was madly in love with Edith, so he said. Edith was aquiver with a new excitement that she thought must be the real thing at last. Was this love? Or was it not rather the kind of attraction of male to female that was released by touch and pressure as she sat upon his lap? Whether or not the fascination which started with physical stimulation ever could become real love in a fuller sense would depend a great deal upon Edith and Chris. But in itself, sex attraction alone is not love.

The second thing that causes one person to become suddenly drawn to another is that he or she reminds him of a previous loved one. This is very common. It is what often lies back of that sudden feeling of recognition and response that may spring up without warning. Across a crowded room he sees her, and he says to himself, "That's for me." She meets him at a party and within an hour she feels she has known him all her life. What probably has happened is that he sees in her some similarity to another woman whom he has loved (his mother perhaps, or a childhood sweetheart) that makes him feel just as he did in the older relationship. He does not consciously recognize the likeness. If he did, the emotional response would not be so intense. But his feelings behave as they used to with the-woman-he-sees-in-her. Of course she very likely is not at all like the woman she reminds him of. But that does not affect the way his emotions respond.

Terry found herself violently attracted to a boy that she did not even like very much. He was crude and clumsy and not at all the kind of boy she enjoyed being with. But his hair curled down around his temples like that of a favorite uncle of hers and she could hardly keep her eyes off him. As a little girl, she used to sit on her uncle's lap and run her fingers through his hair while he fondled her and told of how he would wait for her to grow up and be "his girl." When the uncle died in the War, Terry was desolate. She mourned so hard that her parents became worried and sent her to camp for a season. She gradually "forgot" her uncle, until he came back in a surge of feeling for a boy she hardly knew. Even then she did not at first recognize her uncle in her fascination for the boy. In fact, as soon as she became aware of the nature of the attraction, the fascination passed as suddenly as it had come.

These things occur quite normally to most of us from time to time. They are nothing to be ashamed of, but rather to be understood as irrational attractions to some part of another person that trips off some half-forgotten response. It is somewhat like detonating an explosive charge. The bomb is there with all its power locked in, waiting to be released. Along comes just the right combination, and BANG, the whole thing goes off in one terrific explosion. The response was built up in the past and only has been released by this new person who set it off. Such experiences usually catch us by surprise and are difficult to understand at first.

A relationship that starts out with a great deal of feeling of "falling in love" in August is often nonexistent by the time Christmas rolls around. Infatuation based upon physical attraction may develop into more lasting love if the two personalities have a great deal in common. The emotional excitement of infatuation more often is as fleeting as fireworks or thunder and lightning storms.

Infatuation and love are not the same thing. Infatuation is apt to be sudden, impulsive, and fragile. Love grows out of mutual association into a steady, long-lasting sturdy affection.

Love feelings are almost always a mixture of many different types of response and reaction. As we have seen, love is a language that speaks in many ways. When we feel strongly about another we are apt to have all our reactions to that person intensified. We not only love him or her but we also feel strongly in ways that are definitely not loving.

Irene loved Sam. But at times he so irritated her that she hated him. We might say that she hated him because she loved him. People who do not mean anything to us can rarely upset us, but as soon as we become emotionally involved, all our feelings seem to enter into the picture.

It is the persons whom we love who can hurt us most deeply. We are vulnerable to them just because we do love them. This means that love is often coupled with resentment, sometimes with frustration, and not infrequently with bitterness and despair.

Strangers can do things of which we disapprove without its bothering us very much. Acquaintances can act in distasteful ways and we are not upset. But let a loved one offend and we respond at once, for the loved one belongs to us and we to him. What he does matters to us so much that we are far more critical and much more emotional when he is concerned than we are about persons for whom we do not care.

Mixed-up love feelings are therefore to be expected. As we mature, we gain more insight into our feelings. In the meantime, we can be assured that love is frequently confused with many other feelings. "Pure love" is usually an idealization of our feelings for some person whom we neither know well nor see very often.

LOVE is not all that matters

Since love feelings are so unpredictable and so often mixed up, we can scarcely rely on them alone as a basis for a permanent relationship. Love may be enjoyed and understood and taken in its stride, but it cannot be used as a compass to guide the rest of our lives.

You might liken your love feelings to the motor in the car. It provides the energy that is needed to move the car, but the motor cannot steer it. So with you, your feelings push you, but your head must do the steering.

Love is not enough to marry on. Many other factors are fully as important if a marriage is to succeed, as you shall see in a later chapter. This does not mean that marriage without love is advocated! What it does mean is that you are capable of loving a great many people, only a few of whom would be suitable marriage partners.

LOVE comes not once but many times

One of the most unfortunate myths in romantic folklore is that love comes only once in a lifetime. The fiction is that if once we love and lose then we are left loveless forever after. Nothing is more false. Any person capable of loving another has the capacity of loving not once but many times, not one individual but many persons.

For any normal man or woman there are many possible partners with whom a fine marriage could be worked out. Second marriages have been shown to work out remarkably well, indicating that at least two loves are possible. As a matter of fact, most of us could learn to love almost any congenial person of the other sex. You can count on love developing if the rest of the relationship is satisfactory. But love is the first to leave when the going gets rough, if there is little else in the situation to hold the two together.

This is what the Chinese proverb refers to when it likens the ideal of romantic love as the basis for marriage to the putting of a hot kettle on a cold stove and expecting it to boil. The old Chinese method was for the parents to pair off two likely persons who in all probability scarcely knew each other until their wedding day. This is like putting a cold kettle on a hot stove, where in time it could be expected to boil. The interesting thing is that the old Chinese family was remarkably stable, and that our modern American marriages break up at alarming rates. One reason is that we expect too much of love.

LOVE does not have to lead to marriage

Not all love leads to the altar. In a lifetime you love many persons, as you have seen. Yet you usually marry only one. Unfortunately, many young people feel that when they love someone, something must be done about it. That is not at all wise. Just because one feels affection is no reason that he must have an affair with or get married to the loved one. Love feelings can be enjoyed for themselves, for the warm radiance they give to all friendships, without necessarily leading into a lifetime contract or a temporary "adventure."

UNDERSTANDING
deepens love

You can know that orange juice is full of vitamin C, and still greatly enjoy the taste of it. You can understand all about nutrition and yet have a good appetite for dinner. Knowledge does not hamper enjoyment. In fact, the more we know about anything, the greater is our capacity to enjoy it. This is especially true of love. As we come more and more to understand it, we feel it even more deeply and meaningfully. That is one of the reasons that wise people seek insights into their love.

"WHY do I love you?"

Lovers frequently wonder why they love each other. The strange power of love baffles them. They ask each other, "Why do I love you?" This is a good question and it can be answered, at least in part. There are real reasons that one person loves another. As these reasons are understood, the love quite often grows stronger still. Only if the attraction is not love at all but merely a passing fancy, will it weaken as it is understood.

You love each other oftentimes because you meet each other's needs. Janice is effervescent and flighty. She loves Dan partly because he is always so calm and stable. He loves her partly because she is so peppy and full of life. They are good for each other, in that each meets some real need in the other.

As you satisfy each other's need for response and belongingness, you give your love a chance to grow stronger still. Everyone needs to feel wanted, desirable—that other people like to have one around. When two persons give each other this sense of being someone special, then each strengthens the love feeling in the other.

There are many reasons that you love some persons more than others. They are all interesting, and they are worth understanding better. The more you know about why you love and are loved, the better you know yourself. The more insight you get about yourself, the better you can manage your life and work out your happiness. Ignorance is not bliss. Insights lead to satisfaction.

LOVE need not be entirely blind

Love is blind only until its eyes are opened. Love at first sight is somewhat like the newborn puppy blindly fumbling about with nothing but its feelings to guide it. Comes the day when its eyes are opened, and then it can really see what it has been feeling all along. The trouble with puppy love is that it so often leads to a dog's life! If love is to endure, it must be in terms of real persons and situations. Insights are necessary for permanent affection.

Understanding does not spoil love. In fact, true love does not develop without understanding. When you love you want to be understood, and you want to understand. As you understand each other, you love each other all the more. As you feel understood and loved even as you are, you can relax and know that love will last because it is based upon realities within yourself.

Abiding love rests upon both head and heart. Feelings alone are not enough. Intelligent understandings too are necessary. When two persons can think together as well as feel together, their relationship is much more solidly based than it ever can be upon feelings alone.

SIX
tests of love

How can you test love? you ask. How can you tell if it is the real thing? Is this love enough to marry on? you may wonder. You have seen that there are all sorts of love feelings for all sorts of persons. Realizing that by understanding your feelings you can guide them better, how can you test your love feelings to tell whether they will endure?

Actually there are no answers in the back of the book for questions like this. There is no love-meter that will accurately tell you just what you rate in love, because people are so complex and the forces that attract them are complicated. Surely some day we shall all know more about such things. We need studies that will delve as intelligently into the stars that shine in lovers' eyes as those that have explored the heavenly constellations. But until these investigations have been made, such tests as the following may be helpful.

LOVE is outgoing

Love that lasts does not center in oneself. Self-centered love is childish love that cannot hold up in the give-and-take of grown-up people. The girl who feels that she is in love because he is so crazy about her may love being loved, but she is not truly in love herself. Emmy Lou came in starry-eyed from a date. "He's wonderful. I'm in love. He spent twenty dollars on me tonight," she exclaimed. No doubt she had had an exciting time. But what she felt was not love. She was too absorbed with her own feelings to be really in love with anyone else.

Mature love looks out to others. It is other-centered. The one in love is more concerned about his sweetheart than about his own selfish interests. He does anything he can to make his beloved happy. He actively promotes and encourages whatever will be best for the one he loves. He cares more about the relationship he enjoys with her than about his own pride. She puts him first, too. When a difference of opinion comes up, they are able to work it through understandingly because they love one another.

Lovers whose love is on a lasting basis are outgoing in their interests. They are not just interested in each other. It is as though they were standing side by side looking out into their world and their common future, rather than just facing each other.

REAL love releases energy

Some feelings inactivate one. At times we are so entangled emotionally that we cannot do anything. Our work falls off. We cannot study. We do not want to eat, or do anything. If this continues, the chances are that it is not real love.

Love that lasts is creative. It releases a great deal of energy for work. When a boy really loves a girl, he is eager to accomplish and achieve. He has a double reason for his efforts now. He wants to amount to something for her sake as well as his own. Their common hopes and dreams stimulate them both to be more productive than either of them could have been alone. It is this creative force in love that quite truly makes the world go 'round. Much of our motivation comes from wanting to please someone we love. Our drives and dreams thrive on the wish to live up to the expectations and hopes of those we love.

LOVE wants to share

Love is best known by the desire to share. When you are in love you want to share a great deal with your lover. You want to share your thoughts. You cannot ever get enough of talking through the things that interest you. You want to share your feelings and your attitudes about things. Lovers do not lack for anything to talk about, for both of them have been saving up the choice anecdotes of every hour of the day to share with the other. Everything that happens is of interest when it happens to be someone you care about. It is this sharingness that keeps love from becoming boring and dull.

Try this little simple test on yourself with the one you love right now. It will be more reliable by far than the old daisy-petal trick. Take any newspaper and see how many things you feel like clipping to share with the one you love. If you come up with a variety of items that you are eager to show your loved one, you are much more in love than if you turn up only one or two things in which your interest is lukewarm.

LOVE is a we-feeling

You are in love to the extent to which you think and feel and talk and plan in terms of We instead of I. The person who is only partly in love still thinks in terms of himself and his interests and plans. We knew a man once who bought one ticket for his own honeymoon! This is an extreme example, to be sure, but there are lots of so-called lovers who are almost as I-centered.

When you find yourself thinking about what *we* like, instead of what *I* like, you are growing into love. If you plan in terms of what *we* shall do, what *we* enjoy, where *we* want to go, you are practicing the habits that keep love alive as well as testing its present vitality. Without it the two persons are always separate individuals, each bent upon his own affairs. With it the two are one in the full sense essential for lasting happiness.

YOU must like as well as love

For love to last it must have a solid foundation of genuine liking. You must be able to respect and admire your loved one if you expect to love him or her for very long. If you cannot enjoy each other as two whole persons, whatever your feelings for each other they cannot last.

Of course you will never be proud of everything that the other is and does in all respects, any more than you are proud of everything that you yourself are and do. There is always room for improvement, even in lovers. But unless you can honestly say to yourself, "I *like* this one I love," your love is headed for stormy seas. In fact there are times when it is more important to like than to love another person. In the heat of a disagreement, if you can respect and admire each other you will fare better than if you are held together by some uncritical force that does not make sense.

This is the place where women especially have made mistakes in the past. They have "fallen for" some man who has habits which they detest, and marry him to reform him. We know that that almost never works. People are not reformed after marriage or by marriage. If the woman cannot like the man as he really is she should not marry him, no matter how strong her feelings for him are. For love that lasts does not come in impossible combinations but in sturdy, sensible possibilities that we can live with comfortably.

When in doubt about love feelings, time will tell. The love that lasts is the love that does last. When a summer's romance is over before autumn, it obviously is not the real thing. When a mad infatuation does not survive the first difference of opinion, it quite certainly is not true love. When love feelings come along for a person who is not for you, they cannot persist permanently without keeping you both out of bounds, as we shall see in a later chapter. But when love continues around the calendar, through troubles and trials as well as joys, it may well be the kind that will go on through the years.

There used to be a saying that fitted this principle nicely. It went, "Never marry a man until you have summered and wintered with him." More important than the seasons are the emotional climates that you weather together. When you have seen each other through all sorts of situations that have called forth a variety of feelings and you still love each other, it may well be the real thing. If you have experienced together a wide gamut of emotions—sympathy, anger, resentment, sorrow, fear, hatred, as well as love—so that you know deep down inside how each of you feels under these conditions, then you can be said to know your loved one enough to expect the relationship to endure.

There is no quick and easy trick for testing love that will work reliably. Young people will continue to pull daisy petals and cross out letters in each other's names, seek fortunetellers, read tea leaves, and play all the other games that are such fun. But when it comes down to deciding seriously whether we are really in love or not, we turn to more reliable evidences such as those we have been discussing.

Lasting love is too precious to confuse with any of its dazzling substitutes. That does not mean that we should avoid anything but the real thing. Far from it. But it does mean that when all the fooling around is over, and we want to settle down to a lifetime of loving someone with whom we can be deeply and truly in love forever, we should stop playing games and take the longer, surer tests.

Love –
embarrassment

CHAPTER **4**

or blessing?

ONE OF THE MOST DIFFICULT things that may happen while growing up is to find oneself in love with someone with whom one should not be. It is hard to understand and deal with in itself, and it is made more difficult by not being able to talk about it freely and easily. Other troubles tend to evaporate when you discuss them. Love out of bounds is an embarrassment. It often hurts inside because it is not fully understood and is hard to handle comfortably.

CRUSHES
on members of one's own sex

People are often troubled by attachments to members of the same sex. A general feeling exists that there is something not quite right about a girl's crush on another girl, or a boy's attachment to another boy. This is especially true if the relationship is intense and persists over a period of time.

Some persons are so attracted to members of their own sex that the other sex does not appeal to them. When such a condition becomes chronic, these persons are unable to fall in love, get married, and lead normal lives as a man or woman usually does. That is why parents and friends may become worried when two girls become so very fond of each other that neither of them is interested in boys or dates. That is why older persons are so often concerned about too close friendships between boys, especially when those attachments become all-absorbing.

CRUSHES on persons of one's own age

Luella and Sally have eyes for no one but each other. They go everywhere together. They are almost never seen apart.

When one shows even the most casual interest in someone else, the other is intensely jealous. Lately they so often have been seen to kiss and fondle each other that the home-room teacher had to speak to them about it. Such crushes as this are not unusual among teen-age people of both sexes. But they may mean that the persons involved in the crush are slowed in their development toward more grown-up love attachments.

CRUSHES on older persons

Gertrude was "crazy" about her history teacher. She lived for the hour that she spent in that one teacher's class. She copied the way she did her hair. She spent all her allowance one Friday on red roses which she put on the teacher's desk with a note that read, "With all my love, Gertrude." When it was time for school to close in June, Gertrude wept at having to be separated from her beloved teacher through the summer months. Her love for her history teacher was no less real because her folks scoffed at it as a schoolgirl crush.

Harry worshiped the coach. He hung on every word and carried out every little suggestion the coach made with zealous devotion. He slipped into the gym early in the morning to get out the equipment for the coach. One day when the coach threw his arm over Harry's shoulder in a gesture of friendly comradeship, Harry felt himself shiver all over. Was Harry "in love with" the coach? Well, we do not call it that, do we? We feel that sometimes there is something not quite right in a boy's being fond of an older man that way. And yet this is one stage of development that many boys like Harry go through during their teen years.

It is as though young people getting into their early teens replace the close childhood love they had for their parents with an even more intense feeling for some older person who for a while has the place of the parent, emotionally. This quite commonplace phase of growing up is something to become concerned about only when it persists for a long time and is not replaced by other types of affection. While it lasts it is a very precious kind of devotion, and not to be laughed at or ashamed of.

The first step in getting over a crush is to really want to; and this can be difficult. One of the characteristics of this kind of attachment is its compulsive quality. "My trouble is, I don't really want to get over my crush," said one perceptive teen-ager. In time this particular problem evaporated, as crushes do as soon as the troubled person is ready to move on to more mature relationships.

The young person who gets well into the teens and still is attracted intensely to people of the same sex may need competent counseling help. An understanding counselor can help the young person discover some of the reasons that his or her emotional development is being delayed beyond what is considered normal. Good guidance can assist in opening other outlets and encouraging the too involved person to make new contacts and friendships.

Time itself is an ally in many of these situations, especially for the individual willing to use it wisely. The boy who recognizes his crush on one of his buddies can make honest efforts to become active in sports, mingle with the crowd, engage in social affairs where girls are, and to develop his skills in getting along with many kinds of people at the same time that he is getting over his too exclusive attachment to one person.

ATTRACTION
or rebellion?

Some young people fall in love with persons that their folks will not accept. It may be someone of a different race, religion, or background. It may be a person with a handicap, physical or social. Parents are apt to be shocked and hurt when this happens.

Loving someone who is "different" can be a very real love or a kind of declaration of independence from one's parents. Not many young people recognize the possibility of this element of defiance. It is as though the young person is saying, "I can run my own life now. I will love whom I please."

Carter III came from a family very proud of its origins and background. As long as Carter could remember, he had heard his folks talk about how important it was to love and marry only people "who belong." Then Carter fell in love. And it was with a girl who his folks felt did *not* belong to their set. Carter's family fussed and threatened and fumed, but it seemed only to drive Carter closer to the girl whom he had chosen. Then Carter's father suffered a business collapse. Suddenly the whole picture changed. The family's concern over the failure of business kept them so busy that they hardly mentioned Carter's love affair any more. Strangely enough, as soon as the family ceased criticizing his girl, he found that her appeal for him had lessened. It was as though he loved her just because his family was so opposed to her! Yes, those things happen; especially when a young person is having a difficult time breaking away from family ties, and into his own independence. The more severely a family insists upon one kind of friend or another, the more some young people defiantly fall in love with just exactly the opposite.

Young people who find themselves violently in love with someone who they have been brought up to believe is not suitable for them should take some time to make sure that it is real love and not just something being used to untie one of the apron-strings at home. It very often is, and effective at that!

FALLING
in love with a married man

Very little has ever been written about falling in love with a married man. It is supposed not to happen. Yet it is not at all uncommon, especially among teen-age girls, and even among older women, too. The reasons are understandable.

MARRIED men are older

For the teen-age girl, the married man is usually older and therefore, in her eyes, more experienced and mature. Girls mature earlier than boys of their own age. So it often happens that a girl who is growing up much faster than the boys around her thinks they are childish and silly and finds herself dreaming about the charms of older men. The married men she has contact with—the coach, a teacher, perhaps the principal, or a minister—seem so much more grown up and exitingly mature that her love interests turn to them rather than to the boys of her own age who are still just "children."

Girls may do foolish things in their attachments to older men. They should guard themselves from becoming either too obvious in their infatuations or too deeply engrossed inside themselves. Fortunately, most girls outgrow this stage fairly soon and may look back upon these early crushes with amused wonder. But while emotionally entangled with the older man, it is not funny at all.

MARRIED men seem safe

One reason that so many girls find themselves loving some other woman's husband is that the very fact of his being married somehow makes him safe. Deep within herself a girl may argue like this: "It is safe to love him because he is already married and nothing will come of it." Becoming involved emotionally with an unmarried man, on the other hand, might call for some action for which the girl is not yet ready. Subconsciously she knows it. This is especially true of the younger girl who is not really mature enough for full love and marriage and family life, and still is old enough to need some love expressions and dreams. She can dream about what it would be like to be married to a man already married without having to prove to herself that she could do it. The fact of his marriage protects her.

MARRIED men are lovable

The fact that a man is married is often some indication that he is lovable. At least one woman has found him lovable enough to marry him. Furthermore, being married, he has had a chance to learn to give and to receive affection as a woman needs and feels it. The married man is often more tender, more gentle, more courteous, more expressive of his affection with women than are men who have not had the privilege of living intimately with a woman. They have learned some of the arts of love-making and often carry these over, without their realizing it, into their relationship with girls and women outside of marriage. The married man who is used to taking his wife's arm in a tender, protective way may without thinking do the same with some other girl who means little to him. Yet her response as a woman to his thoughtful tenderness may be out of all proportion to the actual meaning of the gesture.

Married men often feel at home with women, able to talk and think and feel with them in a way that is impossible for less experienced males. The married man, feeling secure with women himself, is able to look directly into a woman's eyes and meet her face to face as a person in a way that is mutually satisfying. A girl feels that such a man understands her. She can get through to him. He seems to listen when she speaks, to care about what she is saying, and to be a companion in a way not usual in the boys she knows, who have had less experience with women.

MARRIED men may be hungryhearted

A man may be married, and yet not have all his emotional needs met within the marriage. Most men, and women too, expect a great deal from marriage. They expect to be completely satisfied in every way by their marriage partner. This is a great deal to ask of any relationship. It is the unusual marriage that does not have its occasional low moments when one or the other of the partners feels deeply lonely, only partly loved, hungry at heart even with the one he loved enough to marry.

Once a man has had the fullness of a woman's love, he learns to expect it and to feel that he has a right to it always. Women are like that, too. When a marriage is not fulfilling all the complex needs of the partners, they may feel so lonely that they seek companionship outside their marriages. A "misunderstood husband" seeks comfort in telling some other girl or woman how his wife does not understand him. A girl, hearing this sorry tale, responds with sympathy. Before she realizes what she is doing, she may be trying to make up his wife's inadequacies with her attention and concern. There is enough of the maternal, nurturing impulse in normal women and girls to want to protect and care for the hurt, the lonely, and the suffering. Then, too, the married man who takes his loneliness-in-marriage outside finds a ready response in the girl or woman who herself is going through some love-hungry moments. It is a case of the hungryhearted seeking and finding each other.

THE romance of unfulfillment is different

Not being able to do something about love makes the romance especially exciting. When one loves a boy of one's own age and kind, who is a possible fiancé and husband, one can date and dream and plan for a common future. One's friends can talk about the plans and one's family may boast. One is free to tell the world about his love and its great promise. It pours out in a thousand ways.

But loving a married man gives no such outlets. It just isn't done. Almost no one can be told about how wonderful he is. There can be no plans that give promise—nothing but dreams that go around and around, tenderly reliving his possible light touch, the way he looks, the way one feels about him, and the utter hopelessness of the affection. Love with no place to go tends to be absorbing, tensely frustrating, full of tender anguish and exciting unfulfillment.

SOCIETY scorns the other woman

In almost all triangles involving married persons, it is the unmarried outsider who is blamed for the affair. Marriage is such a sacred institution that any girl or woman who alienates the affection of a married man is apt to be held in contempt by most people. The girl who wants to punish herself will find that getting involved with a married man is a sure way of doing it. Girls who are going through difficult days in breaking away from their parents may unconsciously get themselves into disgrace as a way to hurt their families. They find that social disapproval falls fast and hard upon the heads of the silly school girls who do it.

FALLING
in love with a married woman

Much that has been said about falling in love with a married man applies to the other combination of boys and men falling in love with married women. Married women are attractive. A married woman has already proved her appeal to at least the one man who married her. She has learned how to love and be loved, to relax into some of the fullness of woman's role in the interplay of the sexes that is mutually satisfying to both.

It is not at all unusual for the growing boy to become very fond of some safely married woman as the first object of his affections outside his immediate family. Of course, every boy has first loved a married woman—his mother! In his growing up, he had to fight off his jealousy of his own father as a rival for his mother's love. When the boy becomes teen age, he not infrequently finds that his affection turns to someone not unlike his mother or perhaps his older sister. Without his being aware that she reminds him of his mother, she calls forth much the same kind of devotion that he has given his mother through the years. The older married woman in this role may play a real part in the boy's weaning of himself from his family.

LONELY married women

Many married women are lonely and hungry for affection and attention. When husbands pursue careers that take them many miles and hours away from their families, a woman can get extremely lonesome waiting for a husband to return. A married woman today is much freer to associate with men in all sorts of settings than was her mother or her mother's mother. In these contacts, often entered into quite innocently in some simple social setting, at work, or perhaps at school, she has ready access to men and boys of all kinds. It may start with a coke shared at a counter, or a drive home after work, or with heads together over some common problem. Before either of them knows what has happened, the boy may find himself yearning to touch her, or perhaps he suddenly discovers that he is in love with her, cannot keep her from his thoughts, counts the days and hours until he will next see her, and longs for some sign that she likes him, too. There may be some impulsive moment when they find themselves in an embrace that puzzles and dismays them both even while they long to repeat it.

The married woman who is already love-hungry may find herself responding to such attention before she is aware of what is going on. One day the boy may have been just a promising student, or pleasant colleague, or friendly companion. The next day she finds that she is entangled emotionally and enjoys responding to his tentative expressions of affection.

CHECKS on his infatuation

The fully mature married woman whose deepest needs are being met in her own marriage does not face the same temptation. She may sense that the boy is fond of her, but she responds to his attention in a kind, impersonal, motherly way that keeps him from getting in too deep and helps him to grow out of his infatuation into the mature love life that is possible with someone more nearly his own age and status.

The repressed woman who has never given a place in her life to her own emotional needs may rebuff the boy's advances in fright or guilt or shame and leave him feeling that he is dreadfully unworthy, that he has been guilty of something sinful in becoming interested in her. Fortunately, boys and men do not often fall in love with severely repressed women. They are far more apt to become involved with a woman who is emotionally alive.

WHAT boys can't tell

A boy may brag about his success with other girls, but he cannot speak of his infatuation with a married woman. He hugs his longing and his affection to himself where it may become absorbing, highly romantic, and keenly frustrating. All that he might express through bragging, praising, planning, is bottled up inside himself in the vicious circle of anguished frustration.

THE
disappointments of forbidden fruit

How do those affairs with married persons turn out? Can there be a happy ending? Can two persons who love each other work things out, even though one of them is already married? What are the possible outcomes of such an affair as we have been describing? Let us count the ways in which these involvements most often terminate.

THE married person withdraws

Most people enter marriage intending to make it work. Marriage means a great deal to most of us, and we back away from anything that severely threatens it. The married person involved in a love tangle outside of marriage has a great deal to lose if he attempts to dissolve his marriage for his new love. He loses his present family and all it means for him. He loses confidence in himself and his ability to make a go of marriage. He feels some shame, too, at breaking up his home and deserting the person whom once he loved enough to marry. If there are children, the problem is much greater. Few mothers can run away from their own flesh and blood. Most fathers feel a binding tie to their own sons and daughters. So in the battle between the wife and the "other woman," the wife usually wins.

The married woman, too, who is caught in the emotional tug of war between promptings that pull her away from home and those that keep her bound to her husband, will usually withdraw from the outside lover and live to see the day when she blushes with shame or smiles with amusement at herself for once being so foolishly tempted.

The fear of what people will say keeps many married partners together when outside interests tempt. The wife thinks twice before she risks her good reputation as a married woman for the almost certain criticism of neighbors and friends if she breaks up her marriage. The married man, likewise, fears not only what his friends will say but what his business associates will feel, if his marriage is threatened by an outsider. He knows that if he does not keep his marriage together, his career as well as his social life will suffer.

The most common outcome is for the married person to sense what is happening in the beginning of an outside involvement and to back out of the emotional entanglement. Any young person who finds himself or herself falling in love with a married man or woman should frankly face the strong probability of being left out in the cold.

THE marriage may be dissolved

In some cases the marriage does not withstand the shock of an outside lover. Usually these are marriages that have already begun to crumble before the new lover came along. Being a party to a broken marriage contract is not an easy role to play. There is always a sense of guilt for both the partner breaking up his marriage and the outside lover.

Human happiness is dependent upon making others happy too. It is extremely difficult to build a happy relationship upon the unhappiness of those that have been hurt or injured by one's intrusion. Emily discovered this to her sorrow. She fell madly in love with a married man who returned her affection. After some months of uneasy discussions, he promised to divorce his wife and marry Emily. The wife allowed the divorce proceedings to go through even though she was deeply hurt and begged Emily to give him up. By the time the divorce decree was final and the man was free to marry Emily, she found that she did not love him enough to go through with it. She reported that the wife's face haunted her and that whenever she looked into her lover's face she saw his wife's tears. She rightly recognized that a marriage built on such a foundation would be too shaky to risk.

ONE exploits the other

Anything that has worth tends to be exploited. People take advantage of a man with money when they can. Men take advantage of a woman's affection, too, sometimes. Teenage girls especially should be wary of both the married and the unmarried "wolves" that are not uncommon in any community. Boys, too, can be exploited by older women. The wise young person recognizes that such things do exist and exercises caution. The lure of "the line" may seem attractive but it does not come from a loving heart, as many a girl has learned to her sorrow. One high school girl dismissed an unwelcome proposition with the comment, "Wouldn't I be a sucker to get hooked like that?"

Fortunately, one or both of the lovers usually outgrow the entanglement and turn to more comfortable and easier relationships. Jim had been in a torment of infatuation for an older married woman for some time. He "ate his heart out" for her. He did badly in his studies. He was sullen and morose at home. He dropped out of sports and school activities. Then, almost as suddenly as he had become involved, he began to come to his senses. He started to date other girls again. His school work greatly improved. He saw less and less of the married woman, until finally one day he realized that he had completely outgrown his infatuation.

Outgrowing an unpromising relationship does not have to be left to chance. A boy or girl, man or woman, can guide his own emotional development if he wants to badly enough. Good counseling helps. Talking over how one feels, what one really wants out of life, what this particular fancy of the moment means to him, perhaps analyzing enough of how the infatuation came about in the first place and getting enough understanding of oneself to see why one got so involved, often is enough to set things right.

A counselor who can help one look objectively at his emotions and see his next step in development may be hard to find. Advice rarely helps. Some people too freely tell us what they would do if they were we. People who might help us, scold or preach or act shocked, and we cannot readily tell them what really counts. Others may reassure us that it's really nothing at all, when deep down inside we know it is something that must be coped with and cannot easily be forgotten.

The good counselor listens to what we are saying, helps us to see ourselves more clearly, and permits us to come to our own decisions. Good counselors may be found in all sorts of settings. Sometimes the person who can hear our confidences and give us most help is an especially trained guidance worker. It may be a teacher with whom we feel we "click." Sometimes it is a minister, or a coach, or parent who knows us well enough and trusts us fully enough to give just the perspective we need in feeling our way out of emotional tangles.

GETTING
over an infatuation

Well-to-do families have a ready prescription for their young people who get involved in unpromising affairs. They send the afflicted one for a trip abroad. The theory is that new sights and scenes, the exhilaration and excitement of a long journey will make the infatuation fade away. This remedy works in a large number of cases. For most of us the treatment would be too costly to consider, and we must find simpler and cheaper and more accessible ways of freeing ourselves from our emotional tangles. Keeping busy is one of the best policies when feelings are confused. It is when we idly brood over our troubles that they become more troublesome still.

Recreation in various forms gives real release of energy and feelings and is re-creating in a true sense. This is particularly true when it is enjoyed with other congenial people. The young man or woman trying to heal a broken heart will find that acting as though everything were all right, going out as usual, and going through the motions of having a good time often works in making the heart throbs less painful.

"Time heals all wounds," and the satirical twist, "Time wounds all heels," are a couple of mottoes that point to what we can count on in the future. It is true that most of these emotional involvements are outgrown as we become more mature. If we can be patient with ourselves, with life itself, and get busy at the main job of growing up, many of these wrinkles will iron themselves out in time.

JUST good friends through the years

Cynical fiction has made fun of lovers' becoming good friends. Yet it can be done. For the men and women who care about their homes, their future, their own real happiness and that of the people who mean most to them, this solution of the problem of wandering love is the most satisfactory that can be achieved. Real affection brings with it a great deal of sympathetic interest in the other's welfare and for other people generally. The outpouring of the spirit that comes with love under control can, if the persons care enough to work it out that way, be channeled in warm, diffused, general outlets that may lift the level of living for them and for all their contacts.

Many old-friends-of-the-family—close friends who stay through the years, always there, always interested, always available when needed—had their introduction in mutual attractions that might have wrecked both their lives had they not been wise enough to keep their feelings in broader channels. We need not laugh when a girl says she will be a sister to a boy who loves her intensely, whose deep love she cannot encourage. If he cares for her at all as a person, he too may learn the satisfaction of enjoying her comradeship, her friendship, her affectionate interest through the years, without the necessity of sexually focused love expressions.

Our society has done little to help us learn these more generalized friendship relations between the sexes. In fact, many of the songs and stories in popular circulation scoff at the possibility of fellowship between members of opposite sexes on anything other than a sex-love basis. This is one step forward in our own emotional education that most of us have to learn through actual experience with those we can trust. It is an endeavor well worth the effort. For it means the continuing of a sustaining friendship with congenial "special" people who otherwise would be entirely out of bounds as soon as marriage entered the picture for one or both of the friends.

This solution is achieved through a number of steps. First comes the realization that this love under a cloud cannot continue in its present direction. One or both of the persons may recognize this moment. Next comes the mutual sharing of concern about the relationship, definition of the values involved for one another and for all the other people concerned. This leads to some mutually developed insight on why the attraction developed in the first place. This step is often most helpful, since it can reveal parts of the personalities of the two persons that should be better understood for their future happiness and growth. Counseling is often particularly valuable at this point.

Finally comes the redefinition of the relationship as one in which they can be permanently comfortable as good friends, as congenial comrades, perhaps as friends of each other's families through the years, without the continued threat of the intense feelings that may have brought them together in the first place. This usually takes some face-to-face discussion of what is to be and what is not to be "in bounds" in their future friendship.

Working out such a permanent fellowship takes patience and understanding and a grown-up kind of real love that can withstand the little lapses and the strong tendencies that one or both of them may have to put the friendship on a more personal basis. But this kind of friendship is worth working for. It spells the difference between the man or woman who is afraid to become related to another fine, congenial person because of what might happen, and the outgoing adult who is not afraid of himself, or of life, or of others because his heart and life are big enough for real friendship and fine fellowship as long as he lives.

MANY
you love

Think of all the people that you love. To begin with, there are the members of your family. Then come all the friends of both sexes that you are fond of. Out beyond these are still others. Most people quite genuinely love their doctors, especially when they have been very sick. Many men and women are sincerely fond of their religious leaders. Down through the years hundreds of thousands of persons like yourself have loved great souls like Jane Addams and Gandhi. Millons more have learned to love the Christ. Love is nothing to be ashamed of as it fans out in so many different ways.

Love can be sweet and good if we let it be so. There is nothing to be afraid of in loving another person. As we grow older and more mature emotionally, we find that we are able to love with deep compassion all sorts of people who suffer, even though we may never see them. We may love honestly and warmly the many fine, lovable persons with whom we come in contact. These feelings need not frighten us. They are a part of the opening and outpouring of a soul rich in the fullness of living. Our tasks lie, not in rejecting our feelings or in refusing them expression, but rather in channeling them in ways that are constructive and healthful.

ETHICAL controls

Ethical controls must be learned in every area of life. One may be very hungry and yet not snatch the food from another's mouth. One may need money and yet restrain the impulse to rob a bank or pick a pocket. In growing up we learn to restrain these impulses for more dependable behavior. Love impulses come as "naturally" as hunger. A person may be strongly attracted to another without having to rush into an impetuous love affair. He accepts the feeling at the same time that he controls its expression. Maturing into genuine adulthood involves not only having the feelings that come with maturity but also developing the controls that make one a responsible person. In the same way that we learn not to kick another when we feel hostile, we must learn, too, not to caress just anybody any time we feel like it. Keeping love within bounds involves learning the ethical controls that are expected in our way of life.

LOVE
that blesses

Channeling love feelings is a learned art that takes years to develop to a fine point of genuine effectiveness. As we learn to love freely, and to accept others' affection easily and happily, we become less and less moved to make something of a chance bit of stray affection or attention. We find ourselves increasingly able to give the gifts and do the kindnesses that are within the sphere of acceptable behavior, and to move among others with the glow of being among kindred spirits.

Love is the greatest force on earth. We need it individually and as a world. Like other sources of power, it can destroy us if we do not deal with it constructively. Love can be felt as a spirit of real affection, in which we care for the other(s) as much as or more than we care for ourselves. We can concern ourselves not just with the pleasures of the moment, but with the lasting happiness of everyone involved. This is the love that lifts and enriches and blesses all whom it touches.

part TWO

YOUR

SEX

QUESTIONS

What do you

THE CHANCES ARE PRETTY GOOD that you know a great deal about the facts of life already. You have grown up at a time when movies, advertisements and other popular media deal with men, women, and sex quite openly. You are at an age when your own maturing is of central interest to you, and should be if you are to develop a sense of yourself that you can live with. You quite probably have talked with your classmates and friends about the relationships between men and women and where babies come from, as well as various sex problems that have come to your attention. Some of this sex talk probably was enlightening. Much of it may have been misleading, confusing, off-color, or simply not true. As much as anything else right now, you may be interested in a straightforward clarification of the facts of life that will satisfy your curiosity, allay your fears, and give you a clear sense of what it is all about and what to do about it.

National surveys of American young people indicate without question that the great majority of today's youth want to know more about sex. They want to get clear the

want to know?

basic facts of life. They want to understand their own sex feelings. They want to be reassured that what they are going through is normal. They are eager to understand how the two sexes differ physically, psychologically, emotionally, morally, spiritually. Most of all they are trying to learn the behavior that is appropriate for their age and their time. So if you have questions like these, you are no more curious than most other teen-agers these days.

PARENTS
and sex education

It is possible that you have been able to get reliable answers to your questions about life from your parents through the years. Long before you were school age, you probably asked about the differences between boys and girls, where you came from, and how you were born. As you grew up your questions became more personal, and may or may not have been answered to your complete satisfaction in your own family.

In a nationwide study of where parents think their children get their ideas about love and marriage, most of the mothers who responded said that they were glad to talk over intimate questions of life and love with their children at any time. But a considerable number volunteered the information that even though they thought they *ought* to discuss the facts of life with their children, they actually found that they were tongue-tied when confronted with their children's sex questions. Many of the mothers admitted being uncomfortable and uneasy in talking about the personal side of life with their own children. Some of them recognized that their embarrassment stemmed from their own inadequate sex education from their parents. As one mother put it, "In my growing-up years we just didn't ask. We simply guessed at answers and put two and two together on our own."

Young people today credit a somewhat larger percentage of parents as the source of their sex education than was true a generation ago, according to comparable studies of youth in the late 1930's and the early 1960's. When the American Youth Commission surveyed 13,528 representative young people in the study *Youth Tell Their Story,* published in 1938, some 30 per cent said that they had received most of their sex education from their parents. Surveys since 1960 have turned up around 40 per cent of the parents credited by their children for their sex education. Considerably more girls than boys say that they get their sex education in their own homes, in both the recent studies and those of more than twenty years ago. But few reported surveys have yet reported as many as half of the girls received their sex education from their parents.

DIFFICULT areas for parent-youth discussion

When Marvin Dubbé asked college freshmen what they found most difficult to discuss with their mothers and fathers, he discovered that the greatest reticence was in the intimate areas of life. Some 85 per cent said they could not discuss sex with their parents; 80 per cent named petting as impossible to talk over with their mothers and fathers. Love, courtship, and marriage were only slightly less difficult for these first-year college students to discuss with their own parents. One reason for the difficulty quite possibly may be that these young people felt that it was not necessary to talk over these areas of their lives with their families. Quite as likely a cause is the wall of silence that is built up between parents and youth in many homes over which it is not easy for either generation to climb, especially in the areas of more meaningful and emotionally explosive concern of both adults and youth.

Now when young people have more freedom in their relationships with each other, parents are more apt to disapprove of their behavior than was true in earlier times. Professor Koller finds that many more of today's mothers disapprove of their daughters' dates than was the case when mother was herself a girl, or than it was in grandmother's time. Mother's disapproval may itself be a block to communication with her sons and daughters through the teen years, unless something is done to encourage the generations to keep in touch with each other.

PARENT-youth panels

A promising approach to the problem of intergenerational contact is the parent-youth panel that is finding its way into many a community program. It is based upon the principle that some things are more easily said in a group than in the emotionally charged atmosphere of parent-child conflict. The process is a simple one. A group of young people and parents get together to thrash out some of the hot spots of their differences. To implement their discussion, articulate members of each generation are chosen to serve as a panel. The areas of greatest friction and disagreement in the community at the time are selected for the agenda. These may include such questions as hours for school parties to be over, the all-night prom, going steady, control of drinking at teen-age affairs, use of the automobile by dating couples, or whatever is an issue in that place at the moment.

An effective moderator is essential for the success of such a panel. His, or her, role is to encourage all the different points of view to be freely and completely aired, to keep the discussion rolling with the full participation of all panel members, to help the group as a whole have its say on any issues that are discussed, and to encourage the development of a consensus on those questions in which there is unanimous agreement, and of a clear statement of difference in those in which no immediate agreement is possible.

Some communities have formalized their specific statements of agreement in a Parent-Youth Code or similarly named document that is duplicated and circulated among families with teen-agers in the community. Sometimes the local paper publishes the code. In some communities it is printed in the high school print shop and distributed at the PTA meeting, with a further opportunity for discussing the items that are included.

The value of such a code is not only in the guide itself but also in the process of parents and young people airing their differences and getting through to each other. Either in the individual family or in the community at large, it helps to keep communication systems open, especially in the hard-to-discuss areas of life.

SEX
education in religious settings

Churches of all denominations and faiths agree that sex education is best done in a religious atmosphere. Some Christian churches and Jewish temples review the facts of life and the principles of morality with their confirmation classes, in recognition that youth wants to know and should be instructed about what it means to become men and women in the adult congregation.

The Roman Catholic church has Pre-Cana conferences for engaged couples. Many Protestant denominations encourage sex education and preparation for marriage as a part of their youth programs. Special series for teen-age boys and girls are offered in church camps, conferences, and local church programs from time to time. But the sum total of these offerings does not affect a large number of youth, according to national surveys. In 1938, only one per cent of the youth reported the church as the source of most of their sex education. Studies since 1960 find fewer than three per cent of today's youth crediting their religious leaders with their sex education. Scout leaders, doctors, nurses, and other responsible professional persons are of help to equally small percentages of today's teen-agers.

You may be one of the lucky few to have had a good course in school in sex education, family living, and the relationships between men and women in marriage and family life. You may have had a unit in Home Economics that helped you understand what it means to be a girl and what is expected of women in the home. Or, as a boy, you may have been helped by your coach or physical education instructor in learning more about yourself.

Some schools include education in growing up as a regular part of the curriculum through junior and senior high school. There are a few schools that have integrated programs from kindergarten through college in human growth and interpersonal relationships. Texts, films, models, and other resource materials are available for teachers who want to cover this kind of material.

When Oregon parents and teachers were polled as to whether the school should have sex education as part of its program, an overwhelming 95 per cent approval of such courses was registered, across the state.

The Golden Anniversary White House Conference on Children and Youth held in Washington in 1960 made a number of recommendations for schools to assume more responsibility along these lines:

> That family life courses, including preparation for marriage and parenthood, be instituted as an integral and major part of public education from elementary school through high school.
>
> That educational institutions and communities provide systematic training, with sound and practical materials, in the developmental changes and problems of early adolescence for all parents and future parents, as well as for physicians, teachers, and others who work with young people.
>
> That schools, religious institutions, youth-serving agencies, and all other community agencies co-operate to create a favorable atmosphere for understanding the dignity and sanctity of the role of sex in human relationships.

Unfortunately, up to this time, there has been very little increase in the number of young people who get what they need from the schools. In 1938, 8 per cent of the young people studied by the American Youth Commission gave the school as the source of their sex education. Since 1960, studies have found about the same small percentage of teen-agers crediting either teachers or school counselors with teaching them what they need to know about themselves and each other in these areas of central concern.

Since sex is such an explosive subject, many teachers are afraid to handle it forthrightly. School administrators fear public disapproval of such courses and report the difficulty of finding adequately prepared teachers to handle the more sensitive areas of adolescent interest in the relationships between the sexes.

The result is that although many educators are aware of student needs in this area, few schools offer effective programs. All too many dodge the major issues completely. One community reporting promiscuity among its junior high school youngsters and an unprecedented number of unwed mothers in the senior high, asked an authority in this field to come and give "a nice little talk to the girls about families, but don't mention sex."

Until parents and young people can convince their principals and superintendents of schools that they want effective sex education made available for all the community's children, few teachers will have the courage to risk their jobs and reputations in trying to be as competent in this field as they are expected to be in other subjects.

OTHER
children as sex educators

When we asked PTA members across the country where they thought their children were getting their ideas about love and marriage, 22 per cent of them mentioned other children as their sons' and daughters' sources of information. Some of these influences were considered good, and many were not so good. Good or bad, these parents recognized the importance of other children in introducing ideas, attitudes, and feelings about sex to their children.

Youth themselves, in even greater percentages, name their peers as the major source of their sex education. In the 1938 American Youth Commission study, 66 per cent of the boys and 40 per cent of the girls said that they got most of their information about sex from people their own age. Studies in more recent years have found between one-third and one-half of both boys and girls naming friends their age as their chief source of sex education.

The unfortunate thing about other children as sex educators is the nature of the "education." Those boys and girls who talk most about sex are apt to be those whose knowledge about it is incomplete. Their interest in and preoccupation with sex often indicates a poor orientation as to what it is all about. The dirty story or the off-color joke is a distorted introduction to the facts of life. With few facts to guide one, thinking gets twisted, and feelings are confused, until one is worse off than ever the more "gutter talk" one hears.

The young person who wants to get facts straight and clean, goes to a wholesome source for his knowledge. He does not have to resort to snorts and snickers with his friends for the crumbs of information he can get. He talks things over man to man with a respected adult, or he gets a good book and "does his homework" for himself.

BOOKS
on the facts of life

There has been an encouraging increase in the percentage of young people who get their sex education from books and other reading material. In 1938, only one in twenty-five representative American young people named books as the source of their sex education. Studies since 1960 have found one of every three boys and one out of four girls saying that they got most of their sex education from reading they had done.

One reason why such a real increase in reading as a source of sex education is noted within recent decades is the number of clear, factual books that have become available on the facts of life for young people. A generation and more ago, a young person had a hard time digging out of dictionaries and medical books what he wanted to know about himself and the processes of growing up, falling in love, getting married, and becoming a parent. Now, there are a number of books that clearly answer young people's questions about these things in good, wholesome ways.

Parents who themselves are too uncomfortable with their teen-agers' questions can now put a good book out where their sons and daughters will be sure to find it. Sometimes, their youngsters are pleased to find Mother or Dad interested in such things, and discussions blossom over a jointly read passage. Parent-youth panels may use sections of such a volume as starting points for their considerations. There are teen-agers who put such a book into their parents' hands as an introduction to the questions and concerns that youth and adult may have been avoiding. The written word is objective and speaks for many persons, and so is acceptable where a more personally intimate tête-a-tête might not be.

Teachers who care about their students make it a practice to provide a variety of reference materials to supplement whatever texts are being used in the courses they teach. Librarians stock such materials for the use of responsible students in school and community. Church school libraries, conference and camp book tables, and religious presses abound in just this kind of material these days.

YOU
do not have to guess

There was a time when very little was known about the facts of life, and the processes that lead to marriage and family life. Then a person had to guess what it was all about, or to take without question some of the old wives' tales that may or may not have been based upon reality.

Fortunately for you, a great deal now is known about how human beings are conceived, born, grow, mature, and live through their lives as men or women. In recent generations there have been great advances in the biological and medical sciences that tell us about the physiological processes of growing up and functioning as men and women, husbands and wives, fathers and mothers.

Advances in the social sciences tell us even more about the ways in which we behave as members of families and of other groups in our society. Social science research and clinical evidence have broadened and deepened our understandings of the ways in which we find our friends, function in groups, go on dates, find particular persons attractive, get serious about certain special individuals, fall in love, marry, and work out the many relationships we share with other people in our lives. It is upon these biological and social scientific findings that materials in this volume are based.

There is nothing wrong in wanting to know about life and your part in it. If you have questions about your own development, your feelings, and your relationships with the people who are important to you, you are showing normal intelligence about the development that is expected in persons of your age.

There is nothing to be ashamed of in wondering about sex and its many manifestations in life around you. When you raise questions about mathematics or science or history, adults around you quite probably are pleased with your interest and go out of their way to encourage you to learn all you can about these subjects. If adults clam up and do little to try to answer your questions about the development of human beings and their mature relationships with each other as men and women, their silence simply means that these are things about which they themselves are not completely comfortable.

You are fortunate if you have responsible adults in your own family, school, or church with whom you can discuss the facts of life and what they mean for persons like yourself. You may be lucky enough to find yourself in a group of boys and girls or parents and youth who are exploring some of the areas of personal and social confusion with candor. You may be one of the many young people who occasionally joke with friends about things that you pretend to understand much better than you really do.

You quite possibly picked up a book like this in the hope that it would spell out for you many things about which you are not sure and take up one by one the questions that are normal and to be expected at your time of life. Lots of the material in the chapters that follow you already know. For you these sections will be in the nature of a review and a chance to reassure yourself that what you thought was so, actually is.

If something is discussed that you have not known before, that is all to the good. For now you know, and who is going to guess that you have not known all along?

What
happens
as girls

become women?

MATURING IS A PROCESS THAT takes place over a period of years. It is not a matter of being a little girl one day and a grown woman the next. The changes come so gradually that even a girl herself may not be aware of some of the earlier stages of her growing up.

VARIATIONS
in maturing

The age at which a girl begins to mature depends upon the individual. Some girls begin to show definite signs of growing up early in the third or fourth grade. Others may still be "little girls" when they reach high school. Many girls in this country have begun to look and act very much like young women before they reach their teens. Studies have shown that the majority of girls in grade-school graduating classes are already growing into womanhood.

Some girls mature very early and begin menstruating when they are only nine or ten years of age. Other girls may be so late in starting their growing up that they do not menstruate until they are fifteen or sixteen. Such widely varying ages are normal, and the age of growing up is not important except in the way girls and their families and friends feel about it.

Early-maturing girls who grow up quickly face some handicaps. Just because they look big, they often find that more is expected of them than of some little girl who may be the same age but who looks much younger. Growing up before the others of one's age and grade imposes the additional difficulty of not having one's friends quite ready to share one's new interests and activities with her.

Research studies of what girls growing up are interested in show that those girls who are already well into their maturing process are much more interested in grown-up matters like relationships with boys, hairdo's, fashions, and love stories than are the girls of the same age who are not yet very far into their process of maturing. This means that the early-maturing girl is ready for dates and fun with boys and dressing up and acting like a young woman before her friends are.

The late-maturing girl finds that many of her classmates are already dating when she begins to be interested in boys. She may not think that this is an advantage, but it often is. The girl who does not become overly interested in boys too soon may have a chance to learn about a wide variety of things that the boy-crazy girl misses. She may do better in her school work and go on for more education than her early-maturing sister gets. Most important of all, she has more time in which to find herself, to discover the kind of person she is and what she wants to make of her life. Such a girl gets a chance to develop a sense of her own identity as a person before she settles down into domesticity.

A timetable of girls' development

Just as there is no one time at which all girls start to develop, so there is no one month or year at which all girls are completely mature. The length of time spent in the process of growing up varies widely among girls, yet eventually almost all emerge as grown women ready to fall in love, marry, and have families of their own.

Generally speaking, larger, well-nourished girls tend to start growing up earlier and to complete their maturing before their smaller sisters do. This does not hold, however, for the girl who has a tendency to be fat, for her development is usually slower and later that that of heavier girls.

Yet for all girls, regardless of when they start, how fast they grow, and when they round out their maturing, there is a regular sequence of growth changes that can be predicted. It is as though each girl were a train making a scheduled run between two points—girlhood through to womanhood. One may be an express train and rush through in record time, reaching womanhood long before her more slowly moving friends. Another girl, quite as normal, may stop for a while at various stations along the way, and not move so rapidly even between stations.

PUBERTY

Research has shown that both the slowly maturing and the fast-growing girl pass through the same general sequence of growth changes in this "run" of physical maturing called *puberty* (pew'-bur-tee). Puberty may be defined as that period of rapid physical development that marks the end of childhood and the beginning of maturation.

THE
sequence of changes in puberty

AN initial slowing down

The first sign of a girl's growing up is, paradoxically, a slowing down of her physical growth. Perhaps she has had her height measured on the doorjamb every birthday since she was a little girl. When she was very small, at two and three and four and five, the intervals of growth in height between birthdays were quite long and she noted proudly "how fast she was shooting up." From the time she started to school, somewhere around her sixth birthday, she grew about the same amount every year for two or three years, more or less. Then somewhere around her tenth birthday (or earlier or later depending upon the girl) there came a time when she noticed that she had grown hardly at all for six months to a year or more. Perhaps her mother worried and suggested her taking a tonic or eating more for breakfast. What was probably happening was that she was in the initial slowing down which is the first indication that she is about to develop into womanhood. It is as though nature now slows down her activities in order to make the mighty burst of speed in growth that is just ahead.

THE pubertal growth spurt in girls

Even before a girl begins to menstruate, she gains rapidly in height and weight. Within a year or two she may become as tall as her mother. The first growth is in the long bones of her body. Her legs lengthen, her arms stretch out of her sleeves. Her feet and hands get big. This stretching *up* period is the beginning of the growth spurt at puberty.

Next comes the filling *out* period when the girl's body rounds into the full figure of womanhood. Her face acquires more grown-up lines. Arms and legs round into curves, replacing the straight lines of little girlhood. Most dramatic of all are the changes in her body as the breasts develop and the hips widen.

BREASTS and brassieres

Breast development is apparent quite early in the girl's maturing. As her breasts become larger and fuller a girl is sometimes sensitive about such obvious signs of growing up. For a short time she may want to avoid tight dresses that reveal the new lines of her developing bust. Fortunately many girls are proud of these signs of growing up and learn to wear clothes that enhance rather than play down the ripening lines of maturity. Some girls, impatient with the course of nature, add to the curves of the breasts by using what are popularly known as "falsies"—padded forms that fit over the breasts and make them appear fuller than they really are. If a girl is concerned about her breast development, she will do well to consult her doctor rather than resort too quickly and uneasily to makeshifts. Given time enough, nature usually endows a girl with the fullness of womanhood that is suitable for her.

Selecting brassières that give some support without being uncomfortably binding is relatively easy these days. Bras come in many sizes, measured in inches around the largest circumference of the bust; for example, 30, 32, 34, 36 are popular sizes. The bra should fit snugly without feeling tight when a girl breathes, laughs, or bends over. The fullness of the breast is accommodated by varying cup sizes of brassières. The A cup is for the small breast, the B cup for the medium breast, the C cup for the full breast, and the D cup for the very rounded breast. Many textiles and styles are available, from the sheerest nets and laces to the heavier fabrics. Some uplift quality is usually desired. Easy washability is imperative. Straps which have a strip of elastic at front or back usually wear better, without pulling out, than those with fixed, inflexible ends. The same holds for the fastenings at the back. A piece of elastic at least an inch or two in length adds considerably to both the comfort and the wearing quality of the garment.

HIPS and girdles

As a girl's hips broaden into mature lines, it becomes possible to wear a skirt, as is not feasible on the thin straight lines of the little girl. The skirt so popular with high school girls literally hangs from the top of the pelvic bones and is held up because of the difference between the circumference of her waist and of her hips.

Some girls become self-conscious about the fullness of their abdomens and may wear girdles to hide the roundness of the "tummy." This is rarely necessary except with certain extreme styles or under a doctor's orders. It is better to flatten the abdomen by strengthening the abdominal muscles than by depending upon external support. Part of the pleasure derived from wearing foundation garments, such as elastic "panty girdles," is that they give a girl such a grown-up feeling. As long as they are not unduly restrictive, such garments do no harm. They should be selected, however, from those types and fabrics which can be easily laundered, since they need fully as frequent washing as do other underthings.

SKIN troubles and care

One big change that comes with growing up is in the nature and functioning of the skin. Oil and sweat glands become excessively active now. And the odors of the mature body are more pronounced than those in children. This means that girls must learn new ways of caring for their maturing skin to keep themselves, clean, sweet, and attractive.

Excessive secretion from the oil glands, especially of the nose and other parts of the face, may accumulate into a little hard pellet with a grimy top, known as a blackhead. When the pores become infected and filled with pus they are called pimples. These skin troubles, so common in adolescence, are known among doctors as *acne* (ack'nee).

The best means of avoiding or clearing up such conditions in their usual forms is plenty of warm water, soap, and a clean washcloth. It is not enough to throw a little cold water on the face night and morning or to use a cool, wet cloth lightly. Now, when oily secretions mingle with the dust and soil from the outside, it takes warm soapy water and conscientious washing to keep the face clean. A girl whose skin does not respond to careful cleansing but remains blotchy or broken out should consult her school nurse or family doctor.

Hair now needs more frequent shampooing than it did when the girl was little. The oil glands on the scalp, designed to give the woman's hair the gloss that can be so attractive, often secrete more oil than is needed and make the hair anything but pleasant. Greasy, stringy hair left too long without washing not only looks dirty; it smells unpleasant and is hard to manage. Girls growing into womanhood learn that frequent hair brushing and shampooing help greatly to give them the "crown of glory" that women have always cherished.

Body odors, now more evident, need attention too. It is necessary to make sure that certain parts of the body, especially under the arms and between the legs, get a warm, soapy bath every day, even when an all-over bath is not possible.

But a sponge or tub bath or shower does not give complete protection from unpleasant odors all day long. It is good practice, therefore, to use a mild deodorant under both arms immediately after washing. Among the many good deodorants on the market, the best one for you is one that keeps you smelling sweet between baths, does not stain your dresses or sweaters, and above all does not irritate your armpits. A little experimenting among the more common brands will help you to choose a deodorant that is safe, effective, easy to use, and not too expensive.

THE appearance of grown-up hair

One of the early signs of growing up is the appearance of hair in places on the body where childish down grew in girlhood. These new hair patterns occur under the arms (*axillary* [ak'si-le-ree] hair), between the thighs in the pelvic region (*pubic* [pew'-bik] hair), and on the legs. As the girl matures, the hair in these places becomes thicker and darker, and eventually when she is well into puberty it curls in an unmistakable kink.

The hair under the arms often shows when girls wear short-sleeved blouses, bathing suits, or formal dresses, so most girls keep it shaved off. There are many *depilatories* (dee-pil'ah-tor-eez) (hair removers) on the market; some are effective and safe, and others cause soreness to sensitive skin areas. Girls usually find that a safety razor or an electric shaver is effective in removing the hair not only from under the arms but also from the legs. Regular shaving under the arms or on the legs does *not* make the hair grow coarser, as was formerly thought, but simply makes the hair feel "bristly" when it is not kept closely shaved. If the hair on the legs is not profuse enough to show, it may be wise to let it be, since infrequent shaving will result in hair ends that stick out through hose.

Pubic hair first appears as a few scattered dark, straight hairs, then in a thicker mass of coarse, dark hair in a somewhat tangled curl. In women this hair is in the characteristic pattern of a triangle low in the front of her abdomen, with the straight edge of the triangle up and the point downward between the thighs. Since pubic hair does not interfere with a girl's usual activities, it is usually left alone except for careful washing.

WOMAN'S
monthly cycle

The most dramatic of all the changes in the pubertal development of girls comes at the peak of their growth spurt when they begin to have periodic menstrual periods, or menses, or "monthlies," as they are sometimes called. Because *menstruation* (men-strew-ay'shun) is so important, and tied in with so much that is uniquely womanly, let us discuss it in some detail.

WHAT menstruation is

Menstruation is the normal, periodic appearance of a bloody discharge from the genitals in maturing or grown-up

What Happens as Girls Become Women?   93

PLATE I   *The Endocrine Glands*

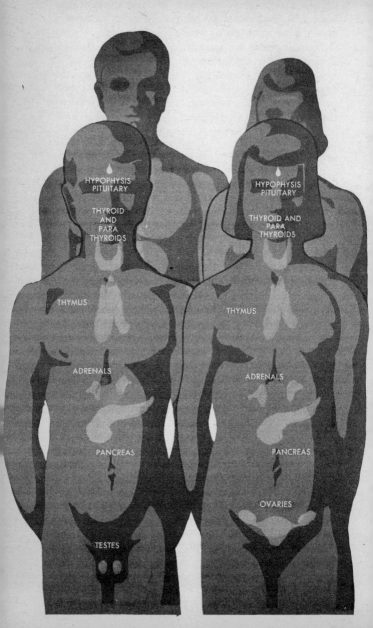

women. It first occurs in girls somewhere between their tenth and seventeenth birthdays. It begins to disappear when a woman reaches her change of life, or *menopause* (men′-o-paws) sometime in her forties. It is closely related to woman's ability to bear children, as described in detail in the following paragraphs.

HOW ovaries function

Deep in the lower pelvis of a girl or woman are two small organs called *ovaries* (o′-va-reez). These organs, about the size and shape of almonds, have two functions. One function of the ovaries is to produce the female sex hormones that make a girl a woman and maintain her womanliness throughout her life. This function lies dormant during girlhood. At the beginning of puberty the ovaries are stimulated by the "master switch," the *pituitary* (pi-tew′-it-err-ee) gland, which lies at the base of the brain almost in the middle of the head. With the increased secretion of the hormones from the pituitary and the ovaries, all the changes characteristic of womanhood begin to take place: the growth spurt, the adult hair forms, the rounding out of the body, the maturing reproductive organs, and, of course, menstruation.

The second function of the ovaries is the production of ripened egg cells. These appear, one each month approximately, throughout the woman's life from puberty to menopause, when the ovaries gradually cease functioning. The human *ovum* (o′vum), as the egg or female cell is called, is so tiny as to be practically invisible except under a microscope. It is not at all like the egg you had for breakfast except, of course, in its ability to produce a human baby in the same way that the hen's egg might have produced a baby chick. Like the hen's egg, too, the human ovum only rarely gets to grow into a baby.

OVULATION

This process of giving off a ripened human egg, or ovum, is called *ovulation* (o-vu-lay′-shun). It occurs in the mid-

ALL PLATES *Museum of Science and Industry, Chicago*
PHOTOS *by Vories Fisher*

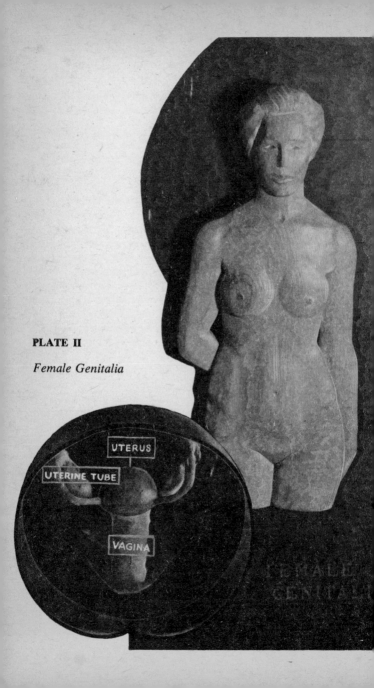

PLATE II

Female Genitalia

dle of the menstrual month, about halfway between the menstrual periods. Since the egg is so tiny and since it is released up inside the girl's body, there is no practical way by which a girl may know just when she is ovulating. Usually there is no pain, no fluid released, no sensation at all accompanying ovulation.

As you know, all mammals have two parents. Most of the plants, animals, birds, and fishes—trees, cats, cows, horses, dogs, canaries, goldfish and all the rest—as well as people must have fathers as well as mothers. The egg from the mother must be fertilized by the sperm cell from the father in order for reproduction to take place. Fertilization occurs in various ways in the different species. In all of them it is most delicately arranged.

In the human being, the ripened egg is released from the ovary deep in the lower abdomen. Only one tiny egg is produced at a time (except in one kind of twinning, as we shall see later). Since it is very important that the egg not get lost and that it have a chance to come into close contact with any sperm cells that may be available, it is caught up in the funnel-like end of one of the *Fallopian* (fa-low'-pee-an), or *uterine* (yoo'-ter-in) *tubes,* one of which lies near each ovary on either side of the lower abdomen. The egg moves down this tube into the uterus.

THE uterus or womb

The *uterus* (yoo'-ter-us) is a pear-shaped organ a little smaller than a fist. It hangs in the midline of the lower pelvic cavity with its large end upward and the smaller neck, or cervix, downward. The uterus is the muscular organ in which the baby grows and is sometimes called the womb. On the inside of the uterus or *womb* (woom), is a soft, cushiony lining called the *endometrium* (en-doe-mee'-tree-um), which thickens and fills with blood whenever a ripe ovum is expected.

If there are live sperm cells in the uterine tubes while a ripe ovum is there, one of the sperms may enter the egg, thus fertilizing it. This process of sperm-and-egg's uniting is called *conception* (kon-sep'-shun), or *fertilization.*

An egg must be fertilized if there is to be a baby. The fertilized egg then moves down through the remainder of

PLATE III

The Menstrual Cycle

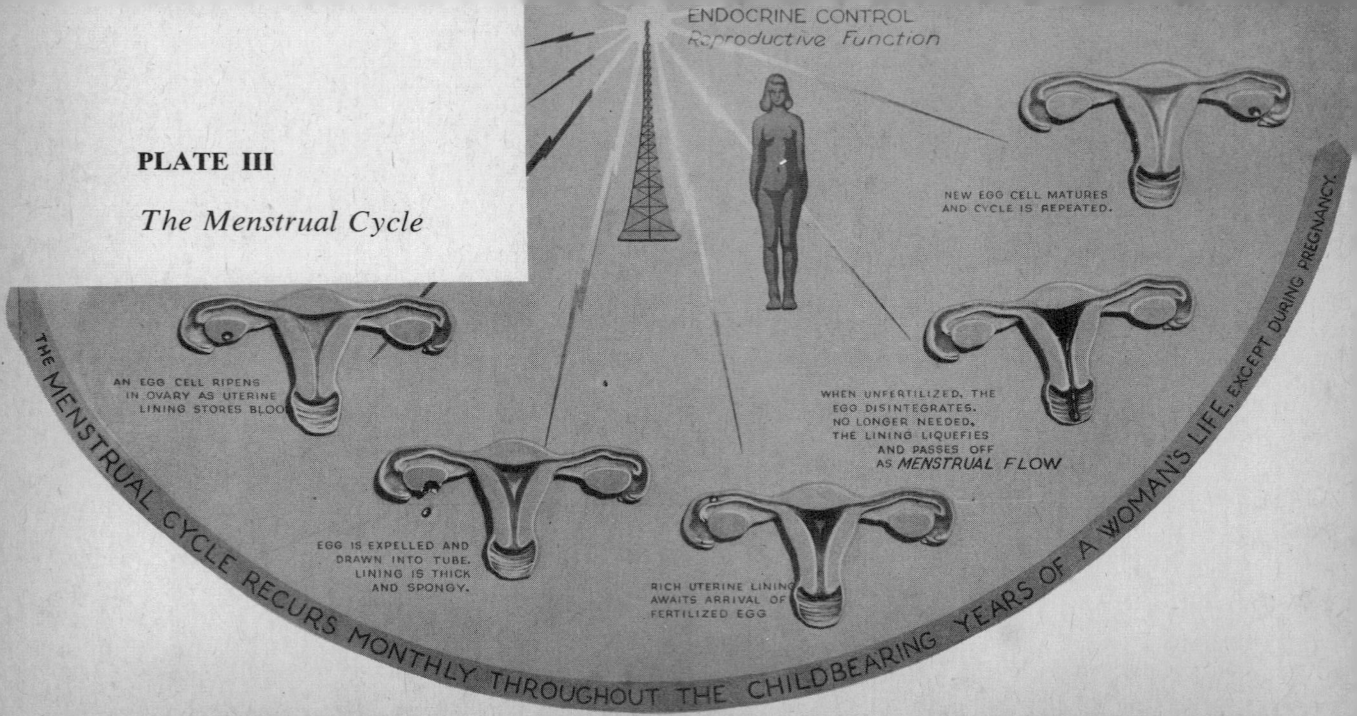

ENDOCRINE CONTROL
Reproductive Function

THE MENSTRUAL CYCLE RECURS MONTHLY THROUGHOUT THE CHILDBEARING YEARS OF A WOMAN'S LIFE, EXCEPT DURING PREGNANCY.

AN EGG CELL RIPENS IN OVARY AS UTERINE LINING STORES BLOOD.

EGG IS EXPELLED AND DRAWN INTO TUBE. LINING IS THICK AND SPONGY.

RICH UTERINE LINING AWAITS ARRIVAL OF FERTILIZED EGG.

WHEN UNFERTILIZED, THE EGG DISINTEGRATES, NO LONGER NEEDED, THE LINING LIQUEFIES AND PASSES OFF AS *MENSTRUAL FLOW*

NEW EGG CELL MATURES AND CYCLE IS REPEATED.

the Fallopian tube and becomes imbedded in the nourishing lining of the uterus. There the *embryo* (em'-bree-o), as the fertilized egg now is called, grows for nine months or so, finally to be born as a new baby.

Most of the time, of course, there would not be sperm cells in the Fallopian tubes. In order for sperm cells to be up in the woman's tubes, she must have recently experienced sex intercourse in which there was no interference with the sperms' journey up out of her vagina into the uterus and tubes.

The *vagina* (va-ji'-nah) is that part of the woman's reproductive tract that opens to the outside of her body. Its entrance is in the pubic region between the opening of the urethra and the anus, in a separate opening of its own. It lies between two sets of folds, sensitive to touch, called the lips, or *vulva* (vul'-vah). The vagina is a soft, flexible, sleevelike tube which stretches easily both in length and in diameter. It serves both as the woman's organ for sex intercourse and as the channel through which the baby is born.

Before a girl marries and begins to have sex intercourse, there is often a cufflike membrane, partially closing the lower end of the vagina. This is called the *hymen* (hi'-men) or, as people sometimes say, "maidenhead." It is just a fold of membrane that can be stretched, so that it is not a barrier to sex relations when the woman is ready to marry. It is wise to go to a physician for a premarital examination before marriage in order to make sure about the hymen and to prepare adequately for the other aspects of physical adjustment in marriage.

If the egg enters the Fallopian tube when there are no sperms present, which is most of the time, it is not fertilized. Since it cannot grow into a baby, it dies. The uterus, however, has been getting itself ready for nourishing an embryo ever since the egg began to ripen. Now it has a lining gorged with the extra blood supply ready to feed a baby-in-the-making. Since conception did not take place, the special preparations serve no purpose. Consequently, a small portion of the inner lining is shed, and the blood vessels lose a little of the blood that was to have nourished the growing embryo. This mucous material and blood makes up the menstrual flow.

OVULATION, then menstruation, alternating

These two functions, ovulation and menstruation, occur in turn every month. An ovum ripens and is discharged, and two weeks later, more or less, menstruation begins. If we count the first day of menstruation the first day of the menstrual cycle, then ovulation may be expected to take place somewhere near the middle of the cycle at about the fourteenth day. Menstruation may be expected to begin again at about the twenty-eighth day of the cycle. It is not always as regular as this sounds, even in a mature woman, and in young girls just beginning to menstruate, irregularity in the monthly cycle is not at all uncommon.

MENSTRUAL regularity

All sorts of things may upset the regular rhythm of the menstrual cycle. A cold in the head, being chilled through, getting emotionally upset, going through some exceedingly exciting experience—any of these may delay or hurry a period. It is nothing to worry about. After menstruating a year or more, most girls find that their periods establish themselves in a way that is fairly predictable. Regularity may be expected to come with maturity.

Menstrual periods usually occur every twenty-eight days or so. Just as normally, however, some girls menstruate every twenty-six, or every thirty or thirty-two days. By keeping a personal calendar in which the first and last days of each menstrual period are checked, a girl can keep track of the length of her monthly cycle as well as the duration of the individual periods. It is wise to do this, so that planning for special activities may be arranged at times of the month when the menstrual period will not interfere.

THE menstrual flow

The amount of blood and mucous discharged in the menstrual flow differs a great deal from girl to girl. Some girls menstruate just two or three days. Others menstruate a week or more at a time. Usually a girl menstruates four or five days. The flow starts with a pinkish bloody discharge, which darkens and becomes more profuse at the end of the first or the beginning of the second day of menstruation. From then it tapers off until, in the last day or so, the flow may be only a show of blood. Actually that word "flow" is a misnomer, since only a few tablespoons are discharged. The discharge develops an unpleasant odor as it accumulates outside the body. This calls for changing the menstrual pad often enough to keep it from becoming smelly or so moist that it may chafe. Dusting a little deodorant powder on the clean pad helps to keep it sweet. When it is all right to use tampons, external discomfort and unpleasantness are avoided.

NAPKINS or tampons

Modern girls are fortunate in having neat disposable materials for menstrual use. Women used to have special cloths or "napkins" which had to be washed between wearings and which were far less convenient than the disposable menstrual pads so much in use today. Many reliable, comfortable, and inexpensive pads are available. A good menstrual pad should be thick enough to give protection, soft and comfortable, especially at the edges, and easy to put on and take off. They are much less expensive bought by the box than individually although, of course, the individual dispenser is a convenience when the period starts before it is expected.

Menstrual pads are usually fastened to a special little belt that holds them securely in place. The menstrual belt (or sanitary belt as it is sometimes called) should be elastic, so that it will fit snugly without being too tight around the waist or abdomen, and should have fasteners that are handy and unbreakable. Safety pins are sometimes used to fasten the pad to the belt. Even more effective and comfortable are the patented fasteners of plastic or metal.

Tampons are small rolls of highly absorbent material which can be pushed up into the vagina to soak up the menstrual flow. They are a great convenience in that they are up out of the way, do not bulge under bathing suits or sheer dresses, do not feel uncomfortable, and do not chafe or smell as soiled pads may.

Tampons may not give complete protection from spotting when the flow is particularly heavy. Furthermore, some people feel that tampons should not be used by unmarried girls. A girl who wants to find out whether it is all right for her to use these internal methods of protection may consult her doctor, who will advise what seems best for the individual girl.

SAYINGS about menstruation that are not so

There are so many old wives' tales about menstruation that it takes a smart girl to know just what isn't so. Some of the more ridiculous of these weird superstitions that still persist, in spite of all science and experience to the contrary, are listed here.

Old Wives' Tales	*The Fact Is, Science Says*
Menstruation is an illness.	Menstruation is a normal, natural function.
Go to bed when you menstruate.	Decrease more strenuous activities the first day or so.
If you shampoo your hair while you are menstruating, it will stop your flow.	Just be careful not to get chilled during your period.
Don't drink cold water while you are menstruating.	Drink all the water you want, any time.
You mustn't take a bath while you are menstruating.	Wash and bathe more frequently during your period, so you'll feel sweet and clean.
Menstrual blood is "bad blood."	Menstrual blood is as good as any you have in your veins.
Loss of menstrual blood weakens a girl.	There is actually an oozing of only a few spoonfuls at each period — not anywhere nearly enough to weaken a girl.
Plants tended by a menstruating girl wither and die.	Of course not. What could menstruation have to do with your gardening ability?
Milk poured by a menstruating woman will sour.	All milk sours in time, but menstruation has nothing to do with it.

You will hear many more bits of advice and folklore about menstruation. Some of them are definitely not so and never have been. You will be wise not to believe any of them until you have checked their truth with your doctor or someone else who knows about these things.

Yes, let's face it, there is sometimes some discomfort at menstrual time. A girl's breasts may become sensitive and her emotions may be more unstable just before her menstrual period, as she experiences what is known as "premenstrual tension." There may be a nagging little backache just before the period starts, often accompanied by a dragging, heavy feeling in the lower abdomen. Occasionally there are pains that girls speak of as "cramps." All of these are relatively normal symptoms of the beginning of menstruation. Any of these discomforts are made worse by feeling sorry for oneself, being scared, or dramatizing one's condition. Menstruation is a universal thing among women. It is perfectly normal. It need not be unpleasant when the woman has learned how to take care of herself both physically and emotionally.

As the time for your period draws near, let up just a little in your more strenuous activities (no ten-mile hikes, or twenty-mile canters, or marathon rollerskating just then, thank you) but keep a normal schedule of rest, exercise, work, and play. Try to get a good night's sleep just before and after the first day of the period. Avoid anything that will chill you through and through: ice-cold showers, being out unprotected in the rain, or sitting with wet feet through class after class, or staying in swimming overlong.

During your period, take more care than usual to keep clean. A warm bath, a quick sponge-off under the arms and in the pubic region at least once a day between baths with soap and warm water, followed by your usual deodorant, will allay even the most persistent odors (your sweat and oil glands are apt to be more active now too, ever notice?). If your hair needs shampooing, wash it. Just be reasonably careful to dry it in a warm room, out of drafts, where you won't get chilled.

What you eat is important, too. If you are constipated, the heavy large intestine may add to the congestion and feeling of "fullness" in your lower pelvis. Take more than the usual amount of liquids, especially milk and fruit juices, plenty of salads, fruits, vegetables; ease up on heavy, rich, starchy things. This will not only help you to feel better but quite possibly will help you to keep your complexion looking better, too.

Above all, be glad that you are a girl and don't start feeling sorry for yourself. You'd be a lot sorrier if you never did menstruate, but remained without the normal manifestations of being a growing-up and grown-up woman. Perk yourself up when a period is on its way. Dress just a little more prettily than usual. Walk as though you loved life. Hum a little tune to yourself. Smile a little wider than usual. Go out of your way to be pleasant to others. Before you know it, you'll have yourself convinced that you really do feel glad to be alive, and YOU.

Of course, if you really are laid low, if you "can't stand the pain," if you can't drag yourself out of bed, then something is the matter in the way either your body or your mind is taking this menstruating business, and it will be wise to consult a doctor in whom you have confidence. He may prescribe some exercises to prevent or lessen the pain. Quite possibly he'll try to help you feel a little happier about being a woman. Way down deep, you may be resenting being a girl or you may be rebelling against getting grown up, and this may be what makes you feel so miserable. Doctors today are wise to see that how we feel about things is quite as important as the thing itself. Our minds affect our bodies more than we know in things like this.

LEARNING
to be a woman

Girls are born female. Nature endows girls with the physical potentialities of becoming women. The basic physical characteristics that make girls forever different from boys and women different from men, that make it possible for a girl to menstruate, to marry, and to have children of her own—these things are her essential *femaleness.*

Femininity, on the other hand, is learned. Most of what goes into making a woman act and behave and feel like a woman is learned as she grows up—as a little girl, as a budding young woman, and as the mature, full-grown woman. Learning to love and be loved, for instance, is part of growing up (and it is mighty nice, too!). Learning to enjoy boys as persons, to like men without being afraid of them on the one hand or being too overwhelmed by them on the other, learning to enjoy the fine arts of being a real woman, with all the satisfactions and challenges that lie before women today—these skills are important, and they are for you to learn.

These tasks of growing up go on through the teen years in a complexity of bewilderments, try-outs, and practicing. New ventures into ideas, into activities, into new relationships, cause one to ask, "How did I do?" "How can I be better next time?" "What does this mean?" "How important is this for me?" Such self-ratings can become confusing. You can easily get lost in tangled thoughts that go around and around and lead nowhere. This confused mental state is often responsible for the moodiness of youth. You want to be alone, to feel, to think through your own feelings. To the family or friends you may seem blue and morose and secretive. But you can be assured that it takes time and patience and working on to be a full-fledged woman. And what is more worth your best efforts right now?

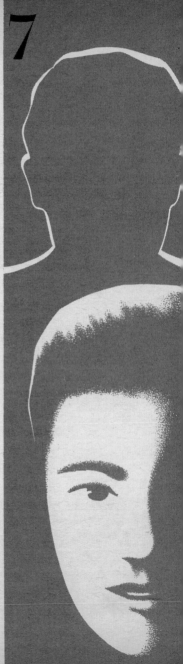

CHAPTER 7

*How
do boys
grow
up to
be men?*

IT IS SOMETIMES HARD FOR BOYS to get all the facts about physical maturity. A boy who wants straight answers may find it difficult even to ask the questions he is wondering about. He discovers that many adults cannot talk frankly about these things, perhaps because they too were always just supposed to know. Some modern dads and mothers make a real effort to explain the facts of life to their boys and girls. Even then a boy sometimes feels embarrassed in bringing up certain questions, because he assumes that he either should have known the answers long ago or shouldn't have asked them yet. There comes a time, too, when he wants to checks his facts and get some outsider's version. This is normal and is to be expected.

Of course, boys talk it over with each other, but even that effort is not completely satisfactory. The stories that boys of one's own age tell are apt to be full of implications and innuendos. Maybe a boy sees through them and maybe he doesn't. Then, too, the other boys usually do not have all the facts straight. There are so many superstitions and half-truths that before a fellow knows it, he has swallowed a lot of stuff that just isn't true. So the time has come to go over the main outline of what happens when a boy becomes a man, what the various changes mean, and—most important of all—what a boy can do to assure his emerging into full manhood with the ideas and habits and feelings of an adult.

WHAT
makes boys men?

At the moment in which you were conceived, about nine months before you were born, you started down the path to manhood that you have followed ever since. Your father's sperm cast the deciding vote that made you a boy, with all the potentialities of becoming a man. Way back then began the development of the special organs of reproduction that will someday make it possible for you, too, to be a father.

TESTES do double duty

The key to your maleness is the pair of *testes* (tes'-teez), or *testicles* (tes'-ti-kls), that hang in a sac from the lower end of the abdomen. These two oval bodies, each usually less than two inches long and one slightly larger than the other, are the manufacturing plants for all the millions of sperm cells that will be produced through maturity. In the yards of tiny tubules (approximately one-half mile of them!) compactly arranged within each testis, develop the ten to thirty billions of *spermatozoa* (spur-ma-toe-zo′-ah) that are produced monthly in the normal male. Each of these tiny sperm cells contains within its body, or head, the entire endowment that heredity may pass on to a possible child of yours. Each microscopic sperm is equipped with a hairlike tail that is capable of propelling that sperm over a considerable distance of moist tissue. Those boys fortunate enough to have had classes in biology or to have had access to a miscroscope have perhaps seen the motion of the thousands of spermatozoa in a single droplet of fresh semen. The production of these swarming hordes of spermatozoa, from the time a boy first matures until he is quite an old man, is one function of the testes.

The other big contribution of the testes is the secretion of the male hormones that make and keep a fellow a man. All the changes that take place at puberty and that are characteristics of a full-grown man come about because of the action of the special fluids produced by and released from the testes throughout life until old age. These hormones have little direct connection with the production of sperms, as it was formerly thought. They go right on being released directly into the blood stream regardless of how little or how much active sex life a man has. Our grandfathers feared that the loss of *semen* (see′-men), the fluid which contains the spermatozoa, somehow meant the loss of manhood. Fortunately this is just not so. The active hormones essential for his maleness are not part of the semen and therefore are not ejaculated, but rather go directly into the blood stream from the testes themselves.

Another false notion that still prevails is that boys must have intercourse to develop normally. This is not at all true. Maturation of the sex organs and functions proceeds according to the individual's growth schedule. Virility and manliness are not dependent upon intercourse or other premarital experimentation.

In the normal development of the boy child, the testes

PLATE IV

Male Genitalia

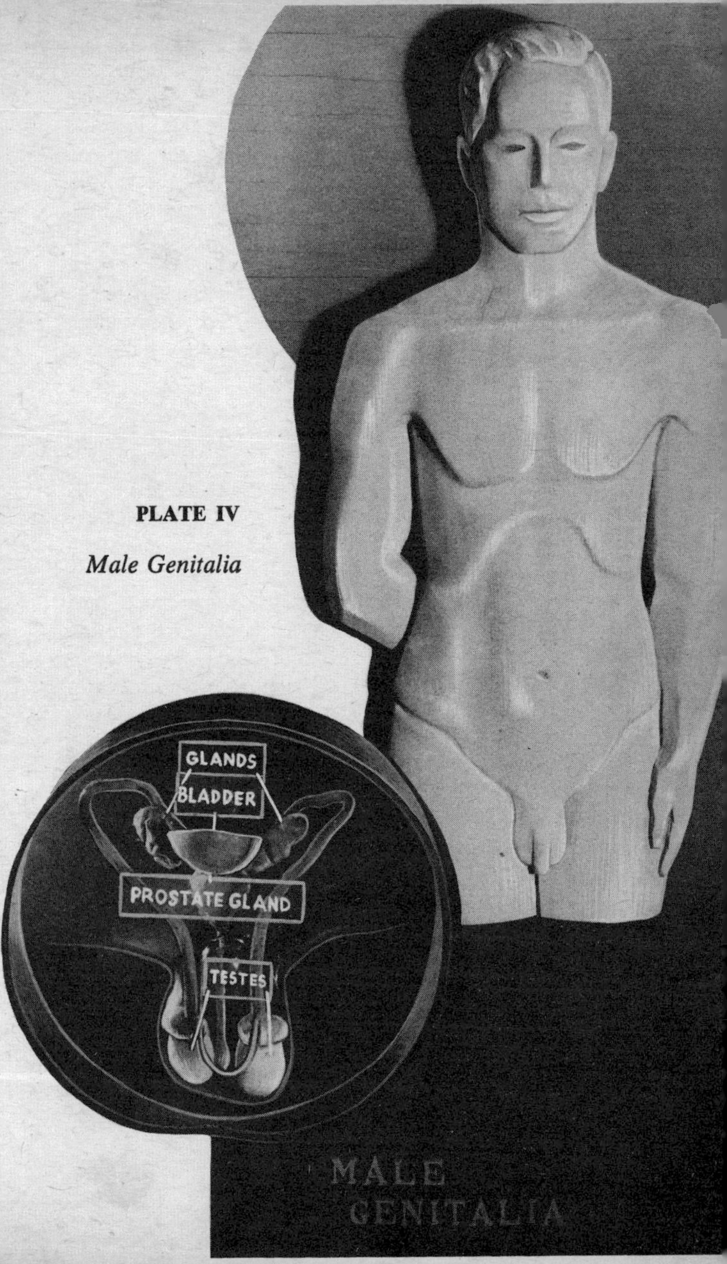

GLANDS

BLADDER

PROSTATE GLAND

TESTES

MALE
GENITALIA

form in the abdomen and just before birth descend into the special sac, the *scrotum* (skro'-tum), which hangs outside the body. Sometimes, for one reason or another, one or both of the testes may not descend. This does not mean that the boy is any less a male, but simply that his testes have not come to their proper place within the scrotum. The boy with one undescended testis is not affected adversely except perhaps in the way he feels about it. Both of his testes go right on producing the important male hormone that makes and keeps him a mannish man. The one descended testis is quite capable of producing enough live, active sperms to make him a father. The undescended testis does not produce live sperms, because it is too warm in the body for sperm production.

SCROTUM sac and thermostat

The testes normally hang in a skinlike sac attached to the lower abdomen. This soft, thin-walled pouch is a very sensitive bit of male machinery. It is sensitive to touch and it responds remarkably to heat and to cold. As the temperature goes up, the scrotum stretches and hangs low, away from the warm pelvis. When it is cold, the scrotum contracts and lies close to the heat of the body. The thermostatic control within the scrotum helps keep the testes two degrees cooler than the rest of the body, which is the necessary condition for sperm to develop.

As a boy matures, the testes increase in size and weight, and the scrotum enlarges to accommodate its contents, the testicles (testes). Men feel more comfortable when the scrotum is supported by a jock strap during athletic activities. This is especially important when the sport exposes one to physical contact that might injure these organs.

THE penis

Down through history, the *penis* (pee'-nis) has been known as *the* male organ. It hangs in front of the scrotal sac suspended from the lower front abdomen. It contains the *urethra* (yoo-ree'-thrah), which runs the full length of the penis. The upper portion of the urethra passes through the prostate gland. When the urethra is functioning sexually,

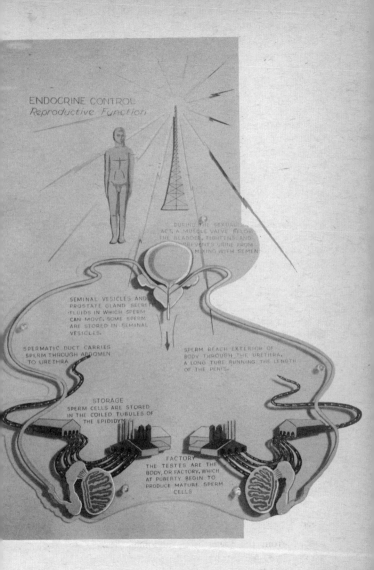

PLATE V

Reproductive Function (Male)

its urinary function is automatically restricted, so that the urinary and sexual functions are separate in male physiology.

When sexual excitation occurs, a multitude of changes take place in the male. One is the release of an alkaline fluid that precedes and forms part of the semen. This neutralizes any possible traces of acid urine in the urethra. As the man or boy becomes sexually excited, blood rushes into the spongy tissue that makes up the bulk of the penis. The normal outlets for the blood supply of the penis are reduced, and the extra supply of blood in the myriad spongy caverns makes the usually soft, flabby penis hard and firmly erect at an angle from the body. This manifestation is preliminary to the ejaculation of the semen, although it frequently and normally occurs at other times.

The normal penis varies greatly from person to person in length—both flaccid and erect—in diameter, in general contour, and even in the exact place of the opening at the end. A boy may go through great anxiety because his penis is different from others. As with noses and ears, there are many shapes and sizes, all within the range of the normal. Then too, boys who are slow in developing in their early teens may be unduly worried because their sex organs do not grow quickly enough to satisfy their anticipation of full-grown organs.

In the normal male, a secretion of *smegma* (smeg'mah) from the head of the penis accumulates and should be regularly cleaned away. This is apt to be particularly true in boys who have not been circumcised. Circumcision is the removal of enough of the foreskin from the end of the penis to expose the rounded *glans penis* at the end of the organ. Circumcision is often performed in the baby boy as a religious rite or for cleanliness' sake. When it has not been done, the boy must take especial care to push back the foreskin far enough to clean the end of the penis when bathing.

INTERNAL connections

The route that the sperms follow is a remarkable one. They develop in the testes located within the scrotum. From there they pass through a labyrinth of microscopic tubes in the *epididymis* (epi-did'-im-iss), an elongated mass at the back of each testicle, composed of the tubes of that organ wound together. Here the tails of the sperm begin to lash as they become motile. From the epididymis they enter the *vasa deferentia* (va'sa def-eh-ren'-shee-ah), small, thick-walled, convoluted tubes about two feet long—one from each testicle, connecting the testes with the internal organs of the male.

Each vas deferens extends into the abdominal cavity, up around the bladder, and through the *prostate* (pros'-tate) gland. This is the gland which sometimes causes trouble in the middle-aged man by growing to such a size that it compresses the urethra and causes a number of unpleasant symptoms, like inability to urinate freely, until adequate medical attention can set things right again. But to go back to those vasa deferentia. Near their entrance into the prostate are two outpouchings called seminal vesicles, one on either side. Nearby, too, is still another gland, called *Cowper's* (Koo'perz) *gland* for the man who first noted it. These are all concerned with the formation and release of the fluid part of the semen that carries the sperms out in each ejaculation. Each vas deferens enters the upper end of the urethra, which goes through the length of the penis to the outside. Thus we see that a single ejaculation brings sperms up out of the scrotal sac, into the body, and out through the penis. The pathway taken by the urine is much shorter and simpler, because the bladder opens directly into the urethra. The opening is guarded by a sphincter muscle which the little boy learns to control and which remains automatically contracted in sexual excitation.

THE pituitary gland

At puberty the *pituitary* (pi-tew'-i-ter-ee) gland, deep in the middle of the boy's head, throws the master switch which sets all the male mechanism, present from the beginning, into its active phase. Hormones, those chemicals which are carried by the blood to all parts of the body and govern the way our bodies function, change at puberty from the balance characteristic of little boys to the equilibrium of manhood. The pituitary is the pace-setter. Its secretion of hormones into the blood activates the hormone development within the testes, and puberty is under way.

BOYS'
physical changes at puberty

CHANGES in height and weight

One of the first signs of puberty a boy notices is increase in height. He shoots up rapidly and may gain more inches in a single year than for several preceding years. This lengthening-out process is the more striking because just before it occurs there is almost no increase in height or much in weight for six months or even a year.

As the boy gains in height and weight, he may become as tall as, or taller than, his father; yet he will find that he is not so strong as his dad in many ways and that he tires more easily. This is because strength follows size in the developmental sequence. An adolescent boy who looks big and strong actually is not able to do a full man's work. The development of the heart, the lungs, and the muscles themselves takes place over a period of time and does not rush into full capacity with the first increase in actual size. This is why a teen-age boy often fatigues easily and needs to rest at frequent intervals. It is also why health experts advise plenty of sleep during this period.

Following the lengthening-out phase comes the broadening and filling-out stage of growth. Shoulders become broad and manlike. The beanpole slimness of the young "sprout" fills out into the full chest, the firm arms and legs and torso of manhood. Feet and hands attain mature proportions oftentimes before the rest of the body and seem to be outsize for a while. Even the face undergoes marked growth as the little-boy lines give way to maturity. The external sex organs increase in size and weight, and at different rates in different boys.

HAIR in new places

Hair where no hair grew before is one of the noticeable signs of maturing. A boy begins to watch eagerly for signs of this new badge of manliness on his face. As soon as the soft down begins to coarsen enough to give an excuse for a shave, he feels assured that he is on the way to maturity. Other areas show hairy growth, too. The armpits, the pubic area around the genitals, the chest and legs—all are sites of new hair growth. Such hair comes in first in a darker, coarser version of the light down that was there through childhood. The boy is now changing from pre-pubescence to pubescence, or *puberty*. As maturing continues, this hair loses its straightness and takes on a decided curl. It is at the stage when the pubic hair begins to curl that some authorities say the boy emerges from pubescence (puberty) to postpubescence (after puberty).

Since boys are proud of the hairy growth that comes with maturing, little attention is given to its removal except, of course, the ritual of shaving the face, which becomes an important part of the young man's daily routine. It is usually some time before it is necessary for a boy to shave daily, although he is often so pleased with the prospect that he uses any energetic bristle as an excuse. Hair under the arms, on the legs, and on the chest is customarily not removed by the male.

SKIN troubles

Sweat and oil glands, especially on the face, work overtime during puberty, with resulting blemishes, pimples, and blackheads, called acne. The best help is soap and warm water, cleaning the skin often enough to keep the oily deposits to a minimum. Facial blemishes during the teens are nothing to feel embarrassed about. They are a sign that growth is going on at a rapid pace and the skin has not yet become completely adjusted to the new order. Persistent skin troubles may be relieved under a doctor's care. A diet of plenty of fresh fruits, vegetables, and milk and a minimum of fatty foods may help to keep this condition down.

Deodorants are for men, too. When a man perspires freely he finds that regular bathing may not be enough to keep him freshly clean all the time. Therefore, many men use a deodorant in the armpits immediately after washing or bathing. This may be in the form of an anti-perspirant powder, roll-on, lotion, cream, or a liquid deodorant. The form does not matter. The important thing is his willingness to protect his associates from the unpleasantness of body odors.

Voice changes are sometimes embarrassing. A sudden, unexpected shift in pitch from high to low and back to high again can be most disconcerting. The fact that this may happen just when a boy is trying hardest to make a good impression makes matters all the worse. Nervous tension, anger, embarrassment, trying hard to be very calm when inside a person is seething with feeling, all add to the excitement that is so frequently associated with the voice that cracks. Fortunately, this phase does not last long, and the voice that emerges in its new low register forever distinguishes one as a man.

"WET dreams"

Nocturnal emissions are a sure sign that a boy is maturing. These "wet dreams" come usually when he is asleep and are frequently associated with dreams about girls or sex play. What actually happens is that the semen that has been developing is discharged during sleep. There is no cause for alarm. Emissions are not a sign that a man is losing his "manhood," as an old superstition had it. Nor are they a sign of wrong thoughts or actions. They are simply and surely indications of a boy's maturing, and nothing more. A boy need not feel embarrassed by the stains on his pajamas or bed linen. The chances are very good that his mother fully understands.

Young people of both sexes often ask, "Do boys have anything like menstruation?" The answer is, of course: "No, boys do not have anything that parallels menstruation in girls." They have no uterus and they do not prepare periodically for pregnancy, so there can be no shedding of the uterine lining as in menstruation. However, if the question is phrased, "Do boys have a discharge that is somehow connected with their reproductive development as is the girl's menstrual discharge? then the answer is, "Yes." The seminal emission is the release from the body of reproductive products that have no further function at the time, in the same way that the menstrual flow is the discharge of special materials for which there is no further use. The seminal emission in the boy is not the periodic occurrence that menstruation is in girls. Emissions come whenever the semen has accumulated to the point where nature releases it. The frequency with which boys have seminal emissions varies greatly, and it is not important one way or another. Since the wet dream is over in a matter of moments, there is no problem of special preparation for it, or care afterward, except for the body cleanliness that should be routine.

ADOLESCENT
boys' emotional changes

More puzzling than physical changes that occur during puberty are new feelings that often catch a boy unawares.

STORMY times with parents

Like David in Chapter One, Jim was having an argument with his mother one morning. The issue really wasn't important, but somehow Jim felt strongly about it and before he knew what he was doing, he found himself shouting at his mother. Then, without warning, the shouting ceased and he found himself in tears. Still angry, embarrassed, and puzzled most of all by himself, he dashed out of the house. What was the matter with Jim? Nothing serious, just that he experienced one of the stormy moments that come from time to time as one grows up.

As a boy begins to look more and more grown up, and as people around him sense his increasing maturity, there comes a forceful urge to put away childish things and to launch out on one's own. This means, among other things, a breaking away from childhood dependencies upon one's mother and father. Parents, even the best of them, are sometimes slow to realize that their children are growing up and that they want to be treated as adults. On the other hand, adolescents frequently behave as though they were still just children. Teen-agers often find this frustrating, and even deeply humiliating. They are apt to burst forth with an angry "You just don't understand!" or to shout some other rebellious retort in their thrusts for independence.

But becoming angry at parents, who usually are still pretty important to a boy, makes him feel guilty and sorry all at once. What happened to Jim happens to many others:

angry shouting in a burst of independence one moment and tears of remorse, frustration, anger, and guilty regret the next. Then, of course, the tears themselves make him feel that he has not stood his ground. He wishes he might have handled the situation calmly and with poise, "like a man." He is ashamed to have cried in front of his mother, and so his feelings are in a tangle indeed.

The more we know about the meaning of growing up, the more we realize that it is not a steady, even maturing, but rather a series of spurts and dips. Especially is this true of one's feelings. It is normal to want to be free, to run one's own life, and to fight for one's independence. Yet there is often a strong desire to avoid responsibility. One wants the childhood securities represented by one's parents and home folks. One wants to grow up and one doesn't. The sudden gesture of defiance is often followed by a lunge back into the family circle or into old childish ways (tears or teasing or cuddling up as one did as a youngster). This seesaw progression out of childhood into adulthood is usual and should not be a cause for concern. As development continues, more and more poise is acquired and a new equilibrium is established at home on a more grown-up basis. But it takes time, and it has to be worked on.

FRESH, new feelings about girls

As a boy gets into his teens he begins to experience new reactions to certain special girls and to the whole male-female relation in general. He may suddenly discover a girl who sets his mind whirling, who occupies his thoughts day after day, whose slightest glance is heaven, whose handwriting makes the shivers run up and down his spine, whose touch is exquisite pain and pleasure in a strange new combination. Whether this may be some new girl who has just moved into town or the same girl he played games with as a kid, his feelings about her are new and strange.

Spontaneous erections come now without warning or apparent reason. Any number of things become sexually stimulating and exciting to the teen-age boy. Normally, the tension subsides without the boy's having to do anything about it.

Love feelings often are a peculiar combination of tenderness and roughness. A boy may think and feel very tenderly about his special girl of the moment. He may dream of protecting her and taking care of her and saving her from danger. He may want to do some special kindness and in some thoughtful way show her his devotion. And then some evening when he is kissing her goodnight, he finds that his tenderness changes suddenly into something fierce and strong and intensely exciting. If he is a sensitive fellow, he may be dismayed by "the brute" in him that turned a chaste kiss into something that he had not contemplated and very probably frightened the girl. But as he grows up, he learns that a man's love for a woman is compounded of such elements. Part of the task of maturing is to learn to recognize and cope with just such diverse feelings, so that one's relationships with girls may become increasingly manageable and mutually satisfying. This is never easy. It takes practice and patience and a willingness to understand oneself and others to reach the point where love feelings inspire and motivate and give the positive lift to life that they are capable of, in both men and women.

LOVE-MAKING in dream life

Many boys are troubled about the frequency and content of their sex dreams and fantasies. Those who have been brought up to think that sex is somehow unclean and unworthy may feel guilty when they find themselves thinking sexy thoughts and dreaming of all kinds of sexually tinged situations. Boys should know that this is part of growing up. In the same way that most girls, if they are honest with themselves, admit that they dream of being pursued and loved and caressed by boys, so boys during the teens act out in their dream life the whole drama of love-making, with many shifts of scenes and characters and all sorts of modifications and elaborations. The best way to keep these preoccupying fantasies to a comfortable minimum is to be physically active and mentally occupied. The boy who is genuinely interested in music, or active in sports, or a leader in group activities is less apt to be bothered by sexual fantasies than the one who remains by himself, out of activities with others. As maturity brings more and more congenial partners of the other sex and love feelings deepen to a more permanent basis, much of this love energy goes into plans for future marriage and family life, and for getting established as a full-fledged member of the community.

THE
tasks of growing up

Growing up has never been easy. Becoming an adult in the complex world of today is full of complications and confusions. One has to find himself in so many ways at once! A boy has to come to terms with his own changing body that is new in size and form, function and potential, as he becomes a man. He has to feel comfortable in his own skin in order to find manhood fully satisfying. This means accepting and understanding himself as a unique human being with both strengths and weaknesses, assets and liabilities.

Growing up involves establishing himself with the other boys and men as an accepted member of the male community. Becoming a man means that a fellow has to learn to love girls as persons without having either to fear them or to exploit them. As a boy matures he must be able to love one girl in particular in ways that are mutually satisfying and deeply rewarding in a permanent sense. These are the foundations upon which his marriage will be built some day.

During the teen years a boy must decide whether he will continue on in school and get the best education he can to develop his talents and abilities, or drop out and sacrifice his future for a jalopy or a makeshift job. For these are the critical years when a boy is determining what his life as a man will be like—either as a competent person with skills to sell, or one of the poorly trained fellows for whom there are all too few places in the modern-day working force.

It is during the second decade of life that a boy heads toward the work that will give him status as man. This involves choosing and training for the kind of occupation that has a future in it through the years to come. It should be something in which he has interest and native ability. It should be a field for which there is a likelihood of employment when he is ready to start work. And it should be the kind of work that he feels is worth doing.

As a boy leaves his childhood behind, he searches for the meanings of life as he knows it. The more he learns about the world in which he lives, the more he needs to have it make some kind of sense to him personally. So he searches for the meanings of life, and for its religious and philosophical bases. One of the tasks of growing up is becoming more fully at home in the universe.

But most of all a man-in-the-making needs to find himself, and to answer for himself the question, "Who am I?" In this quest for self, for the meanings of one's life, its directions and its purposes, he finds the peace of mind that makes possible choices and decisions that otherwise would plague and torment him.

Talking things out with a responsible person whom you can trust helps a great deal in thinking things through. Just putting your feelings into words often helps to make things come clear for you. Boys who have someone to confide in, someone to share their deepest anxieties and their highest dreams, someone who understands without scoffing or ridicule, find that moody spells are not so baffling after all. This is why some schools realize the importance of having especially trained guidance persons on the staff whose job it is to help with the tangles that are a normal part of growing up.

Where do

babies come from?

THERE ARE SO MANY SUPERSTITIONS and folk tales mixed up with the facts of life that only an unusual young person knows what is and what is not true about reproduction. It has long been a tabooed subject. Adults have been reluctant to talk about it even among themselves. Parents were often not given the true facts as they grew up, and so they find it hard to talk about it with their children. The confusion has continued from one generation to the next.

You may be fortunate enough to have grown up in a home where frank answers were given to your questions. Many young people have had different experiences, however. Their parents have avoided their questions with such replies as, "Wait until you are old enough; then you will understand." Or they may have been given the answers that babies grow under cabbage leaves, that the stork brings them, that they come from the doctor's black bag, and other stories that parents have used to put off children's questions.

There are teachers, nurses, doctors, ministers, and wise adults of various professional backgrounds who in recent years have been willing to help youth separate fact from fiction in the story of human creation. Young people who have had the advantage of such guidance often do not realize how hard it is to get such knowledge otherwise. Books may be written on the subject, but often the library does not have them; or they are kept out of sight in conformity with the taboo that still exists in some places against reading or discussing such things. Other young people may be a source of information, but they too are often mixed up and full of questions themselves. Those who give the impression of being well informed are frequently quite confused, but they do not know it. Piecing together information with the help of dictionary and encyclopedia

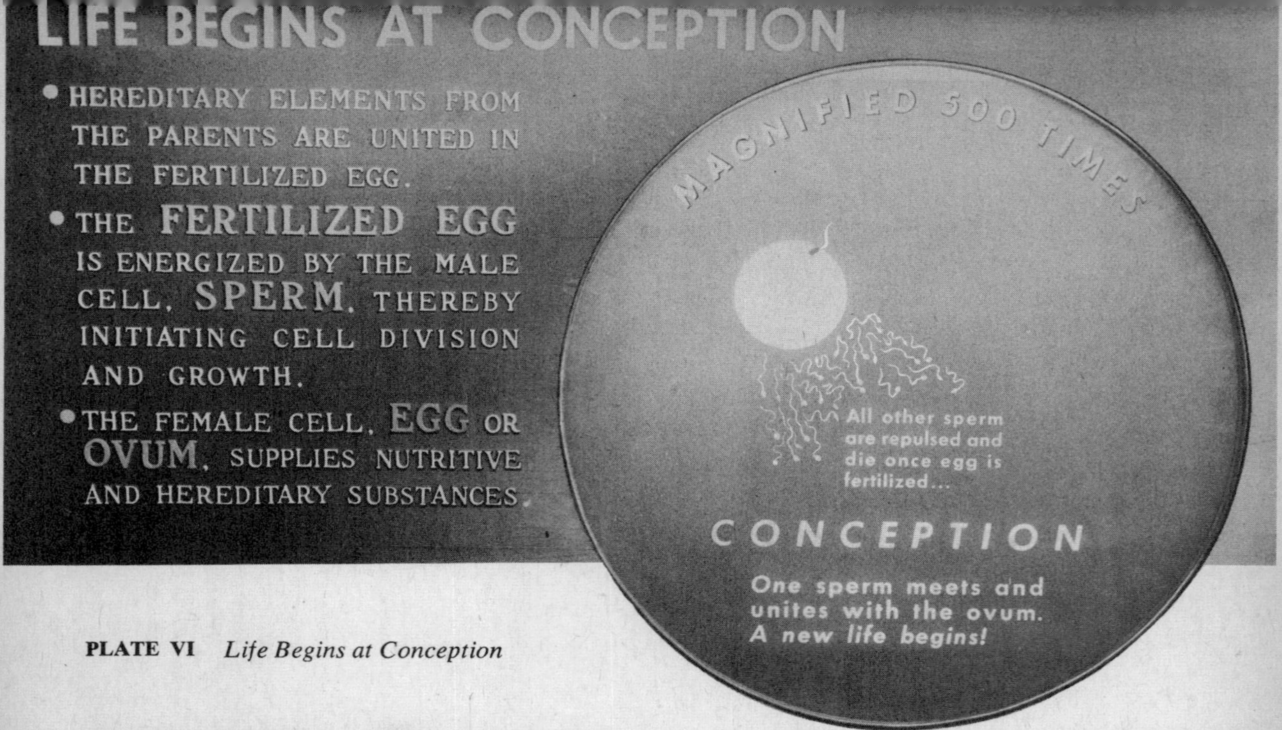

PLATE VI *Life Begins at Conception*

is pretty sketchy at best. Because we agree that there should be straight answers to honest questions, let us summarize point by point the facts about reproduction.

HOW
a new life begins

The truth about human reproduction can be presented very simply in these three statements:

1. A baby starts when a sperm from the father joins an egg within the mother's body.
2. Babies grow in their mothers in a place called the uterus, or womb.
3. When the baby is ready, after growing in the mother's body for about nine months, it is born through her vagina.

WHERE father cell meets mother cell

The mother's contribution to the new baby is the ovum, or egg, which develops in one of her two ovaries. This egg is released from the ovary, usually one each month, into the Fallopian tube which lies close by. The Fallopian or uterine tubes are small tubes bridging over the ovaries on either side to the uterus in the midline of the lower pelvis.

Fertilization, or conception, is the entering of the sperm into the ovum. It takes place in the Fallopian tube soon after the woman has ovulated (released the ripened ovum) and not long after the sperms have been deposited in the upper end of the vagina. In order for conception to take place, everything has to be just right—both male and female cells must be there at the same time, both actively ready for fertilization.

Sperms are deposited in the vagina during coitus (sometimes called sexual intercourse, or marriage relations, or mating). This occurs when the penis is inserted into the vagina and the semen, containing millions of sperms, is ejaculated out of the penis into the vagina.

Not every act of intercourse results in fertilization by any means. Fertilization depends upon the precise timing that brings the sperms into the tubes when a ripened ovum is there, freshly released from the ovary. No one can tell in advance whether conception will take place. Some couples start a baby very easily and others do not. There is a wide variety of reasons, including the delicate balance of hormones in both man and woman, the physical structure or condition of the reproductive organs, and how the two persons feel about each other, about having a baby, and about sex in general. Sometimes couples are married for years and eagerly await a baby which does not come. They may be discouraged about having a baby and adopt a child, only to discover a few months later that they are to have one of their own at last. Other women find themselves pregnant after a single coitus. When a baby will get started for a particular couple is not easy to predict.

HOW
a baby develops in its mother

After the egg has been fertilized in the tube, it travels down the tube into the uterus. There it lodges in the lining of the uterus, called the *endometrium* (en-doe-mee'-tree-um), which has been in preparation for possible pregnancy since the last menstruation (as we saw in Chapter Six). Here the fertilized egg undergoes its amazing growth from the size of a dot hardly big enough to see to the newborn infant of about seven pounds.

Soon after the fertilized egg, or *embryo* (em'-bree-oh), as it is now called, reaches the uterus, elaborate development and specialization of growth take place. Out of the embryonic tissue grows the *placenta* (plah-sen'-tah), which is the organ of attachment between the baby and mother. This fastens itself into the uterine lining and serves as the two-way food and waste-disposal exchange for the baby throughout pregnancy. The placenta connects with the baby through the *umbilical* (um-bil'-ik-al) *cord* fastened at one end in the placenta and at the other in the baby's *navel* (nay'-val), or *umbilicus* (um-bil'-ik-us) (the "belly button" of child language). Through the placenta and cord pass all the food that the baby needs for his growth during the nine months he lives in the uterus. Through the same system the baby's waste products pass out into the mother's blood stream, to be released through her lungs and kidneys.

During the nine months the *fetus* (fee'-tus) not only

PLATE VII   *How the Fetus Lives and Grows*

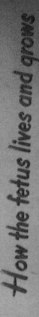

How the fetus lives and grows

EARLY IN PREGNANCY

THE PLACENTA DEVELOPS.

THROUGH THE PLACENTA

THE MOTHER

SUPPLIES HER FETUS

WITH MATERIALS

FOR LIFE AND GROWTH

AND DISPOSES OF WASTES.

AT BIRTH

THE PLACENTA,

NO LONGER NEEDED,

IS DISCARDED

AS THE "AFTERBIRTH."

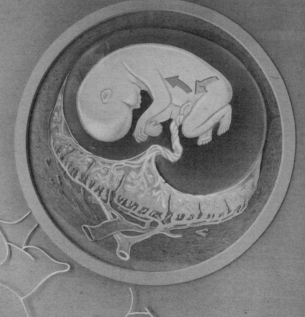

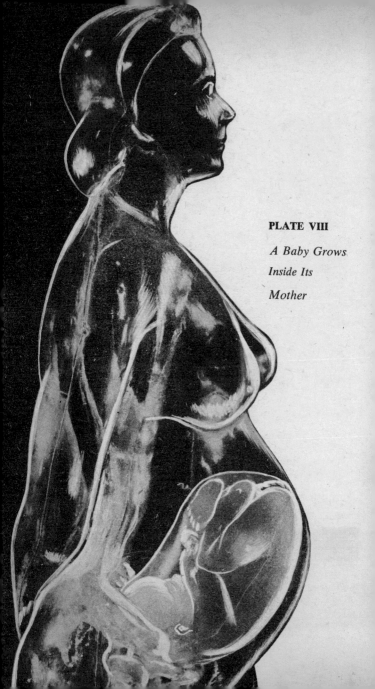

PLATE VIII

*A Baby Grows
Inside Its
Mother*

grows in size but it also develops into a human child. From the single fertilized egg comes the full human equipment with which the baby is born—arms and legs complete with fingers and toes down to the last perfect little toenail, eyes and ears, nose and mouth, heart and brain and lungs and blood, and all the thousands of other specialized parts that make it possible for him to maintain life on his own. Never again in that person's lifetime will he grow so fast or develop so much as he does in those first nine months within his mother's uterus.

HOW
a baby is born

Approximately nine months after the baby starts growing in the uterus, it is ready to come out. The mother is first aware of the approaching birth of her baby by little painful contractions across her abdomen. These pains, which are called labor pains, are caused by the stretching of the neck of the uterus, the *cervix* (sur'-viks), so that it will be big enough for the baby to come through. Normally the cervix is a firm band of muscle at the lower end of the uterus. The stretching of these muscles takes quite a while in most women who are having their first baby, and usually only a short time for women whose many children may have left the cervix relaxed and elastic. *This first stage of labor,* lasting anywhere from a few minutes to as much as twenty hours or more, goes on until the cervix is open wide enough for the baby to come through.

The second stage of labor pushes the baby through the wide-open cervix and the vagina to the outside. It is accompanied by bearing-down sensations in which the muscles of the uterus literally push the baby out through the cervical opening. The pain is more intense at this stage and is usually relieved by some anesthetic.

Doctors find that some women who know how to relax, who do not fear childbirth and are not afraid of pain, have their babies more quickly and with less discomfort than do those who become tense and frightened. Most people today believe in making childbirth as comfortable for the mother as is possible without endangering the health of baby or mother. The doctor usually eases the mother's pain, using his judgment as to what will be best for her and her baby under the circumstances. You may have heard of some drugs and techniques that are in use today—caudal anesthesia, saddle-block, hypnosis, guided relaxation (or what is called "natural childbirth"). The kind of general or local anesthetic used is really not too important, for the pain is not so great that a woman cannot stand it and as soon as the baby is born a woman quickly forgets the discomfort she has been through in the joy of having her baby in her arms.

Far more important than pain relief is the care the mother gets before, during, and after the birth of her baby. The number of maternal and infant deaths has been greatly reduced in recent years by the improvement of such obstetric care. There is no substitute for adequate prenatal supervision, to make sure that everything is all right, and for good doctoring and nursing at the time of the baby's birth. That is why so many babies today are born in hospitals where well-trained doctors and nurses are ready to do what is necessary to insure a healthy baby and a happy mother.

When the baby is born, it draws air into its lungs by gasping or crying. The umbilical cord is tied in two places and cut through between the knots, so that the baby is then completely on its own. The fraction of an inch of cord left on the baby soon dries up and sloughs off the navel. The rest of the cord emerges with the placenta, to which it is still attached.

The third stage of labor is the birth of the placenta, or "afterbirth" as it is often called. The uterus contracts as it did in pushing out the baby, and this loosens and expels the placenta. The doctor usually makes sure that all the placental tissue has come out, so that danger of the mother's excessive bleeding may be avoided. Within a few days after the baby is born, the mother may be up and around, and six weeks afterward she is entirely back to normal again.

The baby in the meantime has begun to breathe and to cry and to suck, and to make a place for himself in his family circle. Anyone who has had recent contact with a new-born baby knows how soon and how loudly he can make his wishes known to the rest of the household!

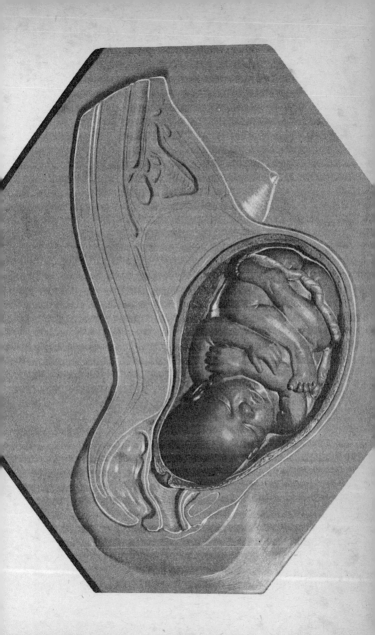

PLATE IX *The Baby Is Ready to Be Born*

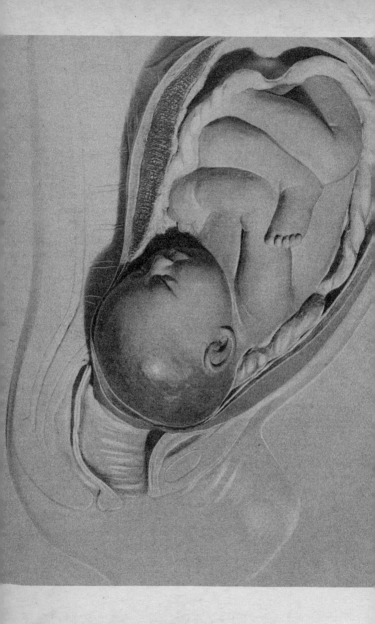

PLATE X   *Early First Stage of Labor*

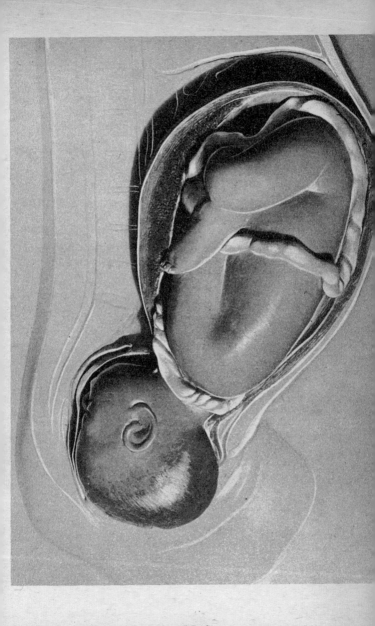

PLATE XI *Early Second Stage of Labor*

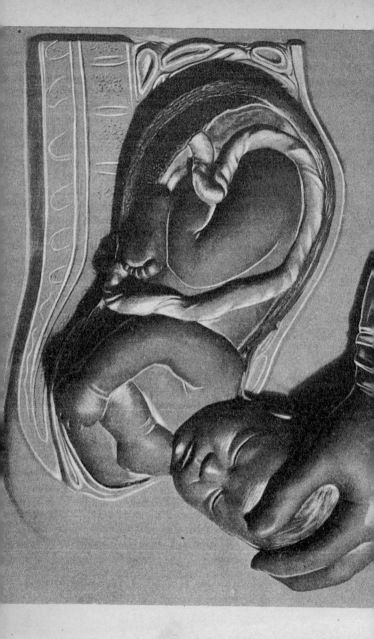

PLATE XII *End of Second Stage of Labor*

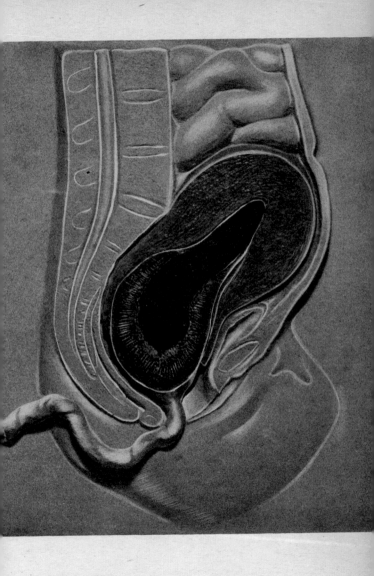

PLATE XIII *Third Stage of Labor*

PLATE XIV *The Newborn Baby*

In the birth of a baby through *Caesarean* (se-zayr'-ee-an) section, instead of the baby's being born through the natural passages, it is lifted out of an opening cut in the mother's abdomen and uterus by the attending doctor. This operation is indicated when the mother's pelvis is too small or when other conditions make natural birth dangerous for baby or mother or both. It is not quite so safe as natural childbirth for either mother or baby.

HUMAN
heredity at work

All that a baby inherits is determined by special small bits of protoplasm in the germ cells. These special determiners are called *chromosomes,* or "color bodies," because of their tendency to take up the color when subjected to certain dyes. Every living thing, both plant and animal, has a specific number of these chromosomes that determine heredity within that species. The human being has forty-six chromosomes, made up in twenty-three pairs. In every cell of your body, the nucleus contains these same forty-six chromosomes— all, that is, except the egg and sperm cells, which have only twenty-three chromosomes, as we shall soon see.

Strung along these rodlike chromosomes are many protein molecules, like beads on a string. Each of these chemical packets, or *genes* (jeens), is responsible for a particular characteristic. There is a gene for eye color, for instance; another is a determiner for a given texture of skin, another for curly hair, another for tallness, still another for the tendency of the skin to freckle, and so on and on through many thousands of individual characteristics.

These chromosomes, complete with their elaborate collection of genes, have come *through* your parents on both sides. They did not precisely come *from* your parents. That is to say, your mother inherited a particular set of chromosomes from her mother's line and from her father's line. These lay dormant in the egg cells within her ovaries until it was time for the egg (the one that was to become you) to mature and be fertilized. The one sperm (out of the two hundred million there) that fertilized the egg at the time of your conception contributed its part of the combination of genes that was to be yours. That sperm might have had any of the multitude of chromosomes available from your father's side of the family. Thus you got a completely new deal in heredity.

You, for instance, may have a body build like your father, but you may have your mother's coloring, and perhaps your grandfather's small hands, and maybe your great-uncle Ed's high forehead. Occasionally you will hear people say, "He's just a chip off the old block." But actually that is never so. However much a child may look like one parent or the other, he actually is a unique combination of characteristics, only some of which are shared by his parents. Of course, since he is more closely related to his parents than to his other forebears, the child resembles them more frequently than he does more distant relatives. But both child and parent share the ongoing stream of heredity in the continuing germ plasm.

DOMINANCE

Not all characteristics get the same chance of showing up in the new individual. Some genes are dominant and have more chance of being represented in the new baby than do others, called recessive. For instance, suppose there is a gene for blond hair that came down through your mother's side of the family. But supposing the gene on that chromosome found itself paired with a gene for black hair from your father's side of the family. Then you would have black hair instead of light, for dark hair is dominant over light. One of your children, however, could have light hair if the light-hair gene in your line is paired off with a light-hair gene in your mate's. So, too, a gene for brown eyes paired with one for blue would be dominant, and the baby would have brown eyes. Curly hair is dominant over straight, and so it goes.

But how, you may ask, can you have blue eyes when your father has brown ones? That is easy to explain. You have blue eyes because the genes for eye color from both the male and the female lines that you happened to get in the sperm and egg that united to form you were *both* for blue eyes. Your father may have brown eyes, but remember that you do not inherit *from* him but through him. The eye-color gene in the particular sperm that went to make you *must* have been for blue eyes. Far back through his family there were, quite possibly, all kinds of eye color, and you happened to get the blue eyes in the chance sorting out of eye-color genes in the sperm that started you.

In our melting-pot society where there are few "pure strains," the chances are one in four that a given child will have a recessive characteristic rather than the dominant one of the pair in the parents. Technically most of us humans are *heterozygous* (het-er-oh-zy′-gus), that is, we have genes for two varieties of every single characteristic within the same individual. The genes that make up the new baby come from the chance selection, out of all the possible genes, of those that make up the particular sperm and egg that unite to start the new individual.

INHERITED and acquired characteristics

Many people are greatly confused about just what is and what is not inherited. They say, for instance, "Ethel is moody, just like her Aunt Jane," or "Tom has a terrific temper, exactly like his father's." Strictly speaking, neither moodiness nor temper is inherited. They are learned or acquired as the person grows up. It may be true that Tom's temper is much like his father's but, if so, it is because Tom has learned to respond like his dad, and not from anything passed on from father to son in the germ plasm. In other words, inherited characteristics are those that are determined by the genes. Examples are tallness, skin color, eye color, bone structure, etc. They are *genetic* (je-ne′-tik), we say. Acquired characteristics are those picked up after the new individual is formed. Examples of acquired characteristics are mannerisms, way of speaking, language, emotional habits and attitudes, and all that a person learns from conception onward.

TENDENCIES, not finalities

Actually what one inherits is often the *tendency* to become this or that, not the final characteristic itself. A girl, for instance, may have the tendency to put on weight and have a round, full figure. By careful diet that girl can control her figure to pleasant healthful proportions. Or she can become fat—and blame it all on heredity.

Musical ability is inherited, but John does everything he can to get out of music lessons and never really learns to play, while Van develops his musical talents and becomes a great pianist. Intelligence is an inherited capacity that is greatly influenced by the willingness of the person to develop it. And so on through almost everything that a person is. Many potentialities are present as inherited tendencies that await their development by the person himself.

WHEN abnormalities occur

Some inherited (in the genes) and some *congenital* (kon-jen'-it-al (acquired before birth) abnormalities appear from time to time in human beings. For instance, some babies are born with six toes instead of five. This is a characteristic inherited through the genes. Other difficulties occur because of faulty development before birth (such as cleft palate) or from injuries at birth (such as certain types of cerebral palsy). When certain drugs such as thalidamide are administered early in pregnancy, there is the possibility of abnormalities occurring in the developing baby-to-be. Many of these abnormalities that used to cripple for life can now be dealt with effectively by good medical and surgical care. Even more important is the attitude of the child and his parents toward the problem. If the people concerned have wholesome, healthy feelings about the difficulty, it never assumes as great proportions as when the person feels rejected or abused because of it.

BIRTHMARKS

One hears a great deal of nonsense about prenatal markings and so-called birthmarks. One of the most common superstitions is that the frightened mother "marked" her unborn baby with the image of her fear. Another is that the mother was hungry for some particular kind of food she could not get while she was pregnant (strawberries, for instance), and lo, when her baby was born, there was a bright red strawberry on the child's body! This is all sheer nonsense. It is true that we all have some skin blemishes and sometimes they are quite large and pronounced. They come, however, not from prenatal marking but from the way in which areas of the skin tissue developed in that spot. There is no way by which a pregnant mother's thoughts or feelings can influence her unborn baby. There are no connections between her nervous system and the baby's—merely the simple cord and placental attachment through which only fluid food and waste products can pass.

THE miracle of normality

When you consider how infinitely complex the human body is, how many millions of cells make it up, how elaborately interrelated the thousands of specialized parts are, how many things can go wrong, you marvel that any of us are as normal as we are. The birth of the normal child is truly a miracle, more wonderful than most of us realize.

BOY
or girl

What determines whether the baby is to be a boy or a girl? There are two kinds of sperms, those which produce girls and those which produce boys. Both types of sperms are just alike except for one chromosome. Every sperm has twenty-three chromosomes, its contribution to the forty-six that the baby is to have. The other twenty-three come in the mother's ovum. The twenty-third chromosome in about half of the sperms is just like its mate in the ovum. It is called the X chromosome. A female child results when an X-chromosome-bearing sperm and an X-chromosome-bearing ovum join to make a fertilized egg. In the other half of the sperms that the father produces, the twenty-third chromosome is much smaller and quite different in appearance from its X chromosome partner-to-be in the ovum. It is called the Y chromosome and determines the sex as male. Thus when a Y-chromosome-bearing sperm joins with the X-chromosome-bearing ovum, an XY combination is made, which is the formula for maleness, and a baby boy develops.

Thus
    X (ovum) plus X (sperm) equals XX (girl)
While
    X (ovum) plus Y (sperm) equals XY (boy)

No one knows for sure why one kind of sperm fertilizes the egg one time and the other kind of sperm another time. Something must operate besides pure chance bcause, although there are theoretically the same number of each type of sperm, more boy babies are conceived than girls. More boys are lost before birth, and yet about 105 boys are born for every 100 girls. If it were pure chance that determined the selection of the sperm, there would be on the average 100 males for each 100 females born.

SEX determination

Dr. Landrum B. Shettles, studying human spermatozoa, has been able to observe consistent differences in the head of sperm. One type is larger and more elliptical (probably the X) than the other, which is smaller, rounder, and more numerous (by inference, the Y). It is possible that the male-producing sperm, being smaller, travels faster than the female-producing sperm, and gets to the ovum in the tube first. The X sperm possibly outlives the Y sperm and so has more chance of producing girl babies later in the ovulatory period.

This would explain Dr. Sophia J. Kleegman's clinical observations in artificial insemination. She reports that if intercourse or insemination takes place just before ovulation, then there a predominant number of boys; if intercourse or insemination takes place longer before ovulation (2 days or more) there are a predominant number of girls. By carefully studying time of ovulation, the sex of the child may be influenced—but only before conception.

Although it has been a subject of interesting speculation through the ages, no method has yet been perfected for foretelling the sex of the baby before it is born. Perhaps this is just as well. The important point is that parents accept happily whichever sex they get. Fortunately, being a girl or boy does not make too much difference in the status or advantages or privileges given the person. It is the kind of boy and the kind of girl that really counts.

About once in every eighty-seven pregnancies, not one baby but two are born. Each set of twins is one of two kinds.

IDENTICAL twins

Identical twins are formed by the splitting of the fertilized ovum early in its development, so that two individuals rather than one grow from the single fertilized egg (one ovum plus one sperm). They are *always* of the same sex, and they resemble each other in every inherited respect. They must be exactly alike, for they have identical chromosomes and so share a common heredity.

When identical twins are joined at birth they are popularly called "Siamese twins" for the famous Chang and Eng born in Siam (now Thailand) in 1811. Joined twins sometimes can be successfully separated by surgery. They are always identical.

FRATERNAL twins

Fraternal twins, on the other hand, are no more alike than any other brothers and sisters, except that they have been "wombmates" in the uterus for nine months before birth. They are formed by the fertilization of two ova by two sperms, making two fertilized eggs. Both became implanted in the uterine endometrium and they grow into twins. These can be both boys or both girls or one of each. They may or may not closely resemble each other, because each has his own personal set of chromosomes and develops according to the blueprint of heredity laid down in his own particular gene combination.

But what about triplets? or quadruplets? or quintuplets? All multiple births take place according to some elaboration of the two kinds of twinning described above. Theoretically, any combination is possible.

DETERMINING twins ahead of time

Twins can be detected before birth. The fetal heartbeat can be heard from about the third month of pregnancy on.

If the doctor hears more than one heart beating in the mother's abdomen, he knows that more than one baby is developing. Nothing that the doctor or anyone else can do will make twins if none are there, or send them back after they have started!

Most twins are born one after another, since the uterus tends to empty itself completely once the birth process is under way. Some instances have been reported in which the second twin was born some days after the first had arrived, but this is not at all usual.

TWINNING in families

The tendency to have more than one baby at a time runs in families. Females in some families tend to mature more than one egg at a time. If there are two ova in the tubes at the same time, the chances are that both will be fertilized if one is, and so fraternal twins are a possibility. Fraternal twinning therefore seems to run in the mother's line. Identical twinning, or the tendency for the fertilized ovum to divide and develop more than one baby, is not so well understood. It may run in either the father's or the mother's line.

PREMATURE babies

Not all conceptions result in fully developed babies. Some are released from the uterus before they can possibly live on their own. Others are born prematurely but, with expert attention and care, they can survive.

A full-term baby develops in the uterus for about nine months. Babies born ahead of time with a possibility of surviving are known as *prematures* (pree-ma-tures'). Thanks to advances in medical and nursing care, they have a much better chance of living now than used to be the case. Yet prematurity is still the most frequent cause of infant death. In most hospitals, a premature infant is usually kept in an incubator where there are constant temperature and the best possible conditions for the baby. It may be necessary to leave the baby in the hospital until it is strong enough to do without this specialized care. Premature babies who survive the first critical weeks and months of life can grow to be just as robust and healthy as any others, and usually do.

No one really knows just why labor starts before it is time for the baby to be born. Women used to think that overexertion or a fall might dislodge the developing fetus from the uterus. And that may be one factor. We know, however, that nature has provided a rather remarkable shock absorber for the baby in the *amnion* (am'-nee-on) and *chorion* (kor'ee-on), membranes forming a double sac filled with water in which the unborn baby floats until it is time for it to come out. Any fall or blow is cushioned by the water surrounding the baby so that he does not get its full impact. These membranes break just before birth in what is popularly called the breaking of the bag of waters.

ABORTIONS

Miscarriage, the sudden emptying of the pregnant uterus before the baby can live, has been experienced by many women. Doctors call this *spontaneous* abortion and can only guess why the baby did not continue to mature. The usual explanation is that the fertilized egg was in some way defective and incapable of carrying through to term. There are probably some other reasons why pregnancy is interrupted spontaneously.

Another kind of abortion is that which results from the intentional emptying of the pregnant uterus. This is a criminal offense in most states, unless it is done by a doctor to save the life of the mother. Even then it is considered a sin by some church groups. Since the purposive killing of the unborn baby not only destroys its life but also may endanger the health of the mother, any abortion is a serious affair. When the abortion takes place under illegal conditions, the mother all too frequently does not get the care she needs, and suffers subsequently.

It is understandable that an unmarried girl may become panicky when she learns she is pregnant and feels that she just cannot go through with having her baby. Childbirth outside of marriage is not often a happy experience. When it occurs it is important that everything possible be done to see that the baby receives loving care. Many communities provide for unwed mothers more adequately now then used to be the case. Parents are sometimes willing to see a girl through an unwanted pregnancy. Placement of babies in adoptive homes where they will have love and care is arranged by child welfare agencies. Of course, the best way is to wait until a baby is really wanted before starting it!

THE
Rh factor

Since 1941, when the Rh factor was first discovered in Rhesus monkeys (for whom it is named), there have been hundreds of articles on the Rh factor in human blood. Many of these discuss the possible damage that may be done to the fetus in the mother whose Rh blood type is incompatible with that of the father.

Approximately 85 per cent of the white population of the United States have Rh positive blood. That is, they have blood containing one or more Rh factors. The other 15 per cent have Rh negative blood containing no Rh factor. Actually there are several varieties in the Rh family, but the percentage above is roughly correct.

When both mother and father have the same Rh blood type there is no difficulty. When the mother is Rh positive all goes well. But when an Rh positive man and an Rh negative woman have an Rh positive child, then there may be trouble *if* Rh positive blood cells from the fetal circulation escape into the mother's blood stream. There they may stimulate the mother's blood to produce antibodies capable of destroying the Rh positive blood cells. These antibodies may enter the fetal circulation and attack the baby's blood cells, producing *erythroblastosis* (i-rith-roe-blas-toe′-sis), or *hemolytic* (hee-moe-lit′-ik) disease, with jaundice, anemia, and general swelling as symptoms in the baby. Such babies may die as they near term, or soon after birth; more often they survive as perfectly normal children.

In spite of all the public concern, erythroblastosis is not very common. Although 15 per cent of all white women are Rh negative; only 1 in 200 babies are born with this disease. The incidence is lower than might be expected, because other conditions beside the Rh factor must be present in order for the disease to develop. There must be some leakage of the fetal blood cells into the maternal circulation in the placenta. (Normally the circulation of blood in the baby and in the mother is kept separate, each within its own blood vessels.) Even then, this difficulty practically never affects the first-born. It is only after antibodies have been built up in the mother's blood by previous pregnancies that the baby may be affected. Nineteen out of twenty Rh negative women will *never* have an erythroblastotic child.

Modern treatment of this disease has greatly increased the survival of babies that are afflicted. Now fewer than 10 per cent of erythroblastotic babies are dying, in contrast to 30 per cent mortality as recently as in 1950.

NORMAL
pregnancy

The woman who has been having sex intercourse begins to suspect that she may be pregnant when one or more of the following symptoms occur: (1) she misses a menstrual period; (2) she feels nauseated in the morning; (3) she has sensations of feeling faint; (4) her breasts become sensitive; (5) she urinates more frequently than usual. These first signs of pregnancy can be confirmed by the doctor's examination quite early in pregnancy.

PREGNANCY tests

When it is very important for a woman to know whether or not she is going to have a baby, she can consult with the doctor about obtaining a laboratory test, whereby the pregnancy can be detected much earlier than is possible in the routine examination. Though it is not 100 per cent accurate and reliable, such a test helps a great deal in early diagnosis of pregnancy. Sometime after the third month of pregnancy, the baby itself makes further tests unnecessary. It moves and kicks, and the doctor can hear its heart beat.

PRENATAL care

Modern expectant mothers go regularly to the doctor every month or so throughout their pregnancies so that routine

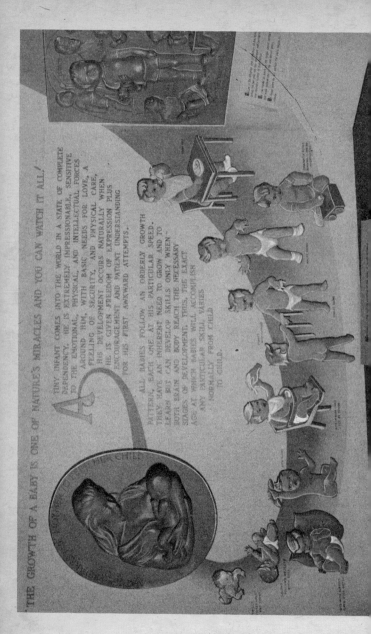

PLATE XV   *The Growth of a Baby*

checks may be made of the baby's growth and the mother's health, and specific advice about diet, clothing, exercise, and general care can be given. Plans are made for the delivery and the care of the baby after birth. Thus, by the time the baby is about to come, everything is ready for it and the family is eager to welcome the newcomer.

Having a baby is a wonderful experience. The mother and father may truly feel that they are partners in creation. Such a fundamental experience brings deep satisfactions and a warm sense of fulfillment that is like nothing else ever experienced.

THE
development of a baby

"The growth of a baby is one of Nature's miracles and you can watch it all!" said the famous Dr. Aldrich, as quoted in Plate XV. The tiny newborn arrives in a state of complete dependency. He has basic needs for food and love and a secure place in which to grow. He thrives under loving care and grows rapidly to take his place as a responsible member of the family.

The pictorial sequence of child growth from the nursing infant to the sturdy two-year-old, in the accompanying plate, tells a story that is worth some serious study. It is important to know that (1) all babies follow an orderly growth sequence; (2) each one develops at his own particular rate; and (3) the exact age at which babies accomplish any particular skill varies normally from child to child.

You were once the rapidly growing, dramatically changing infant that needed freedom of expression and patient, understanding care. The time is not far distant when you will be watching this same miracle of growth in your own children. Your children's development will depend to a large measure on the kind of persons you and your mate have been, are, and are becoming. For growth is a lifelong process for all of us.

CHAPTER 9

What about those sex problems?

THE SEX SIDE OF LIFE IS FULL of problems for young people. There are several reasons for this. Only among enlightened people can sex be openly and helpfully discussed. The taboo that has kept it out of most discussion makes it difficult for young people to get the understanding they need to grow up into satisfied members of one sex or the other.

Most young people have a strong urge to be "normal," to be assured that they are all right. Since people differ widely one from another in all respects, it is understandable that wide differences exist in sex development and activity, too. Because these differences are not clearly understood, young people are frequently worried lest some phase of their own sex life may not be "normal."

During the teens sex powers reach full development. There is often an urgency for sex expression that is hard to control. The dilemma of having strong urges for sex expression at a time when few outlets are encouraged becomes a baffling one for many young people.

Furthermore, young people today have far more freedom than in former years. A young person's conduct today is largely his personal responsibility. Parents no longer closely supervise one's dating. Young people are more frequently exposed to potential danger and, unless adequately prepared to meet it wisely, are more often likely to make mistakes.

GETTING
into trouble

Having a baby before one is married is commonly known as "getting into trouble." When people use this phrase in general conversation, it usually does not infer any of the many other troubles that confront growing youth, but almost always refers to the pregnancy of an unmarried girl. This attitude of the general public increases the seriousness of the problem. The criticism to be faced by the young person "in trouble" is so severe that real understanding of the persons involved and sensible planning for their welfare are difficult.

There is an erroneous assumption that it is the teen-age girl rather than the older female who most usually gets into trouble. But Dr. Clark Vincent's research study *Unmarried Mothers* (Glencoe, Ill.: Free Press, 1961) points out that the greatest increase in the illegitimacy rate in recent decades has been among women between twenty-five and thirty-four years of age. In the United States in 1958, for instance, 79 per cent of all illegitimate births were to females eighteen years of age or more.

Regardless of the age of the unwed mother, her plight is an unhappy one. Getting into trouble has inevitable consequences for the girl, her family, her boy friend, her unborn child, and the larger community.

WHY girls get into trouble

The more common reasons why a girl becomes pregnant before she is married are: (1) she wants a baby out of wedlock as a way of "getting back at" her father or mother; (2) she does what she sees others doing; (3) she is starved for affection; (4) she impulsively gives rein to her feelings and does not practice restraint; (5) she does not know enough about the facts of life to protect herself; (6) she may have been the victim of an unscrupulous boy or man. Let us look at these one by one.

Leontine Young published a remarkable study of unmarried mothers. Out of her personal experience with hundreds of girls in trouble, and her study of thousands of records of others, she helps us to understand their problems probably better than they do themselves. She finds unmarried mothers in every walk of life, rich and poor, educated and uneducated, intelligent and not too bright, in their teens, their twenties, and even older. Perhaps her most startling discovery is that having an out-of-wedlock child is *not* something that just happens. The girl usually does it on purpose. The great majority of the unmarried mothers studied wanted to have a baby without a husband. In fact, the men in most of the cases were not particularly important to the girls except for the purpose they served in getting the girls pregnant.

Why should a girl deliberately get into trouble? According to this study, because she consciously or unconsciously is seeking revenge upon an overly dominating mother or a strongly hated father. Most of these girls come from homes dominated by their mothers. Having a baby without being married is a girl's way of evening an old score against her mother at the same time that she declares her independence from her by doing what only grown women are supposed to be able to do—have a baby.

The spiteful rage that a girl in trouble feels for a dominating, abusive, or rejecting father is expressed through the one act that will show him that he no longer runs her life. The fact that her behavior hurts her more than it does him is another instance of "cutting off your nose to spite your face." Nevertheless, such motives account for a great deal of baffling human behavior. Some of the other reasons that girls get into trouble may be easier to understand. But, none is more frequently found in actual cases than this first one.

A girl who grows up in a family in which her mother and older sisters play around with men in a promiscuous fashion will possibly follow their example and become involved in affairs with men. Certain families regard these things much more lightly than do others. In some homes it is not uncommon to find the mother of the family caring not only for her own children but also for those already born to her unmarried daughters. Some girls grow up in surroundings in which they are early exposed to sex experiences. Lou Anne, for instance, lived with her widowed mother who supported them both by money she got from men. When Lou Anne became pregnant it was from doing what her mother had taught her to do. Many young people get out of such family situations as soon as they can and build good lives for themselves. But some are not so fortunate.

The girl who is starved for affection may accept the attentions of boys and men as a kind of gratification of her need for loving. Many love-hungry girls will do anything just to be caressed. They have grown up feeling they were not wanted, that no one really cared for them, that they were rejected by their families. As they mature they tend to turn to men and boys for the love they have missed at home. They go all the way rather than risk losing the man's love. The pity is, of course, that men rarely love these girls in a real sense but only use them to gratify their sexual impulses at the moment.

Some girls are so impulsive that they get into trouble. A certain type of emotional immaturity, of not being adult in a responsible sense, frequently leads to behavior that results in an unwanted pregnancy. Viola was that kind of person. She was a creature of strong desires and lusty appetites. All her life she had snatched what she wanted without considering the consequences. As soon as she was old enough to be attractive to boys, she gave complete rein to her feelings and did not stop the behavior that led to her pregnancy. Not until she was waiting for the birth of her baby did she get the counseling guidance that helped her come face to face with herself and start the process of growing up emotionally to the place where she could act as a reasonable, sensible person.

It sometimes happens that young people do not realize the force of sexual feelings before they have become too strong to curb. Sex feelings are so compulsive that they must have the respect of any young persons who want to avoid "getting into trouble."

Even in this enlightened age, some girls are still so ignorant of the facts of life that they find themselves pregnant without any real awareness of what has happened. This is especially true of the very young girl who has had no previous introduction to the facts of her own development and the relations between the sexes.

Unscrupulous men and boys may attack or seduce girls and women into sex relations that lead to pregnancy. One hears of instances of rape in communities where girls are attacked as they return home from school. Even more common is the subtle playing upon the girl's emotions until she voluntarily permits the man to use her body for his sexual gratification. For this reason, wise parents do not want their daughters out alone in certain neighborhoods and advise them against riding in cars with strange men or going with boys or men to hotel rooms, motor courts, or other places where they would not be protected from possible sexual attacks.

Getting into trouble is not a pleasant experience for a girl. At best it is disillusioning, often painful, and a poor introduction into womanhood. At worst it can wreck her whole life and make her feel so like "damaged goods" that she never afterward can love and be loved by a man worthy of her devotion. Society tries to safeguard girls from such circumstances by rules and regulations designed for their protection. When a girl defies these safeguards she places herself in a highly vulnerable position. Better by far is willing conformity to the standards of one's culture, based upon one's intelligent awareness of why such restrictions are important.

THE BOY in the case

Little has been written about the teen-age boy who causes a girl to become pregnant before marriage. Often he, too, is in real trouble and needs the help and understanding of those who know him. Boys get into such jams for much the same reasons that girls do, with the added factor of the greater urgency of sex desire that they, as males, experience.

Some boys have an irresponsible attitude about their sex behavior. They claim a right to any gratification they can get—"If a girl gets into trouble, why, that's her fault; she let me, didn't she?" Such an attitude toward women, toward motherhood and life, and toward their own behavior is poor preparation for the fulfillment that comes with deepening love and respect for girls, the ability to love and be loved in its fullest sense, and all that goes into a happy marriage and family life. Some boys who are promiscuous and sexually irresponsible before marriage tend to continue these habits after marriage. As might be expected, the result very frequently is instability and unhappiness in their homes.

Other boys are much more sensitive about their responsibilities to girls. When something happens that messes up the girl's life, the boy feels involved, too. He reasons, "I got her into this trouble; the least I can do is to help her out." Wilfred found himself marrying a girl for whom he had no affection because he felt that it was the only fair thing to do. It meant stopping his education and taking a job he didn't like. The irony of it was that after their marriage he found that he might not have been the father after all. There were several other possibilities. He had simply been the one who had succumbed to her tearful pleas to be rescued from "the fate worse than death." On the other hand, it occasionally happens that a "shotgun wedding" does work out happily. In such instances it usually is a mature and responsible love that has drawn the two persons together.

The boy who stands by and sees the girl with whom he has been familiar having to leave school, be dropped from clubs, scorned by those who were her friends, often feels like a heel. His own sense of guilt is hard to bear. Whether he is exposed as the other parent of the child-to-be or not, he knows what he has done and may need help in regaining his own self-respect.

Sowing wild oats so often means the harvest of a crop of thistles that boys today are increasingly recognizing sex behavior to be a matter of responsibility for both sexes. The old double standard of morality made the girl entirely responsible for her chastity and left the boy free to behave as he would. The trend now is in the direction of boys and girls together facing their mutual privileges and responsibilities in their relations with each other.

PREVENTING
conception

Not every act of intercourse results in pregnancy. As we saw in Chapter Eight, this is true even if the couple do nothing to prevent conception. But unless reasonable precautions are taken, a woman may become pregnant in any single sex act. The prevention of conception is known as *birth control,* or *contraception* (kon-tra-sep'-shun). This is not only a personal but a social question. It is a matter of great concern to several religious groups, notably the

Roman Catholic Church, which considers it a mortal sin to use any artificial means to prevent conception. It is also a medical question, since there is no absolutely perfect method of contraception; but several methods work satisfactorily when prescribed by a competent physician.

Since the advent of oral contraceptives, some ill-advised girls report carrying in their purses "anti-pregnancy pills" to use if there is danger of their going too far with their boy friends. Since these preparations are ovulation repressants and must be taken regularly on twenty specific days through each month, swallowing any number at the time of exposure could not possibly be effective. There are only two foolproof ways of avoiding pregnancy: refrain from intercourse, or follow a medically prescribed and supervised regimen.

STERILIZATION

Some people confuse contraception with sterilization. Contraception is a temporary, immediate effort to prevent the union of egg and sperm. Sterilization, on the other hand, is an operation that renders the male or the female incapable of ever having children. It is permanent and usually irrevocable. For the man, it consists of tying off or severing the tubes that lead from the testes. For the woman, it involves cutting the Fallopian tubes so that no further ova may ever reach the uterus. Such an operation performed by a competent doctor does not interfere with normal sex functioning and feeling, but it does permanently render the individual incapable of having children. It is a very serious step, to be entered into only with real responsibility.

Some states permit the sterilization of hopelessly substandard humans, such as idiots and the criminally insane, so that future generations may be protected from eugenically unfit persons and society may be relieved of the burden of helpless dependents. Even with such socially worthy objectives, there is general recognition that sterilization procedures are not to be taken lightly by either the individual or the state.

PROSTITUTION

Prostitution is the business of offering a woman's body for the sexual gratification of men for money. Women who engage in this "profession" are called prostitutes or, commonly, "whores" or "women of the street." They may approach men on the street or may operate in houses of prostitution presided over by a "madam" who runs the establishment. Such houses of prostitution are often in a neighborhood called a "red-light district." Persons who find girls and women to serve as prostitutes are called procurers, or pimps. They often take advantage of a girl's running away from home or getting into trouble to lead her into prostitution. The girl herself may keep only a portion of her earnings from men. Most of the money goes to support the persons who run the business.

Variations on the prostitution theme are found in: (1) "the easy make," who will do anything a fellow wants for some trifling gift; (2) "the call girl," who is available to men attending conventions or doing business away from home; and (3) "the B-girls," who encourage men customers to buy drinks in bars and occasionally are willing to slake their sexual thirsts as well.

Prostitution is outlawed in many communities, as it should be. Not only is it bad in itself, in that it capitalizes on the exploitative impulses of man and enslaves woman, but it also is a basic factor in civic corruption and a common breeding place for venereal disease.

VENEREAL
diseases

Diseases transmitted by sexual intercourse are called venereal (ve-neer'-ee-al) diseases. The two most common, *syphilis* (sif'-il-is) and gonorrhea (gon-or-ree'-ah), are separate diseases caused by different germs. They are usually thought of together because they are both contracted through sexual contact with an infected person. Both syphilis and gonorrhea can be cured by early diagnosis and care under competent medical attention. Neither yields successfully to home remedies or to concoctions that may be sold over the counter or passed from friend to friend. These diseases can be so serious, if left to their natural course, that intelligent people today recognize the importance of preventing them if at all possible and of taking immediate steps to get adequate medical attention after exposure. This involves medical attention after *any* sexual intercourse with a person who may be infected.

Since no one can tell by looking at another whether or not he or she has one of these diseases in an active form, the only sure protection is in restricting sexual intercourse to marriage. Premarital examinations in which both bride and groom are given tests that will disclose the presence of such infections are now required in many states.

SYPHILIS the great masquerader

Syphilis is a unique disease. The first symptoms are so slight as not to be noticed in some cases. A little sore, or *chancre* (shang′-ker), appears at the point of infection, usually on the genitals. Some time later there may be sore throat, white patches on the mucous membrane of the mouth, perhaps a skin rash, and headaches. These symptoms may escape the attention of the infected person or be passed off as some slight disability. After this second stage passes, the *spirochetes* (spy′-ro-ketes)—little corkscrewlike germs that cause syphilis—burrow deep into the body tissues and lie dormant, oftentimes for many years. The final stage of the disease may appear twenty or thirty years after the original infection. It is never pleasant and has many forms. If the germs have concentrated themselves in the brain, insanity and paralysis result. Disfiguring sores, blindness, and other distressing incapacities are forms in which this "great masquerader" among diseases may appear.

Congenital syphilis (kon-jen′-it-al sif′-il-is) is contracted by the baby before birth from a syphilitic mother. It is not inherited but is caught by the unborn baby from the mother. However, if the mother has been adequately treated in her early pregnancy, the disease can be halted so that it does not affect the baby. Many infant deaths are now prevented by the simple procedure of routine examination of every pregnant woman for possible venereal infection, followed by medical treatment sufficient to save the baby and arrest the disease in the mother.

Cure of syphilis today is quite possible, especially if the infected person gets treatment early. Modern drugs and methods have greatly speeded up the process and give real assurance of complete recovery. The important thing to remember is that early examination and treatment under competent medical supervision is imperative. Now, when most communities of any size have clinics and moderately priced facilities for such treatment, there is no excuse for anyone remaining infected with syphilis. In spite of the availability of treatment, it is a sad fact that the incidence of venereal disease has not yet shown a considerable decline.

GONORRHEA *the sterilizer*

Gonorrhea is one of the reasons for sterility among both men and women. This disease is contracted through sexual intercourse with an infected person. The tiny micro-organism—the gonococcus—that causes the infection, thrives on the moist mucous membranes of the genital tract, where the infection rapidly spreads.

In the female, the first symptom may be an infection of the urethra, causing burning, painful urination, or it may appear as an irritation of the vagina and vulva. From there, if untreated, the infection travels up through the cervix and uterus and on into the tubes. The tubes often become so swollen that the narrow passageway is obstructed or sealed off, thereby sterilizing the woman, since the ova can no longer get through. It is possible for the disease to go on and infect the ovaries, and even to get into the abdominal cavity where death may result from peritonitis. Before these things were as well understood as they are today, women were rendered sterile for life, became permanent invalids, and even lost their lives in the ravages of the disease. Today, early diagnosis and treatment by a competent doctor usually cure the disease before such severe complications develop.

Gonorrhea in the male infects the moist lining of the urethra that runs the length of the penis. If untreated, the infection can spread through the urethra and on through the entire genital tract, eventually closing the vasa deferentia and so rendering the man sterile, since the sperms cannot get through the sealed vasa. Gonorrhea may be checked by adequate medical treatment and a complete cure can generally be assured the man who goes *early* for diagnosis and care.

The eyes of new-born babies are protected from possible gonorrheal infection of the mother by the placing of a medicinal preparation as prescribed by law in the baby's eyes as soon as it is born. Formerly a great deal of blindness in babies resulted from their eyes becoming infected with the gonococci from the mother's vagina. Nowadays we take no chances, and *every* baby is given the eye treatment that will kill any germs of gonorrhea that just possibly might have reached the moist surface of the eyes.

Similarly, persons with active cases of gonorrhea are cautioned not to touch their eyes, and to scrub their hands thoroughly after any contact with their genitals. General hygiene procedures include avoiding moist toilet seats, not handling wet washcloths or towels that others have used, and refraining from drinking from a cup or glass that another person has recently used. At the same time, we can be assured that there is no danger of infection in touching dry smooth surfaces, such as books or doorknobs, even though an infected person has recently handled them. We need not become panicky about a possible venereal infection when we realize that the vast majority of cases result from intimate sexual contact with an actively infected person.

HOMOSEXUALITY

Possibly no word in the English language is as misunderstood as is *homosexuality*. In our society we are so afraid of it and we know so little about it that we are apt to become anxious whenever we hear a whisper of homosexual behavior. The slang words "homo," "fairy," and so on that refer to the homosexual are unfortunate because they are used so loosely and with so little relationship to the facts.

When you stop to think of what homosexuality means and how frequent it is, some of the fear drains off and you want to understand what it is all about. In its simplest definition, homosexuality is the response of two persons of the same sex to each other. *Overt* (oh-vurt') homosexuality involves active sexual contact with a member of the same sex. *Latent* (lay'-tent) homosexuality refers to a strong preference for members of the same sex not directly manifest in physical expression.

Most people at some time in their lives have experienced some kind of homosexual tie. We know, for instance, that it is not unusual for girls to go through a period when they would rather play with other girls than with the boys. The closest friends of many boys in their early teens are other boys for whom they develop deep feelings of affection and mutual satisfaction.

In every community of any size there are men who desire contact with other men and boys. Some of these men actively seek sexual outlets with each other and with younger boys. It is not unusual for a teen-age boy to have been approached in a too friendly fashion by an older man sometime in his experience. When this man is an admired teacher or coach or leader, a boy may either respond to the advances of the older man, or he may be dismayed at being approached. Only if he is aware that such behavior does exist can he be prepared for it and meet it without too much internal turmoil.

The boy who has been approached by an older man in ways that do not seem quite right to him should avoid further opportunities to be alone with this particular individual. At the same time he may confide in some trustworthy older person who can help him to handle the situation. Sound counseling help is also needed by the boy who has been inducted into homosexual activities and has become deeply involved emotionally. He will need to think and to feel his way through the emotional tangle, and this is usually best accomplished with the help of a trained and responsible counselor.

Homosexuality among women is known as *Lesbianism* (lez'-bee-an-ism), and the women who participate sexually with each other are called *Lesbians* (lez'bee-an), after Lesbos, a Greek island in the Aegean Sea which the woman lyric poet Sappho made famous in the sixth century B.C.

You cannot tell by looking at a person whether or not he or she has homosexual tendencies. Common talk assumes that men with homosexual interests are more effeminate in character and less masculine looking than are men whose predominant interests are in the other sex. But this is not necessarily so.

The sturdy, husky girl or the boy with a less obviously masculine voice or build may be so labeled without any basis for it. Nothing is necessarily wrong with either of them. A boy or girl who is teased and taunted about his or her appearance may be reassured and helped by a good counselor who takes time to explore the situation.

There is little evidence that people are born with predetermined tendencies toward homosexuality. We learn to love as we grow up with other people. Sometimes our earliest experiences with people give us little faith in them or in ourselves or in love itself, and so we may develop twisted feelings about others and distorted ways of responding to them. Most of us learn to love and to enjoy responding to the other sex as we develop and find ourselves as men and women. In situations where we are thrown into almost exclusive contact with members of our own sex over an extended period, we may develop abnormally intense interests among them, but as soon as the other sex is again available the majority of us return more or less completely to more heterosexual interests.

Each individual develops somewhere along on a scale of homosexual-heterosexuality. At the homosexual end of the scale are persons whose sexual interests involve members of the same sex exclusively; at the other end of the scale are men and women who are interested primarily in members of the other sex only; in between is the large number of persons of both sexes who at some time in their lives and to some extent find their own sex appealing, but whose capacities for responding to the other sex are also well developed.

Many boys and girls are involved from time to time in "crushes" with members of their own sex. These attachments were discussed in some detail in Chapter Four. We can conclude that although a great deal of shame and guilt are wrapped up in our fears of homosexuality, actually we deal with it best in ourselves or in others when we get over our anxiety and understand it as a not unusual part of growing up.

Homosexuality is not to be confused with *hermaphroditism* (hur-maf'-ro-dit-ism). The hermaphrodite (hur-maf'-ro-dite) is an individual having both male and female sex organs. Upon occasion one hears of such a person being brought up as a member of one sex and later functioning as a member of the other sex. In a recent widely publicized case, the male sex organs were surgically removed leaving the individual who had previously been considered a man with only female characteristics and years ahead as a woman. This is sometimes called "sex-changing," but more accurately could be considered sex clarification, since without the presence of both external and internal female sex organs, no man could become a woman by the removal of his male parts.

MASTURBATION

People used to feel that the handling of one's genitals was a very serious affair. Not long ago many people really believed that a boy or girl who "played with himself" would become insane, or feeble-minded. Some persons still think that masturbation is a sin, to be avoided at all costs. There are those who believe that the boy or girl who masturbates can be detected by circles under the eyes, pimples on the face, or a peculiar look in the eye.

In recent years, intelligent, scientifically minded persons who have studied these things tell us quite a different story about masturbation. They say, for instance, that masturbation cannot and does not cause insanity or feeble-mindedness. It is true that mentally unbalanced, immature, and inadequate persons may masturbate more frequently than normally endowed individuals, but it is not *because* they handle themselves that they are insane.

The evidence is that no one can tell by looking into another's face whether or not he is an habitual masturbator. Circles under the eyes or a shifty look in the eye can mean a lot of things.

Today we know that the tendency to relieve sexual tension by rubbing the genital area to the point of release is a very common practice. Statistical studies and clinical findings indicate that between 80 and 90 per cent of teen-age boys report that they masturbate, and that somewhat fewer teen-age girls also report the practice. With a habit as common as this seems to be, what the harm is, if any, is a very real question.

Psychologists agree that the greatest danger involved in masturbation is that of feeling guilty or ashamed. For instance, one 15-year-old boy says, "Since I was 13 years old, I have been masturbating quite frequently. At first I thought that I would outgrow it, but I am afraid that it has turned into a very bad habit. I still tell myself that I shouldn't do it, and that there is no sense in it, but it doesn't seem to work. At first it gave me a good feeling, but now it's just like eating and sleeping. Sometimes I feel like a narcotic who is taking drugs in order to satisfy his wants."

Such feelings of unworthiness undermine one's self-confidence and make it difficult to take a happy, wholesome outlook on life. This sense of wrongdoing is encouraged by certain religious groups that believe such sex play is sinful. If this is the point of view of a person's religion, he must come to terms with his religious beliefs, himself, and his sex life if there is to be any real integration and wholesomeness in his adjustment.

Some authorities report that a history of masturbation on the part of the woman, and in some cases of men too, makes more difficult the adjustments to the marriage partner later. Some girls who have stimulated themselves to the point of release for years before marriage may require exactly the same type of frictional excitation from their husbands after marriage in order to achieve full release from sexual tension. This may make more complicated the early marital adjustments that even in the best of unions take mutual adaptation to achieve.

Some teen-age boys and girls are so ingrown and retiring that the practice of masturbation is likely to exaggerate their tendencies to withdraw from others. The healthier role involves truly satisfying participation with many other persons of both sexes and all ages in a variety of wholesome activities and in the pursuit of mutual interests. Occasional episodes of masturbation in the life of a person who is alive socially, maturing emotionally, and wholesome mentally seem to have no injurious effects.

Masturbation is an individual affair in a way that other sexual practices cannot be. Premarital or extramarital intercourse very definitely involves other persons. Prostitution is a social as well as a personal concern. Even petting necessitates the involvement of the pettee! The release of insistent sex tensions by self-stimulation, therefore, is the only physical outlet without social consequences beyond the individual involved.

The sex drive differs so greatly in intensity among individuals that some youth may be spared the necessity of seeking some overt release, while others are frequently and insistently driven to some form of sexual outlet. Nature takes care of the accumulating semen in the male by periodic seminal emissions. Even so, the torment of the tensions involved for the boy may be an ever-present challenge to him. So also in certain highly sexed girls the sex drive may prove to be too compulsive to ignore in the years between maturation and marriage.

Here, as in other sex troubles and worries, seeking counsel from some qualified person in whom one has confidence may be helpful. As such things are brought out into the open and discussed frankly and intelligently, they frequently lose their anxious overtones. It is the hidden fears that haunt and corrode the spirit. The more honest we are with ourselves and the more freely we seek adequate professional guidance before we get beyond our depth, the better we feel about these things.

SEX
fantasies and dreams

Young people are often worried by their recurrent dreams and fantasies of a sexual nature. Boys usually dream of some sexually exciting episode during the seminal emission. At intervals through day and night boys and girls alike may find themselves living out in imagination some highly sexual activity, oftentimes in quite respectable surroundings and involving even the most innocent persons. These things are disturbing to many young people who are trying to live according to high standards and moral ideals. They may feel that these fleeting fantasies are unworthy, unclean, inappropriate to their way of life.

Such thoughts, which come spontaneously to all normally sexed persons from time to time, are no cause for alarm or concern. They are but indications of the sexual potential inherent in being mature. Persons who deliberately stimulate such thoughts by shady stories and lewd pictures have the added burden of keeping under control the excitation that builds up under those circumstances. Persons for whom such visitations are unexpected and unsolicited find that the mood frequently passes as suddenly as it came, without undue strain or difficulty.

IF
you get in a jam

You are not perfect. The chances are very good that you have done things of which you are ashamed, which brought pain and unhappiness, and made you lose confidence in yourself. You quite probably have made mistakes that you wish had never happened. But they did. When you have gotten into some sort of sex jam, your life is not necessarily ruined. As soon as you are sorry for what you have done, you can do what you can to make restitution to the other(s) whom you may have wronged. You can ask their forgiveness. You can talk through your problem with some responsible adult in whom you have confidence. Most important of all, you can forgive yourself and make a fresh start in the life that still can be yours.

SUBLIMATION

Sublimation (sub-li-may'-shun) is the channeling of sexual energy into activities other than direct sex outlets. Some people get so much satisfaction in active social affairs, sports, participation in music, art, drama, and scientific endeavors that their sex problems do not become burdensome. Many outstanding persons say that during their periods of greatest creativity they feel little desire for active sex behavior. Authors and playwrights, scientists and musicians, humanitarians and religious workers—all have learned to some extent to sublimate their sexual powers.

The degree of sublimation that a person desires and achieves depends on many factors within his personality. The frequency and nature of the physical gratification he feels the need for is also dependent upon a variety of individual characteristics that range all the way from the nature of his sex drive to his concepts of himself as a person and his basic philosophy of life. In a broad moral sense he is good and right as long as his behavior harms no one else and fosters his own best growth and development.

SEX—
problem or promise

Sex is a part of life. It can be fine and full. It can be painful, restricting, and shameful. Like every other source of power, it must be harnessed or it runs wild and becomes destructive. Electricity wired into your home will light your house, cook your meals, warm your feet, and perform all kinds of miracles. Left unleashed, as lightning, it can destroy everything you care about in one burning holocaust. So it is with sex. If left to run wild, it can hurt and destroy and leave forever scarred all that you hold dear. Or, it can be the basis of the fullest friendship, the finest love, the happiest marriage, and the supreme satisfaction of home and parenthood.

Many years of rich fulfillment are ahead for the boy and girl capable of effectively harnessing their sex drives. The sweetness of really belonging to friends who love and accept and respect you, comes only to those who are learning to curb the exploitative, explosive aspects of sex and to develop its tender, responsible forms of expression. The joy of finding someone to have and to hold as yours forever in loyal devotion, belongs only to those who have developed ways that are essentially monogamous. The rewards of motherhood and fatherhood belong to the parents who love each other deeply enough to be able to let their children go and grow through the years. The deep wells of a person's sex life can bring relaxation, confidence, and personal significance, not as they gush forth in a series of wild outpourings, but only as they are channeled for purposes beyond the moment, and dedicated to meanings that represent the best of which he is capable.

Your sex life is yours to choose. More than ever before in history young people are given the freedom to work out their own behavior and to run their own lives. Your sex worries, your difficulties with sex, are yours to work out with all the help that modern science and religion can offer. Your fulfillment of the sex side of life is yours to achieve, too, with the benediction of all who find life good.

part

THREE

YOUR FRIENDS,

YOUR PARENTS,

AND YOUR DATES

CHAPTER 10

What do
you expect

LEARNING WHAT IS EXPECTED of you by members
of the other sex is the big business of the teen years. When
the time comes that you are ready to date, and go out with
each other, you have to know what is expected of you if
you are ever to be secure with others. Fortunately, there
have been several studies of what teen-age boys and girls
say they like and do not like in each other. These general
expectations probably hold for many young people in communities all across the country.

Since such surveys are only "in general," they cannot
represent variations in expected behavior in certain groups
or among particular individuals. What a fellow in a big-city
gang expects of girls will differ considerably from what a
4-H club farm boy expects of his date. What a girl who
has been dating for several years expects probably will not
be the same as what a girl who has never had a date expects.
With warnings of the many exceptions there are, let us take

of each other?

a good look at what boys and girls tend to expect of each other generally.

WHAT
boys say they like in girls

Lester Crow's study of more than 1,600 boys and girls between the ages of 14 and 17, turns up such characteristics as these in what boys say they admire in girls:

"I like a girl who acts like a girl and not like a tomboy" (14-year-old boy)

"I like a girl who is pretty and talks nice" (14-year-old boy)

"I like a girl who doesn't hang around with a bunch of boys or tough girls" (14-year-old boy)

"I would like her to be of average intelligence" (14-year-old boy)

"I like a friendly smile" (17-year-old boy)

"I like a girl with plenty of good sense at parties and dates" (17-year-old boy)

"I like a girl to be a good dancer, a lot of fun, and to have a good sense of humor at the right time" (17-year-old boy)

"I like a girl to be able to carry on an intelligent conversation" (17-year-old boy)

In Dr. Blood's study of dating preferences on a large coeducational university campus, more than 80 per cent of the men said they preferred a girl who "is willing to join in a group," "is a well-rounded person," and "is a good listener."

The gist of these and similar studies in other schools and colleges gives us a clear impression that boys like girls who are feminine, friendly, at ease in social situations, and pleasant persons to be with.

WHAT
girls say they like about boys

The girls in one high school study had these things to say about what they like in boys:

"I like a boy to be well groomed" (14-year-old girl)

"I like a boy who has good manners and isn't a show-off" (14-year-old girl)

"I like a boy who knows how to get along with people" (14-year-old girl)

"He should be neat and clean, courteous, kind, and considerate" (14-year-old girl)

"I like a boy with intelligence, someone who knows how to talk about other things besides movies and baseball" (17-year-old girl)

"At present I like all the traits my boy friend has: he is considerate, polite, ambitious, intelligent, punctual, kind, thoughtful, complimentary, just affectionate enough; and he has a wonderful personality which allows him to mix well with all groups of any ages" (17-year-old girl)

"I like a boy who is firm and stands up for what he thinks is right" (17-year-old girl)

Practically all the college girls in the large coeducational university (in Dr. Blood's study) said that they personally preferred for serious dates a man who "has good sense, is intelligent" (100 per cent); "is honest and straightforward" (99.3 per cent); "is an intelligent conversationalist" (98.5 per cent); "is willing to join a group and is well poised" (94 per cent); "is appropriately dressed" (90.2 per cent).

In the university study both sexes agree on a number of characteristics they prefer in members of the other sex for either casual or serious dates. There is practically unanimous approval of the person with such qualities as these:

Is pleasant and cheerful	Acts natural
Has a sense of humor	Is considerate
Is a good sport	Is neat in appearance

WHAT
boys and girls criticize about each other

Twenty-five hundred high school students living throughout the United States were selected by Dr. Harold Christensen as representative of today's teen-agers in his study of attitudes toward dating practices. Both sexes agree on liking such qualities in each other as dependability, pleasantness, consideration, and general attractiveness in appearance and manners; but there are a number of ways in which each sex tends to displease the other.

High school boys are criticized by high school girls for being careless, thoughtless, disrespectful, sex driven, and loud. In such tendencies as these, not only did girls mention them as sources of trouble with boys, but the boys generally recognized them as characteristics in boys that warranted criticism.

Teen-age girls in this study are criticized by high school boys for being less natural, more touchy, money minded, unresponsive, childish and flighty than boys. These are qualities that boys mention as particularly characteristic of girls, and that girls admit are more frequent as criticisms of their own sex than of the other.

Review of such criticisms that each sex makes of the other indicates that both boys and girls tend to behave in certain ways that the other sex finds unpleasant. Boys tend to fall short of girls' expectations in being too thoughtless, unmannerly, disrespectful and sex driven. Girls do not measure up to boys' expectations when they appear shallow, touchy, conceited, possessive, and money minded.

Neither boys nor girls like continuing disagreeableness, even in an otherwise lovable person. As one sixteen-year-old girl phrases it:

> I have been going with a boy for over six months, and he says he loves me. I love him too, but every time he's in a foul mood, which seems to be frequent lately, he takes it out on me. He yells and calls me names and makes me want to cry. Half the time he's like this and the other half he's wonderful to me. How can I make him see that when he treats me that way he's slowly killing my love for him?

Further light is thrown on what each sex finds objectionable in the other by a Florida State University study of college freshmen and sophomores. In this exploration of dating behavior, men said that they broke off dating with a girl for such reasons as lack of interest, low morals, or finding out something unpleasing about her. The college girls said that they would stop dating a boy if he showed disrespect for them, if they found out something unpleasant about him, or if he got too serious.

Studies agree that many boys and girls feel insecure, shy, and uncertain with each other. Learning what to expect in a given situation is one way of gaining social poise and overcoming self-consciousness. Let us explore some of the circumstances and situations that arise in any young person's life and see what is commonly expected.

TELEPHONE
courtesies

Telephoning comes into its own during the teen years. The instrument which was used only casually during childhood is jealously guarded by adolescents as a priceless means of communication. Dates are made and broken over it. What to wear and where to go and what to do are all discussed over it. Most important of all are the post-mortems that take place soon after two teen-agers have left each other. These self-evaluations include reviews of what he said, what she said, how they both felt, what they did and how, and a critical analysis of just how things went. Such conversations take time and may sound trivial to an eavesdropper, especially when they come soon after the two have been together for hours. But to young people, the telephone is a friendly confidante of great importance.

HOW to place a telephone call

It is well to master the know-how of telephoning. Since most teen-agers live with their families or in dormitories where they share the use of the phone, certain basic courtesies are expected. For example, when you put through a call, ask at once for the person to whom you wish to speak, giving your name, in this way: "'Hello, is Jane there, please? This is Edith calling." When Jane comes to the phone repeat the salutation: "Hello, Jane. This is Edith." Then give the message you called to deliver. If Jane is not there or cannot come to the phone, you may leave a message for her if you keep it short and simple. Long, involved messages get twisted and are a nuisance to transmit. If you cannot get your message into a few words, leave word that you will call her back later, or that you would like her to call you when she returns. Thank the person to whom you have been talking, and hang up courteously.

Reserve your kidding and teasing for those who appreciate such fooling. Asking Jane's father if he knows who is calling is apt to get you in Dutch with Jane's family and to put Jane on the spot too. Nor is it wise to be too "cute" and full of nonsense with others of the family who may answer the phone. Keep your request and your message short and simple.

HOW to answer the phone

If you are expecting a call it is well to be close by when it comes through. When the phone rings do not quickly take it for granted that it is your call. Give the person on the other end of the line a chance to identify himself before you salute him. Picking up the receiver and saying, "Hi, sweetheart!" just might cause your dad's boss to sputter in consternation!

Your salutation starts best with your identification. You may simply repeat the number of your phone, immediately assuring the other party that the correct number has been connected. Or you can answer the phone by the formula, "Hello, this is the Gaynor residence." Another variation is to say, "Yes? This is John Gaynor speaking."

IF a girl must telephone a boy

In a poll of high-school boys more than two-thirds said that they do not like to have girls call them on the telephone. They feel that this is a boy's privilege, and that a girl seems forward when she phones a boy. They furthermore report that their families tease them about the girls who call them up at home.

Yet there may be times when a girl really must call a boy with an urgent message, to give him an invitation, or to make a request that cannot wait until she next sees him. When such a call is necessary, the girl must be unusually careful to observe the expected telephone courtesies. She should protect both the boy and herself from embarrassment by keeping her call short, and not telephoning him too often.

HOW to hang up politely

After the business of the call has been transacted, some young people hang on to the phone, finding it hard to say goodbye and hang up. If this is caused by a little anxiety lest the other be offended by too abrupt a closing, a few simple formulas can be employed to end the call comfortably. If the other has called you, after the conversation seems completed you can say, "It was nice of you to call me. I'll see you soon." If you placed the call, you can conclude by saying, "I've enjoyed talking with you. Goodbye for now." If you feel it necessary, you can add, "I must run along now." Whatever your pet closing, it is courteous to hang up before unduly prolonging your telephoning.

A telephone call that goes on and on aimlessly, picking up little stray bits of chatter, does not make much sense and may be annoying. Even when the call is going great guns, it slackens off after a while and should be brought to a comfortable close. Some families put a three-minute limit on telephone calls in order to keep the lines free for incoming calls and to give the others in the family a chance to use the phone.

Dorothy's father is a doctor, and it is essential for her to keep her calls to a minimum. She keeps an egg-timer by the phone and allows herself only the three minutes while the sand flows from one end to the other. This practice has helped Dorothy learn to plan what she is to say, and she has become an interesting conversationalist just because she knows that she cannot run on and on. A successful phone call has a courteous beginning, a pleasant main message, and an easy short closing.

GIVING
and accepting gifts

As soon as two persons begin to be interested in each other, they find themselves eager to do things for each other. When one is fond of another, he wants to give gifts and do thoughtful things that will be appreciated. These are impulses that lift any relationship out of self-centeredness into considerate warm-heartedness. Yet it is not always easy to give an appropriate gift. Receiving gifts is sometimes even more difficult. There is an art to giving and receiving that comes with practice.

It may be trite to remind ourselves that it is not the gift that counts so much as the thought behind it; nevertheless, that is the case. No matter how suitable and fine a gift is, it rarely is so much appreciated as the thought that prompted it. Knowing that someone cared is what makes his gifts meaningful. We may be far more deeply touched with some little trinket that expresses a friend's sensitivity to our interests and needs than we are by some impressively elaborate gift.

WHEN gifts are appreciated

At certain seasons gifts are expected between friends. Christmas, of course, is a customary time for close friends to exchange gifts. It is possible then to give a gift to someone who at any other season might be embarrassed by it. Indeed, Christmas giving is so often taken for granted that it may become perfunctory rather than a generous expression of friendship. It does not have to be burdensome.

A gift on a friend's birthday is usually greatly appreciated. A birthday is peculiarly one's own. To have a good friend remember it with a thoughtful present is heartwarming. Certain anniversaries are marked occasionally by gifts. Graduation gifts are common. Going-away presents are usually appreciated. Any special day which has particular significance to an individual may be celebrated with him by the bestowing of some appropriate gift.

Good friends do not have to wait for special days to express their affection with a small gift. Some little thing may remind one of a friend and be given to him with the simple presentation, "I thought of you when I saw this." An article, a booklet, a clipping, a poem, a cartoon, or other item that seems to have some special significance to a friend, may be presented with nothing more than a simple, "This will interest you." Because they are individualized, these spontaneous gestures of friendship are often far more appreciated than the more routine gift giving at established times.

GIFTS that are appropriate

Certain accepted standards of gift giving between friends should be recognized. Among the gifts that young men and women may give each other are books, stationery, pens, pencils, inexpensive jewelry such as pins, earrings, tie clips, cuff links, and the like, or wearing apparel like scarves or gloves. It is not considered appropriate for a boy to give a girl intimate items of clothing like underwear or night clothes.

A gift that is made for the other is especially appreciated. Girls often knit their boy friends socks or mittens or ties or scarves or even sweaters that express their devoted interest quite fittingly. A boy may make his girl friend something that she would enjoy, like a frame for her diploma, a simple case for her books, or a chest for some of her treasures. Such items do not need to cost a great deal beyond the time the boy invests in their construction. Making something special for one's friends is a fine thing to do as long as it does not interfere too seriously with other friendships and responsibilities.

When in doubt about what to give a girl, flowers are usually safe. They are especially prized when some dress-up occasion comes along. When a boy takes a girl to a formal dance, a corsage, or flowers for her hair, is usually expected. Otherwise, he may or may not bring her flowers when he comes. In some seasons and in many places, flowers are so expensive that a boy may not be able to afford them as often as he might like. A girl should not expect him always to bring her flowers. She will enjoy them more, and he will feel them more appreciated, if they are a surprise.

A boy planning to bring flowers which a girl may wear to a dance is wise to ask her ahead of time what she plans to wear so that he can have the corsage that will go with her gown. Boys have been known to arrive at a girl's house with pink rosebuds, only to find her in a bright-red dress. A girl with some imagination can surmount such a predicament. She might change hurriedly into something with which the roses go more attractively. Or she might wear them in her hair, where the clash would not be so pronounced. In either case she is careful not to hurt the boy's feelings.

There are other occasions when a boy may send flowers to a girl—remembering her birthday with them or sending a plant or cut flowers to cheer her up when she is ill. By sending her some little green growing thing in a pottery container that she can keep on her window sill, he may say "Thank you" for some especially appreciated hospitality or thoughtfulness on her part. He can send her a chrysanthemum to wear to a football game, or a gardenia to wear in her hair, or even a single rosebud to mark some special moment in their lives. He can bring her a bunch of spring violets that he picked himself, or share with her some of his mother's late-blooming dahlias. It is not so much what the flower is, or how much it costs, as the fact that he has remembered her that a girl appreciates.

THE cost of a gift

Some inexpensive item, selected particularly for a friend, is often greatly appreciated. An expensive gift may embarrass the recipient, especially if he or she cannot reciprocate at the same price level. It is not considered proper to give a girl friend or boy friend very expensive gifts. Such things as furs, costly jewelry, and elaborate gifts should not be exchanged between friends.

Exchanging gifts sometimes seems like swapping items between two persons. There may be the unfortunate feeling that you have to give the other the same kind of thing at the same general cost as the gift that comes from him. This puts the whole thing on a commercial basis that detracts from the spirit of thoughtful giving.

Another mistake is to try to treat everyone exactly alike. A girl may wish to give each of her boy friends precisely the same thing so that no one of them will feel slighted. One Christmas a boy bought six identical compacts for six girls he knew. Needless to say, when they saw one another's compacts none of them felt personally remembered.

Gift giving should fit into one's budget without breaking the bank for the next several weeks. Extravagant giving is not necessary. It may be embarrassing to the other person as well as to one's own budget. It is not the cost of the gift so much as the imagination and personal thoughtfulness behind it that gives it value.

REFUSING a gift

Sometimes a girl must refuse a boy's proffered gift. Edward tried to give Lee a beautiful heirloom brooch that had belonged to his great-grandmother. Lee could not take such a treasure from him, even though she was deeply touched by his generosity. She closed the box and returned it to Edward with the words, "It is beautiful, Edward. It was wonderful of you to want me to have it. But I cannot keep it. You will realize this, too, when you think about it. Thank you just the same."

Sometimes a girl's parents will insist that she return some gift. That may be hard; but it can be done with a simple explanation that Mother does not think it best that it be accepted. Every effort should be made in such a situation to let the boy know that you appreciate his kindness and his generosity even though you cannot accept the gift itself.

When a gift is received, the courteous thing is to open it as soon as you can, in front of the giver if convenient, and to express your thanks appropriately at once. It is not necessary to gush or rave on extravagantly about the present. It is important that you communicate your real appreciation and gratitude for the other's thoughtfulness, telling, if you can sincerely, how suitable the gift is.

When a gift arrives from an absent friend, your thank-you should go out in the mail within the next day or two. The note should be friendly, warm, and appreciative in whatever way comes most easily to you. It should express your gratitude specifically by naming the present with some fitting adjective, and your thanks for it. A thoughtful thank-you note usually includes some item of interest that assures the giver that you are doing your part to keep up your end of the fellowship. It is not necessary for you to rush out and get a present for the person who has given you one. Better to wait until some especially appropriate time before attempting to return the kindness.

BALANCE of giving and receiving gifts

Persons secure in their friendship do not worry about who gave what to whom, or when. They are not concerned that they keep their giving exactly balanced between them. One may be able to give more often and more generously than the other, without either of them feeling uneasy about it. When you really feel loved you do not need a person's presents to make you feel secure. When you have a grown-up kind of devotion for someone, you want to give to him and do for him as your heart dictates. Extreme stinginess and foolish extravagance both are often marks of insecurity. As persons become more maturely secure they usually find a comfortable balance between the two.

HOW to ask a girl for a date

When a boy wants to ask a girl for a date, there are several rules to follow and pitfalls to avoid. First of all, he invites her specifically for a particular occasion, giving her the time, the place, and the nature of the affair. He says, for example, "May I take you to the game in Hometown Gym at two next Saturday afternoon?" Knowing all the relevant facts, she has a basis upon which to refuse or to accept. In the second place, he is friendly and shows that he really wants her to accept his invitation. He looks at her with a smile while he waits for her reply. If she accepts, he is pleased and arranges definitely for the time at which he will call for her. If she refuses, he says that he is sorry and suggests that perhaps another time she will go with him.

HOW not to ask her

Boys find that girls do not like the indirect approach that starts, "What are you doing next Friday night?" That puts the girl "on the spot." Boys should not act as though they expect to be refused, as Amos does when he says, "'I don't suppose you'd like to go on a date with me, would you?" This backhanded kind of invitation is apt to make the girl feel uncomfortable and is a mark of the boy's feeling of insecurity, too.

Girls do not like to be asked for dates at the last minute. It is no compliment to call a girl up the very evening of an affair. Even if she is free, she may be reluctant to accept such an eleventh-hour invitation. If circumstances have made it impossible to ask early for the date, then go right ahead, of course. Be frank about it. It sometimes happens that a girl has had no other invitation to an affair she wants very much to attend. Girls protest, too, that some boys try to date them months ahead. Beth put her uncertainty about such an invitation this way: "Why sure, Mac, I'll go with you to the Prom next year if we both still think it's a good idea when the time comes."

Since asking a girl for a date is both a compliment and an invitation, a boy need have no fear of using a simple, direct, and friendly approach. He might be surprised to know how eager the girl has been to hear the words he is struggling to say!

HOW
to accept a date

When a boy asks a girl for a date he has a right to expect a definite reply. Some girls try to stall with a "she didn't say yes and she didn't say no" kind of answer while they make up their minds, or perhaps see if a better offer comes along. This is unfair, and a mark of the girl's social inexperience. If for some reason the girl is not sure that she can accept the boy's invitation, she tells him why and then lets him know exactly when he may have her answer. If she must decline, she does so firmly, kindly, with only as much explanation as she feels necessary. She says in effect, "I'm sorry, Jim, I already have a date for next Friday," or "I don't believe I can."

When a girl accepts a date she does it with pleasure, in a way that makes the boy glad that he asked her. This does not mean that she falls all over him, embarrassing him with her exuberance. But she makes clear that she is glad to go with him and that she will be waiting for him to call for her. She usually finds it wise to repeat the time and place, thus letting him know that she understands just what the arrangements are. This practice prevents many a misunderstanding and is always a good procedure.

WHEN
you have been stood up

Sometimes a boy does not appear at the time when a girl expects him. This is embarrassing for her, and she is apt to be annoyed about it. Even so, if she is a loyal friend, she will reserve judgment until she has heard his explanation. She gives him a chance to explain at the very next opportunity. It may have been that there was some misunderstanding about the time. It may be that the boy was unable to come and for some reason could not let her know. Nick was delayed on an out-of-town trip with his father and at the time of his date was many miles away, without even a chance to phone. This happens rarely, but the girl should give the boy the benefit of the doubt until he has had a chance to speak for himself. Even a court considers a man innocent until he is proved guilty!

The boy in the case owes it to the girl to follow through on their arrangement if it is at all possible. If something comes up so that he cannot appear as agreed, he should call her as much ahead of time as possible, letting her know what has happened and what to expect. If he is ill or has had an accident, either he or his mother should telephone the girl. Getting cold feet, or deciding that he does not want to go out after all, is no excuse for not appearing or calling.

Sometimes it is the boy who is left holding the bag on a date that never materializes. This is much less common, for the simple reason that it is the boy who calls for the girl at her home in most cases, and so is on hand to collect her when the appointed time comes. But, occasionally, the agreement is made to meet in some place other than the girl's residence, and she does not appear. Or, upon arriving at her home, he is told she is "out" or "ill," or he is given some other excuse for which he has not been prepared.

In such instances, the girl owes the boy an explanation of her behavior at the earliest possible moment. He is wise to reserve judgment and try not to be too angry or hurt until she has had a chance to tell him her side of the story. If her reasons seem to be good ones, he may then attempt to make another date with her. Should he feel that she is "brushing him off" he probably will acknowledge the situation with as much poise as he can muster, and refrain from ever letting her stand him up again.

Thoughtful persons of both sexes do not subject a date to the embarrassment of being stood up. They make sure that time, place, and function are mutually understood in the first place. Then, if anything comes up that makes it impossible to go through with the plans, the other person is notified, and the date is postponed.

NOT
expecting too much

Datable persons may be more numerous than you think. Too often young people unnecessarily restrict their dating possibilities by unreasonable and unimportant limitations on who is datable. Girls often refuse to consider a boy unless he is taller. This is too bad, especially in the early teens when so many girls are growing faster than boys and are apt to be taller. After all, height is not the whole man.

Boys sometimes demand that the girl be exceptionally good-looking. Looks are not so important as personality in a friendship. Plenty of ordinary-looking girls are interesting companions and may be even more loyal than the school "glamour gal."

A good date is someone you know or would like to know better. He or she is an enjoyable partner in fun. He does not have to be witty or clever to be interesting. She need not be a brilliant conversationalist. When you can relax and not expect perfection either in yourself or in your friend, you are far more likely to have a good time.

COMING
up to expectations

No one expects you to be a perfect date every time. You need not feel that you are a failure because you once pulled some boner in public. You will begin to feel adequate with members of the other sex as you master the few general principles of good conduct that usually are expected. You can make your own list of what these would be.

TEN commandments of good conduct

A Chicago high-school girl won a date with a movie star by submitting the best letter on the topic, "How to Catch a Man Without Running," in which she suggested ten commandments of good conduct that ran like this:

1. Be a teen with taste, dressing appropriately for the occasion.
2. Act like a lady, and he will treat you as such.
3. Be able to enjoy an everyday date as well as the glamour occasions.
4. Don't hang on him too possessively.
5. Don't have him fetch and carry just to create an impression.
6. Make up if you like, but do not try to make over what you are.
7. Be popular with girls as well as boys.
8. Learn to like sports—it's an all-American topic in which boys are interested.
9. Don't be too self-sufficient; boys like to feel needed.
10. Be natural.

Boys' conduct on dates is a mirror image of girls' behavior. It takes two to make a good date. When the boy is suitably groomed and courteously at ease, he not only gives the girl a good time but he is likely to enjoy himself too.

Both girls and boys must learn how to be "smooth" in their dating. None of us is born with the attributes of being a good date. All of us must learn how to conduct ourselves with poise in ways that are expected of us.

CHAPTER 11

Are you ready

DATING BEGINS AT EARLIER ages for many young people than in our parents' or grandparents' time. People used to think that dating should be delayed as long as possible. Going out together was taken more seriously than it is today. When a girl in great-grandmother's time started going out with a boy, it usually meant that wedding bells would soon be ringing for the couple. So, it was generally believed that dating should be postponed until the girl and boy were ready for such a serious step.

Nowadays dating is not considered as a commitment for marriage. A boy and girl may date just for the pleasure of being together, without the community's expecting them to make it a permanent arrangement. Dating has become so generally accepted that a young person may go with several others before settling upon "the right one" in marriage.

for dating?

The ages at which young people begin to date differ greatly. Some boys and girls in elementary school start going together to family and neighborhood outings, church gatherings, movies and clubs, sports and school affairs. Other young people well along in high school, or even in college, are yet to have their first date. How is it that some persons start so young, and others do not begin to have dates until so much later?

THE
"if I only had—" excuses

When others around you are dating, it is easy to give yourself excuses for not having dates. Such rationalizations (good reasons instead of the real ones) often begin with the phrase, "If I only had . . .";

"If I only had good-looking clothes, I would get plenty of dates."

"If I only had a car, I would be dating too."

"If I only had a big house with a rumpus room and a barbecue, I would have no trouble getting dates."

"If I only had lots of money, I could have all the friends I wanted."

These are the obvious things that young people pounce upon as good date bait. But actually the amount of money you have, or where you live may not be so important as how you use what you have. So, let us look deeper into the various factors that influence the age at which you start dating.

AGE
is only one factor

The number of years you have lived is only one piece in the puzzle of your readiness for dating. Many other influences are at work, as you may have guessed. Perhaps you have already discussed the importance of such things as looks, grooming, clothes, money, and other immediate tangibles in datability. Young people sometimes tend to feel that such obvious assets are all that count in getting started. There are other things, not often recognized, that are fully as important in determining the age at which a person gets started having dates.

APPEARING
attractive to others

The way you look is what other people see first. It is not the only part of your personality, but it certainly is important as a first impression. It probably is true that the exceedingly attractive boy or girl has an easier time getting dates than does the less appealing person. But, even though you will never win a beauty contest, there is a great deal you can do to improve your appearance. Being clean and well groomed is attractive in both boys and girls. Choosing clothes that are simple, appropriate, and becoming is worth learning, both for the present and for the years ahead. The best-dressed girl is not the one with a closet full of clothes, but the one who knows how to select clothes that do something for her, and how to wear them well. Both boys and girls can develop the arts of accenting their strong points and playing down their weak ones. The way you talk and walk and carry yourself contributes far more to the impression you make than anything you are wearing, as any clothes model can tell you. If you can throw your shoulders back and stand up straight, with a smile on your face, and a light in your eyes, people are bound to notice you as someone who looks alive and interesting.

MANNERS
and courtesy

You do not have to be stilted and "proper" in a formal sense to appear well. In fact, it is the simple unobtrusive courtesies that are most attractive. Saying such little words as "Please" and "Thank you" and "I am sorry" when they are called for, in easy sincerity, even without thinking, opens doors into comfortable social situations. Remember that boasting and shouting, whining and complaining, pouting and temper tantrums are unpleasant to others generally; and that courteous listening, thoughtfulness, consideration of other people, a sense of humor, and graciousness are always pleasing. Things like this you have probably always known. Now is the time to get them into action often enough and smoothly enough to be ready for the dating opportunities that lie ahead.

HOW
your parents feel about your dating

Some parents are eager for their sons and daughters to go out with others. These parents often send their boys and girls to dancing school and begin giving parties and fostering social affairs during junior high school days. They may be so anxious for their children to do well in making friends that they push their social activities as fast as they can, sometimes even faster than the young persons like. When the boy or girl begins to date early and well, such parents are pleased, and they reward the social success of their children in many ways.

Other parents discourage dating by trying to delay the age at which their sons and daughters begin to have dates. Some fathers say flatly that they will not allow their daughters to have dates until they are at least sixteen years of age. Sometimes parents tease their children so much about their first boy friends and girl friends that dating may hardly seem worth all the ridicule at home. Then there are the parents who expect, and perhaps need, so much help at home that they openly discourage any outside social life that will interfere with family responsibilities.

Parents tend to be more lenient with their younger children than they were with their older ones. The oldest child has the task of building up confidence in his parents. When he has assured them by his behavior that young people can go together without getting into trouble, then his parents relax and allow younger brothers and sisters more freedom. Frequently younger brothers and sisters date at an earlier age, stay out later at night, and obtain the privilege of the family car and other advantages in dating much more easily than the was the case with their older brothers and sisters. These are real factors in the age for dating of young people that, once recognized, can be dealt with accordingly.

AIDS
to dating

THE importance of social experience

The amount of experience you have had in getting along with people makes a difference in the age at which you start to date. Those who have had many opportunities for mingling freely with others seem to be ready to date at an earlier age than those whose childhood friendships have been somewhat restricted. Young people who grow up in social families have an inside track. Through their families they have already made the acquaintance of eligible members of the other sex. Even more important, they have had opportunities to learn how to meet people, enjoy friends, and have a good time without feeling embarrassed and ill at ease.

Young people who have been active in clubs, committees, and other school and community organizations begin to mingle with the other sex at an earlier age than those who have not been active in social groups. They have learned how to get along with others comfortably, so that they are ready for dates with the other sex sooner than those who have not had this advantage.

Getting and keeping dates calls for many skills in one's relationship to others. Introducing oneself into a new crowd, being a loyal friend, patching up disagreements, making decisions or sharing responsibilities with others, and even having a good time—all these are learned skills requiring years of practice with flesh-and-blood people. The extent to which you have begun to learn such things affects the age at which you begin to date easily.

YOUR interests and skills

Some young people are delayed in starting to date because of the solitary nature of their interests. Clair did not begin to have dates until he was of college age. All through his high school days he spent every spare minute out of school with his paints. He was talented and felt the pressure of his teachers and parents for developing his artistic ability. He became a good painter, but he was definitely behind the crowd in his dating skills and experience.

Estelle followed quite a different pattern. She was interested in the young people's organizations of her church and began to be active in them very early in her teens. By the time she entered high school she was recognized as a natural leader and was voted to a class office in her freshman year. She made still more friends as she sat on the Student Cabinet. It was not surprising that she got started early and dated relatively easily from the beginning.

Girls and boys who have learned to do the things that others of their age enjoy, greatly increase their dating chances. It is the girl who can do things who gets invited out to do them. If she can play tennis and golf, dance, swim, skate, or play an instrument, she widens the horizons of her dating circles. Similarly, the boy who has learned to do the things that bring young people together is usually ready for dates at a far earlier age than the boy who has not acquired the skills others share.

Some communities make it easy for young people to grow up socially. The town that provides a teen-age center where young people may meet and enjoy each other in healthful recreation promotes the kind of fellowship that leads to wholesome dating. Towns where the churches have active youth programs foster easy access of one sex to the other in pleasant growth-promoting settings. Neighborhoods where there are frequent parties for various ages and both sexes, with such activities as square dances, suppers, skating parties, picnics, hikes, and other informal kinds of fun, provide the type of social climate in which healthy dating can thrive.

Schools can do a great deal to encourage the right kinds of dating by the attitudes of their teachers and through their extracurricular programs. Many high schools now have courses in the social arts, in boy-girl relationships, and similar subjects. Teachers who by personality and training are able to give good guidance to their students in these personal-social adjustments are a great asset. Schools that encourage the development of such activities as drama groups, special interest and hobby clubs, informal non-competitive sports, forum and discussion groups, and social events that are planned for the majority rather than for the sophisticated and socially experienced minority do a great deal to help young people build friendships with each other.

Today's young people can do a great deal to influence community policies and programs. If your town does not have adequate recreational facilities it is up to you as young people to let your views on the matter be known in places where your suggestions can be effective. This is not a matter for impatient fussing, but rather for the careful drafting of a proposal that meets the approval of a representative group of young people, has the backing of influential older persons, and is submitted in carefully worked-out form through proper local channels.

So it is too with revising church and school programs to meet the youth's needs today more adequately. Church and school policies are being rebuilt for, by, and with their young people. Many of the splendid church programs and school courses on boy-girl relations, courtship, love, marriage, and family life, sex education, and modern codes of behavior, have been developed in recent years as a direct result of articulate groups of teen-agers who made their wishes known.

Your community helps in providing a climate in which it is good to grow up, socially, emotionally, morally. But, it is a two-way process. You can help your community to become the kind of place in which it is good to live. Why don't you talk over some of the changes you would like to see made, with your friends, your parents, your advisers at church and school, your leaders wherever they are?

PERSONAL
maturity for dating

Just as young people grow up physically at different rates, so too they mature socially at different ages. We have already seen in earlier chapters that physical maturity comes at various ages for boys and girls. Now we see that one's readiness for dating may be closely related to the age at which one matures physically.

The early-maturing boy shoots up faster and is taller and more grown-up looking than a late-maturing boy of the same age. It is quite likely that he is interested in girls at an earlier age. The girl who matures at an early age is ready for dates with boys before the girl who is slow in her physical maturation. Not only does she look the part earlier, but she feels the interest sooner.

In general, girls tend to mature at an earlier age than boys. This makes for real dating problems, for girls are ready to date with boys before boys, on the average, are mature enough to be interested in girls.

A common complaint among young adolescent boys is that girls "chase" them and hang around all the time. Girls are frequently concerned about how to get boys pried loose from the gang and interested in having fun in mixed groups. Because boys mature more slowly than girls, they are usually not ready for the kind of boy-girl friendships that teenage girls find most satisfying. This means that for a while the girls take the initiative in boy-girl affairs—an effort which takes some skill if it is to be done well.

DATES
without chasing

One of the most perplexing questions many school girls ask is how to get the boys interested without chasing them. They want to meet certain boys. They want to have fun with them at parties and dances and in clubs. Yet it appears to be difficult to get the boys interested in such things as soon as the average girl wishes.

GETTING acquainted with a shy boy

It often happens that a girl wants to know a boy who seems too shy to ask her for a date. She does not want to appear to chase him, so what does she do? A girl can be friendly and nice to boys without being forward. Merely smiling and saying "Hi" as she sees boys in school helps to make her approachable. She can ask a boy a question about the lesson before class starts without offending, if she does it carefully. Or as a class dismisses, she can leave the room when he does and make some comment as they go out the door together. Such seemingly casual beginnings can grow until the girl and boy easily chat with each other as friendly comrades in school. From there on it is just a short step to interesting the other in something that would be fun to do together.

It is generally agreed that girls defeat their own purposes when they show off in front of boys in the hope of attracting their attention. It is not wise to interrupt a boy who is with a group or to call to him loudly to get him away from his friends. Loud talking and giggling are usually frowned on by boys and girls alike.

SHARING a boy's interests

Girls today share a great many interests with boys. A girl can participate in clubs, sports, musical activities, and a host of other things that will bring her into contact with boys who are similarly interested. These are natural settings for getting acquainted and coming to like one another. When such a boy and girl from the same activity group do get together, their common interest provides a topic for conversation. In fact, they meet because they are congenially interested in the same thing.

KNOWING what to do if whistled at

Boys sometimes cluster in groups and whistle at the girls who pass by. Girls often wonder just how to interpret this kind of attention, and what is the best way to respond. Some girls ignore the whistled salute entirely. Others blush and act embarrassed. Some girls toss back a remark that will cause the boys to laugh. These responses tend to perpetuate the practice and do not help the two sexes to enjoy each other as they might. The girl with poise, who accepts the whistle with a friendly smile that is neither embarrassed nor fresh, often helps the boys to feel that she is approachable without being forward.

Boys who whistle at girls usually are those who have not yet learned to enjoy girls as friends. The whistle is the boy's way of recognizing the girl as a female. If she responds without too obvious coquetry, the boy's interest in her may be quickened. Moreover, he is not scared off by her forwardness nor amused by her fear. In time a girl not only gains the boy's respect for her as an individual but also makes friends among those who are most congenial.

DIFFERENCES
in age

"Is it all right for a girl to date a boy who is a year or two older than she is?' is a frequent question. Boys ask whether it makes any great difference if they date girls younger than they are. Since many school parties are given by members of a certain year or class, this somewhat limits boys and girls to those of about the same age. But for those affairs in which there is more choice it is quite understandable that boys tend to prefer girls somewhat younger than they are. We have already seen that girls mature earlier than boys. The chances are good that girls will enjoy boys a year or two older, and that boys will feel more comfortable with girls a bit younger.

When a girl in high school dates a college man or one very much older than herself, the situation is different.

In doing so she may cut herself off from others of her own age and may miss much fun within the school setting. She may also find that the man has interests more serious than her own. Sometimes the girl finds the older man pretty hard to handle, and she comes back with relief to boys of her own age.

WHEN she is the older

Occasionally you find a congenial couple in which the girl is the older of the two. With so much pressure in the other direction, the girl may feel embarrassed because she is older than her boy friend. She may do everything she can to keep from revealing her age, even to her date. Perhaps it makes the boy self-conscious to know that he is younger than the girl he is taking out. Yet actually, except for the way these two persons and their friends feel about their difference in age, it doesn't matter much. If the boy and girl enjoy each other's company, if they have many interests in common, and others that they are encouraging each other to develop, there is no sensible reason that they should let the difference in age come between them.

The way two persons involved feel about it makes the biggest difference when the girl or woman is the older. If her age makes her feel insecure and afraid she will lose his love, then it becomes a handicap. If her greater maturity increases her security, wisdom, and poise with him, it is an asset, especially if he appreciates these qualities in her and feels comfortable with them.

BLIND
dates

Blind dates are those arranged by one or more go-betweens for two persons who have never met. Sometimes they are fun; sometimes they are dreadful. Young people can avoid some of the unpleasantness of blind dates by requiring the following conditions: (1) The date must be arranged only by a friend whom you can trust. This is important. A real friend knows you and your likes and dislikes. He or she will see to it that your interests are protected and that you are teamed with someone with whom there is a reasonably good chance of a pleasant time. (2) You go only to an occasion or to a place that you are sure about. When you do not know the person with whom you are dating, it is especially important that you be sure of the place and the affair that you will be sharing. Blind dates are not the times to explore questionable places and activities unless, of course, you don't mind a spot of trouble!

EXPECTING too much romance

The very uncertainty of a blind date may make you susceptible to dreaming up too much glamour and romance for it. As you try to guess what your date will be like, you are apt to endow him or her with all the wonderful qualities you have been looking for in the other sex. The girl may dream that here at last will be the *Real He,* the *Mister Right* that she has been looking for all along. The boy, too, may imagine all the lovely, lovable attributes of his *Ideal Woman* in the blind date ahead. Neither fully realizes that the Prince Charmings and the Princess Beautifuls are not often out on blind dates, and that Romance with a capital R rarely pops out at one from behind the unknown quantity of the blind date.

The blind date may be a fine person, well worth knowing, and a grand companion for an evening. It is when we expect to be transported into the Never-Never Land of Romance that we are most often disappointed.

THOSE Risky Pick-Ups

Pick-up dates are always risky. There is no one to vouch for either of the partners. Neither knows the other's real background. People are often not what they seem, and it sometimes is quite a while before they are known for what they really are. By that time, one or both of the persons may have hurt the other. A pick-up can expose you to an immoral person, out not for an innocent date but for any form of unscrupulous exploitation. Such possibilities are real, and their danger is not to be underestimated. It is a foolhardy young person who chances the pick-up date, for safer forms of dating can be arranged.

WHEN
double dates can be good

Double dates are as good as the people who make them. Dating with another couple can add a lot of fun, or it can increase the stress and strain of dating. It depends on the combination. Double dating has grown in popularity in recent years, largely because of the convenience of sharing the car. When one of the fellows has the use of an automobile, he usually has no difficulty in getting some other couple to double with him.

Two couples can have more fun and a livelier time than one couple alone. Four-way conversation is usually somewhat easier to maintain. The give-and-take of the two boys as well as the interaction of the two girls gives a little "extra" to the security of all four. These are real advantages beyond the convenience of sharing an automobile.

DOUBLE-DATING Difficulties

Difficulties are encountered in double dating when the couples are not well matched. If one couple has plans or ideas beyond the interests of the other, someone has to give in. Differences in drinking practices, dancing places considered within bounds, and smoking and language patterns may cause one or both of the couples to be uncomfortable. One of the greatest difficulties may come at the end of the evening if one couple engages in love-making in a way that the other couple does not care for. To avoid embarrassing situations, it is better by far to date only with persons of similar interests and tastes.

Time for getting home at the end of the date may cause problems beyond those encountered on a single date. If one person or one couple wishes to stay out late, it is hard to stick to standards. This is especially true if the nighthawks are the ones with the car. The question of plans for the evening is best decided as the foursome start out; otherwise it is likely to be the more impetuous or demanding ones that influence the party.

Double dates are good if you date with friends you know and like, if you enjoy doing the same things together, if the couples share the same general standards of behavior, and if there is some consensus at the beginning of the evening as to what the plans are and when the party will be over.

BECOMING
more datable

"What is the matter with me?" you may wonder if you do not have dates. Everybody else seems to be talking about their good times—what he said and what she said, and then what they did. It sometimes makes a boy or a girl who is not dating feel pretty much out of things. You may get to wondering if there is something wrong with you that keeps you from going places and doing things with the other sex. You may put on a big act and pretend that you have special friends and admirers (as many of the others do, too). But deep down inside you may be puzzled about what it takes to make friends, to get a date, and why some people seem to do it all so easily while others have to work so hard at it.

You can improve your own datability by following a few simple rules. You are more datable to the extent to which you are increasingly friendly and sincerely interested in others. People truly interested in each other are always good companions. You are a better date as you practice good grooming habits more conscientiously. You do not have to dress extravagantly or dazzle your date with your appearance. But both boys and girls become more interesting to each other when they have mastered the basic rules of cleanliness, appropriateness, and general attractiveness of appearance.

You become more datable as you develop more and more interests outside yourself. The more things you can do and enjoy doing, the more you have to share with others. The more things that interest you, the greater your insurance against being bored or spending a dull evening. Dullness is within yourself, just as good times are. You make your dates what they are by your ability to enjoy a number of things with various kinds of people. As your interests grow, you too grow to the point where you like to do so many things that you can have a good time in countless ways and in all sorts of circumstances.

What do you do on a date?

WHAT YOU DO ON A DATE depends upon a great many factors: who you are, where you live, what the possibilities are, whom you are going with, what you can do, what you like to do, how much money you have to spend, what your parents consider permissible, and above all, the ingenuity and imagination you possess for inventing ways of having a good time.

GOING
out together

Many dates begin with the boy's asking a girl to attend some special affair with him—a sports event, a musical

program, a play, or a school or church or community party. She accepts, and it is a date. These situations are simple in that their success does not depend upon either the boy's or the girl's planning what they will do together. That was decided when the invitation was accepted.

There are times, however, when nothing special is going on for a particular evening. Then a boy may simply ask a girl for a date on Saturday night. When he arrives at her house he may have some idea of what they will do, or he may have not the foggiest idea.

A girl usually prefers to know ahead of time what kind

of date it is to be. Then she can dress appropriately for the activity that is planned. If they are to go skating, she will dress differently from the way she would dress if they were to dance. Bowling requires different clothing from that for a movie date. It may be that the boy just asks her to "a show," meaning that he plans to take her to a movie. When he arrives, they will decide together which picture to see. She will probably be prepared with the programs of the various theaters and will join in the process of choosing the film they both would most enjoy.

SPECIAL sprees

Special occasions sometimes come along requiring unusual recognition. Perhaps it is the girl's birthday. It may be a celebration for the boy's first big advancement, or graduation for one or both of them. Then they will probably want to "go out on the town," instead of just doing the same old things again. In this situation it is wise for the boy to set the stage. The check will be his when the party is over, and prices differ so widely in commercial entertainment that he should suggest something within the scope of his ability to pay. Couples may pool their "special money" for such unusual sprees and share the expense as well as the fun. Sometimes the boy gets tickets for some nice affair and surprises his date with the exciting novelty.

Flowers are not necessary for such a special affair, but are nice if the boy can afford them and the girl enjoys them. The way the two dress depends upon where they are to go and what they are to do. There are few places where formal clothing is expected except, of course, at the formal proms that schools and colleges sponsor once a year or so.

INFORMAL outings

Some of the most enjoyable dates are those spent at picnics, around barbecue fires, swimming, skating, singing, playing folk games, and other such informal outings. Such activities offer better opportunities for getting acquainted with each other than do many of the more formal, dress-up affairs. Either the boy or the girl or both together can plan and arrange for the casual kind of date. Usually other couples are included too, for at a picnic "the more the merrier." You do not even have to invite people in couples for the informal outing. That is why such affairs are so easy for the unattached girl or boy. Not having to bring a date or be escorted by one, both boys and girls feel free to come, even though they may not be dating someone at the moment.

Cook-outs and picnics are most enjoyable when everybody has a hand in them. The fire is made by volunteer fire builders. The food is prepared by those who like to cook. Songs are led spontaneously by the boy or girl to whom the crowd look for such leadership. Because everybody helps, everybody feels "in" and has a good time. Such affairs do not have to be expensive to be a lot of fun, and they go a long way toward helping boys and girls to get acquainted.

THE
first date—a pattern

John calls for Mary at her home at the appointed time. Mary is ready for John and answers the door herself when he rings (he has come to see her, not some other member of her family). She greets him pleasantly and leads him into the living room where her parents are waiting to meet him.

Mary introduces John to her parents by saying something like this: "Mother, this is John. Dad, you remember John plays center on the team." This little lead as a part of the introduction gives Dad and John something to talk about at once. Dad may ask a simple question on how the team is going this season. John is put at his ease and answers, while Mother and Dad relax and enjoy getting acquainted with him.

In a few moments Mary picks up her coat and, smiling at John, indicates that they had probably better be on their way. If John holds the coat for Mary, she accepts his assistance graciously; if he does not, she slips into her coat without comment and prepares for departure.

As the couple is about to leave, Mary turns to her parents and says, "We are going to the double feature (or whatever), you know. We should be home before midnight (or whatever hour seems reasonable)." This announcement of plans and specifying of time for homecoming has a double purpose. It lets her folks know that she is taking responsibility for getting in before it is too late, and prevents them from putting down the parental foot too hard. Further, such initiative on Mary's part lets John know what is expected of him in getting Mary home. If Mary has already talked over their plans with her parents before John has arrived, her last-minute announcement is simply a confirmation for all four of them.

The couple leave, with John opening the door for Mary, while she accepts the courtesy with a smile. When they reach the box office, Mary steps back and looks at the display cards while John buys the tickets. Inside, if there is an usher, Mary follows him while John follows her down the aisle. If there is no usher on duty, John goes ahead and finds seats while Mary follows. Once seated, John helps Mary slip out of her coat and get settled. They enjoy the show without annoying their neighbors with talking, giggling, or other disturbing behavior.

Out of the theater, John may suggest something to eat or he may conduct Mary to the place of his choice. At this point, Mary is careful to let John take the lead. When he asks her what she would like to have, she thoughtfully hesitates until she sees what price range he has in mind. She says something like this: "What is good here, John?" or "What do you suggest?" If John recommends the steak sandwich with French fries, or the double gooey sundae with nuts, this gives Mary the general idea of what he is prepared to spend. If she is friendly and shrewd she may note that John, in his desire to do the right thing, is suggesting something extravagant. If so, she will ask for something that she knows costs a little less. But if John says, "'Which do you like better, coke or root beer?" Mary graciously keeps within these bounds. Over their food, John and Mary talk about the movie they have just seen or friends they have in common or anything that is of mutual interest. As they leave the restaurant, John pays the check and Mary thanks him by saying, "That was good; thank you, John."

Once back at Mary's house, Mary gets out her key, unlocks the door, and then turns to John with a smile. She says, "It's been a lovely evening. Thank you, John," or something similar that lets John know she has enjoyed the date. John replies, "I have enjoyed it, too. I'll be seeing you." Then she opens the door and goes in without further hesitation. Since this is the first date, neither John nor Mary expects a goodnight kiss. So Mary is careful not to linger at the door, which might make John wonder what she expects him to do.

DATES
at home

There was a time when most dates were spent at the girl's home. Nowadays dating in the home is not so common, but it can be interesting.

The date at home ranges all the way from the girl's inviting the boy over to study some special assignment with her over a bowl of popcorn, to the very special party which the girl "throws" at her home. In any case, it is usually the girl who plans it. She has knowledge of what her resources are, what her folks will permit, and what will be best within the limits and possibilities of her home.

Home dates need not be restricted to the living room by any means. The kitchen offers rich opportunities for boys and girls to enjoy food preparation and the fun of eating their wares. One teen-age set spend an evening every other week in one of their kitchens, cooking their way through recipes from other nations. Russian borsch, Italian spaghetti, and Swedish meat balls have all proved popular with both boys and girls. Some of the group prepare a special little symbol of the nation of the evening, to appear at the table while the food is being served. Some of these affairs have been very clever; all have been fun.

Homes with attics or garages or basements lend themselves to informal parties and interesting activities. One high-school girl in New England invited three other couples and her date over to play charades in her attic, with the trunkfuls of old clothes that had accumulated through the generations her family had lived there. A boy in the Midwest fixed up his garage as a gambling casino and had a crowd of boys and girls in for "A Night of Sin," with quantities of stage money for stakes and a jug of sweet cider for the liquid refreshment.

One girl cleaned out her cellar and staged an old-fashioned barn dance on Hallowe'en, complete with apples bobbing in her mother's washtub, corn popping in the furnace, and pumpkins at the windows. Her uncle, in checked shirt and overalls, played his accordion and called the dances; and her big sister topped off the evening with ghost stories by the light of one flickering candle. That crowd of teen-agers did not need a fancy rumpus room for their fun; they had it where they were, thanks to a little imagination on their hostess' part.

Dating activities are limited only by the good taste and the creativity of the persons involved. They do not need to follow the same pattern week after week. They can be widely varied. Dates can be as twosomes or within a crowd. They are best when shared by all the participants. They can be jointly planned or sprung as surprises. They can cost a lot of money or be practically "for free." They can be initiated by the girl or the boy, and can take place either in the home or out on the town. What you do on a date is up to you.

MEETING
the costs of dating

Since it is the man who pays for most dates, it is he who must find the money and plan the date to fit his purse. High-school boys in many communities get part-time jobs which give them some extra cash of their own. The dole from dad can be called upon in an emergency, but most boys prefer some more dependable source of income when they begin to date. A regular weekly or monthly allowance gives a boy a definite amount of money to count upon, but necessitates his budgeting his expenditures to stretch over the entire period and to cover the many "specials" and "extras" that dating so often involves.

HOW girls share costs

Girls often want to help out on the money side but find it hard to relieve the boy of the burden. "Dutch-dating," wherein the girl and boy share the cost, is not a common practice in most American communities. A girl must be extremely tactful. Boldly buying her own ticket or handing him the cash in public may be embarrassing to him. It is usually wise to have the arrangement definitely understood in advance and to give the boy the money before leaving the house. In some cities a girl dutch-dating with a boy at a restaurant can simply ask the waitress to give her a separate check. But this is not yet common enough to risk if one or both of them feel uneasy about it.

Girls have many other ways of reciprocating kindnesses beside actually sharing the cash costs. The entertaining a girl does in her own home often is a quite acceptable way of repaying boys' hospitality. The group parties that girls give for boys are still another way for girls to share the financial burdens of dating.

Occasionally a girl may acquire tickets for some special event, and present them to a boy friend with some simple explanation. Nina's Uncle George came to town and bought football tickets for the whole family. Nina's mother did not want to go and gave her ticket to Nina. It was easy for Nina to call her boy friend and suggest that he come with them to the game. Such courtesies are usually appreciated and go a long way to even up the money outlay.

TIPS on tipping

How much to tip depends on a number of things: the amount of the bill, the kind of place it is, the excellence of the service, and the number served. The usual rule is to leave between 10 and 15 per cent of the amount of the check. A quick coke at a soda fountain does not require a tip at all. A leisurely meal at a really swank place usually calls for a generous tip. If there is a tablecloth, such as there will be in the Pullman diner or in the nicer restaurants, the minimum is twenty-five cents, with the amount increasing as the size of the check and the number served increases. Whatever the size of the tip, it is left unobtrusively under one's plate or on the little tray on which the check has been presented.

It is not courteous for the girl to try to find out how much of a tip her date has left or to comment upon his tipping. That is the host's affair, in which a gracious guest does not interfere.

Others beside the waitress who give service may or may not expect a tip. The Pullman porter does, of course. So, too, does the redcap who carries one's suitcases on and off the train. The usual redcap tip is thirty-five cents per parcel carried. The taxicab driver expects a tip which may vary widely, depending upon the service he has given, but is rarely less than 10 per cent. The bellboy expects some gratuity for his attention. On the other hand, the doorman of the hotel or restaurant usually does not expect a tip except when he has rendered unusual service beyond the line of duty. Similarly, in the United States, it is not necessary to tip the head waiter or waitress, the ticket seller, the usher, the bus driver, the train conductor, the airplane steward or hostess, or the policeman who may give requested information. A courteous "'Thank you" or smile of appreciation is all that is required.

WHAT
to talk about on a date

Keeping conversation rolling is a challenge to most boys and girls. They feel so "special" with each other that the usual things to talk about somehow seem not quite appropriate. He may have no trouble at all talking with other boys; she may be a regular chatterbox at home. But together they are tongue-tied until they "get the feel" of what to talk about with each other.

The topic that is sure to be of greatest interest to a boy and girl is that of Him and Her. This is an area in which they are expert. Each knows his own interests better than anyone else. Each enjoys telling of them. Both like to talk about and to share the things they are fond of. Discovering that they like the same things and have common interests is very pleasant. In fact, looking for such similar interests is a conversational pastime among people everywhere.

Drawing the other person out is most easily done by getting him to talk about himself. The girl who is trying to get the conversation going may inquire what her date is planning to do next summer, where he went last summer, what he does after school, what courses he is taking, what he plans to do when he is out on his own—any subject that will help the boy overcome his uneasiness and begin to talk about the things in which he is interested. This serves a double purpose. It not only makes for a good time at the moment, but it also provides an opportunity for the two to become better acquainted with each other's real interests, hopes, and dreams.

GOOD listening

When someone is talking to you, you have the responsibility of listening to what is being said. Really listening to another person does not mean just being quiet while the other is speaking. There are people who spend the time when others are talking in thinking up what they plan to say next. That does not make for conversation at its best. Listening involves giving one's whole attention to the other, getting not only his words but also his meanings as far as one can.

Genuine listening includes putting oneself in the other person's shoes and getting the feel of what he is saying. You sense what is prompting his words, so you reflect in your interest that you have not only heard his words but that you know something of his feeling. That is what we usually call being "understood." It is highly satisfying to both participants because they are thinking and feeling together.

HOLDING up your end of the conversation

Conversation is something like playing tennis. The ball comes over the net toward you, and it is up to you to bat it back if the game is to go on. When ball after ball falls dead at your feet, the sport palls and interest lags. So it is with conversation. It is up to you to pick up the comments thrown your way and toss them back with enough bounce to keep the conversation rolling. Poor Hy could not do this. His date reported that all he could say in answer to her leading questions was "'Uh-huh" or "Uh-uh." She never dated him again and we can understand why.

You do your part to keep conversation going when you respond and add something for the other to reply to. Using the tennis ball again as an example, this means that you do not just catch the ball and hold it; you get it back over the net with a snap. Specifically, it is up to you to answer the question and end with a question of your own, or a comment that the other can pick up. Taking the weather as a simple illustration, let's see what this looks like.

He—"It's a good clear night, isn't it?"

She—"Wonderful. Did you ever see such a moon?"

He—"We may get a really close look at it in our generation."

She—"When they actually start scheduling trips, do you think you'd want to go?"

There you are, from the weather to his confidential opinion of the space age in four little steps, simply by adding a question to every answer.

NOTHING to fear in silences

There is nothing to fear in silences. Some of our nicest times with other people are the quiet moments when no words are necessary. When ninth-grade boys in an Iowa high school were asked if they liked girls who talk a lot, fifty-eight answered "No," and only thirteen said "Yes." A good conversationalist is not necessarily the one who talks all the time. More often he or she is the sensitive person who listens well and is not afraid of the silences that come along from time to time.

When nothing has been said for a while, either of you can break the silence. No apology is needed. You do not have to say anything about how dull a companion you are and how you can't think of anything to say. Better to say nothing for a moment. Perhaps the girl will break the silence with a little smile and a nice comment on how pleasant the evening is or how she is enjoying the music, or show by some little sign that she is having a good time and feeling happy inside. This increases the boy's sense of security. His tongue may be loosened and conversation may roll again. Even though it does not, it need not frighten either of you.

TIMES when you don't say it

Some things are better not said. Girls and boys learn that dating conversation has certain limits which are wise to respect. Thumper in the Walt Disney film had one thing down pat when he said, "If you can't say anything nice, don't say anything at all." The griper, the groaner, the complainer, is a spoil-sport and a poor date. The boy or girl who runs down other people, shreds reputations right and left, and belittles others' efforts is not a pleasant companion. Being negative and pessimistic is not smart; it is more often the mark of the insecurity of a person not yet quite grown up.

"Nice people don't swear." Profanity adds little to any conversation. There are few occasions when a profane word or statement is nearly as original, clever, or interesting as something that particularly fits that situation, made to order for it, as it were. Boys who respect their friends do not use language that may offend. They realize that such things are not the mark of maturity. Pretending to be tough is little-boy stuff. The really big guy is a gentleman.

Off-color stories set an atmosphere that spoils the enjoyment boys and girls can find with each other as friends. As soon as shady stories begin, the party is immediately divided into the men's and women's side of life, with each being acutely aware of which is which. The tone set is one of biological excitement and emotional uneasiness, in which little wholesome companionship is possible.

Some boys tell slightly off-color stories to see what the girl will do. A girl passes the test when she does not encourage him to continue and yet does not act shocked or goody-goody. She may simply let him know that she got the point, did not like it too well, and prefers getting back to more pleasant conversation. One popular girl just wrinkles up her nose and shakes her head ever so lightly when such a story is told, as if to say, "Something does not smell sweet around here." The boys respect her wishes and tend to keep their language clean when she is with them.

That is not to say that boys and girls should not talk about sex or about each other when they are together. It is all right to discuss dating and dating behavior, love and love-making, and other areas of keen interest to men and women, *if* the tone is wholesome and each respects the other's wishes.

It is not so much what is talked about as the way in which it is discussed that makes the big difference between clean conversation and smutty talk. In general, conversation that deals with people as fine human beings can include almost any topic and yet be uplifting. Banter that belittles and considers men and women as mere biological entities who live on an impulse level can make even the most sacred topics seem degrading.

WHAT
to do about a line

When we are very young, we may take seriously all the sweet things that are said to us. We cuddle the compliments we receive close to our secret selves, and dream over and over again of the moment and the person who brought them to us. But, there comes a time when we are rudely awakened by the realization that not all we hear can be taken seriously. We face the disillusionment that comes with believing a "line" and so we learn other reactions to lighthearted coquetry.

Our first response to being tripped by someone's line is to protect ourselves from being hurt again by such sweet deception. In our distress, we rudely remind the gay deceiver that we know better than to believe such nonsense. We sharply call a halt to gay banter by snapping back to reality any moment that strays away from the cold facts. A boy who handles a girl's line in this way may get the reputation of being serious or solemn, because he tolerates no nonsense. A girl may suffer even more serious consequences in being thought cold and unapproachable.

In time, we try to meet the problem of the idle compliment by "giving as good as is sent." We return the flattery with interest compounded. When a girl asks for attention with her sweet talk, the boy gives her plenty, in words designed to delight her feminine heart. When a boy whispers sweet nothings to her, the girl counters with phrases directed to his vanity as a male. Such practices are common in courtship, and can be a great deal of fun. They require practice to get the degree of smooth suavity the game of wits requires. Experience is the best teacher in meeting the line with a line of one's own. It is worth learning as a device. But, even the most expert verbal fencing is a poor substitute for genuine conversation of sincere people who might really enjoy knowing one another.

Banter, teasing, and idle compliments are fun on a date,

and have a place in friendship. But underneath must run a strong current of sincerity if the relationship is ever to become a sound one. When two persons basically trust and respect one another, they can enjoy a bit of kidding or even some extravagant flattery, because they know one another. The line then becomes a kind of lubricating oil within a smooth-running relationship.

A genuinely friendly girl or boy recognizes a line for what it is, accepts it with a smile, and then goes on into sincere conversation that is, after all, the highest compliment one person can pay another. Men and women with anything to them besides a good line will accept such a challenge, relax from the strain of pretended enchantment, and join in friendly fellowship.

THE
goodnight kiss

In many communities, a goodnight kiss is expected as the customary way of ending a date. It is usually enjoyable to both boys and girls, especially if they both know what it signifies. A goodnight kiss can mean any number of things. It may be the way a girl says "Thank you" to the boy for giving her a good time. It may be a way of saying, "I like you." It may signify their special awareness of each other as dating boy and girl friends. It may be just a way of saying, "Come again." Or it may be a very special token of genuine affection. What it means depends upon the two persons and their definition of their relationship and of themselves.

Most girls, and boys too, agree that the first date is too soon for a goodnight kiss. Girls say that it seems too easy when it closes the very first date. Boys sometimes confess that they will try to kiss a girl the first time they take her out but that they really do not expect her to allow it, especially if she is the kind of girl they respect. Both boys and girls generally feel that a couple should have seen each other long enough to have become somewhat better acquainted than is possible after just one date, before they kiss each other.

How many dates before the first kiss? This is a good question, but hard to answer precisely. It depends upon the person involved, how they feel about each other, how well they know each other, and what kissing means to them. Some couples date for a long while and never are particularly interested in kissing. They may enjoy each other's companionship but do not feel the need of expressing their interest that way. Kathy liked Tom a lot. They had great fun playing together in the school band. Yet she never thought of him as a kissing partner, somehow. Not that he was repulsive; just that he was a pal, a friend, a comrade, whose contact with her was such that kissing him never entered her head. Perry on the other hand had swept her off her feet and she was ready to kiss him goodnight long before he took the initiative.

We must recognize the difference in kisses. They range all the way from the light, butterfly variety that flutters upon cheek or forehead, to the heavy kissing that gets rather deeply into petting practice. There are the tender kisses that boys and girls genuinely fond of each other use in expressing their affection. But what of the other more stimulating kinds? Where do they fit into dating? Just when and with whom are they appropriate?

DO
you have to pet to be popular?

Some grown boys collect kisses and caresses from girls in much the same way that they collected marbles as kids. The game in either sport is to see how high a score can be run up: the more marbles, the better the player; the more kisses, the higher the dating score. The big difference is that they played marbles for keeps, and the kisses are definitely not for keeps, but simply a badge of power.

Petting, and the kind of kissing that goes with it, is not always indulged in by the kiss-collecting Lothario, but it happens often enough for girls and many boys to ask the question, "Do you have to pet to be popular?" Students of high schools and colleges who have voted on the question reply with an emphatic "NO." They say that the most popular students of both sexes are not the heavy or promiscuous petters. They report, too, that the girls and young men who have reputations as petters are not the ones who are most in demand as friends or club members or even as dates, except when someone is out on a foraging expedition.

Some men confess that they will try to fondle a girl the first time they take her out, as a way of testing her. If she lets him pet her, she is labeled "a-girl-who-will"; if she refuses, she is tagged "a-girl-who-won't." This is a crude effort to distinguish between girls in this day of easy freedom between the sexes. In grandma's day every man knew there were two kinds of women, the good ones and the bad ones. He could tell which was which by the clothes they wore and the way they looked at him. In these days it is not so easy to tell the respectable girl from the girl who plays fast and loose, and so boys apply their own simple tests of how much familiarity a girl will allow.

Boys and girls, men and women, who respect one another as personalities may from time to time want to express their affection with some physical caress. But this is a far cry from the indiscriminate handling that goes under the name of petting. If one wants to be popular as a *petter*, one must pet in order to be eligible. But if one would rather be popular as a *person*, promiscuous petting is a decided handicap.

PUBLIC demonstrations of affection

Certain standards of good taste keep thoughtful friends from showing their affection in public. Young people are sometimes concerned about the way some of the couples in their school show no restraint in their love-making. They hold hands in the corridors, kiss in front of their lockers, and openly neck at school parties. The offending couples rarely are aware of the extent to which they irritate and amuse their fellow students. They are usually the more immature, impulsive boys and girls who have not yet learned that there is a place for everything in life, and that even a kiss is better when it is reserved for the times, the places, and the persons that give it most meaning. With experience a man is able to tell a woman he loves her with his eyes; a woman can express her adoration in a hundred little gestures that only he can understand. It is only during the calf-love stage that love-making is open to the herd.

WHAT
to do about a bad reputation

Supposing something you once did was a serious mistake, what can you do about it? Perhaps in one mad, impulsive moment you got yourself into an awful mess. Can you ever live it down? If you have acquired a bad name from some person who in some way was linked with you, is there anything you can do to come out from under the shadow? These questions are not uncommon. They are usually best answered in the following ways.

BEND over backward for a while

Whatever you did (or were supposed to have done) that offended your conscience or your reputation in the first place must not be repeated if you are to clear up your mind about it, and your reputation with others. You must bend over backward and be more careful if you are in the process of cleaning up a habit or reputation. The boy who has been drunk, now cannot afford to touch the stuff. The girl who is supposed to have been too easy, now must be more careful than her Great-aunt Christobel. One little slip and the reputation-makers are ready to snort, "I told you so; you see?" It makes no difference whether you really were guilty of that first offense or not. Once you get talked about, you must be careful never again to make the mistake that caused the gossip.

THROW yourself into worthwhile activities

You overcome a bad reputation by gaining a good one. As you take up really worthwhile activities, associate yourself with public-spirited groups, throw yourself into pursuits that are recognized as worthy, you gradually gain the reputation of being a serious-minded person whom others can count on. In time the past escapade is forgotten, or pigeonholed as a "wild-oats episode," and you emerge with a reputation of being a respectable citizen. Your reputation is built by the way you behave. But the persons who are closest to you are part of your reputation too, as the next question recognizes.

SHOULD a girl date a boy with a bad reputation?

The danger in a girl's dating a boy with a bad reputation is that she is apt to share his poor social rating. This is a heavy price to pay for a date. It may be that the girl goes with the boy because she is defying her parents and making a lunge toward her own independence. She dates such a fellow with an "I'll-show-them" kind of attitude that almost welcomes whatever sorrow may befall her dating him. Needless to say, this is dangerous and often leads to serious trouble.

A girl may date a boy with a bad reputation because she genuinely likes him and has faith in him as a person. She may feel that he has been wronged in what has been said about him and that her dating him will show her confidence in him. She is successful usually to the extent to which her own reputation is good enough to stand the strain of being associated with him. Stella dated Tony, who she felt had had a raw deal and merited a better rating in the community. She was class president and a leader in her group. She was able to bring Tony into her set without endangering her own position. This is unusual but it does sometimes happen—to the lasting benefit of the occasional boy who has been wronged by too hasty public opinion or prejudice.

Standing by a friend in trouble is a mark of loyalty. Having faith in another is a fine thing that should not be discouraged. When the girl is sure that the boy is trying to overcome his unfortunate reputation, she can help him immensely by showing others that she has faith in him. Whether or not she dates him depends upon their own decision as to whether that would help more than hinder.

DATING
a serviceman

Years ago when men in uniform were professional soldiers or sailors, there was the general idea that girls who were seen with them were not quite "nice." Even then that was not true, although enough servicemen took advantage of girls to keep the reputation of the man in uniform a cloudy one.

But now, when almost every boy must serve his term in military service, the question of dating a serviceman is not an easy one for a girl or her parents to answer. They may have some of the old prejudices against the man in uniform that are not warranted now. They may have seen the irresponsible behavior of a few men in uniform that has given a "black eye" to all of them. Or they may recognize quite sensibly that all kinds of boys from all kinds of backgrounds are in uniform today, and learn to judge which ones are datable and which ones are not.

SIZING up the man in uniform

If the girl has known the boy before he went into service, she can decide on the basis of what she knows about him, and how well she likes him, whether he is datable or not. If she meets a visiting buddy of one of her close friends who can vouch for the newcomer, she can be fairly sure it will be all right to accept dates of a certain kind with him. If she meets him at church, or in some other nice place where only people like herself are likely to go, she can assume that perhaps he is the kind of boy who would enjoy coming home with her, meeting her parents, and enjoying a good home-cooked meal with the family. But if she is accosted by a serviceman on the street, at a dance hall, or in some other public place, she has no way of knowing what she may expect of him now, and therefore runs the same kind of risk she would in accepting any pick-up.

WHEN you write to a serviceman

Sometimes writing to a serviceman cheers up the man in service and does no harm to anyone. Sometimes writing to a serviceman can bring only heartache and trouble to him, as well as to the girl. The wholesome type of correspondence keeps within the bounds of the acquaintance of the two persons, and does not presume beyond it. The more dangerous kind of letter is one in which the teen-age girl pours out her heart to some man she hardly knows under the illusion that he is so far away that anything she says is safe enough. The times comes when the man returns home and looks up the writer of such letters, and the outcome can be plenty stormy for him, for her, for everyone involved.

Of course a girl may write to old friends and acquaintances in service. In her letters she may relate all the news that she knows will interest the fellow. She will be careful not to take advantage of his tales of loneliness and longing by assuming that they are professions of his love for her. She is wise to keep the tone of her letters gay, cheerful, and as warm as is appropriate for them as persons.

EXPERIENCE
in dating

When you first started to learn to drive a car, you faced many questions and a great deal of uneasiness that wore off as you got the hang of driving. When you were learning to ride a bike, you probably felt pretty wobbly at times. And then came the time when you pedaled off down the street with not a thought of how you were doing it. So it is with dating. You learn how to do it by doing it. At first you will feel somewhat uncomfortable in new situations and embarrassed in unexpected predicaments. But with experience you polish off the rough edges and become smooth. There is no magic about it. It is just a matter of following sound principles and keeping up your practice, and one day you find yourself comfortably competent in dating situations.

CHAPTER 13

What's the harm in petting?

IF THIS WERE A QUESTION IN mathematics, you could find the correct answer in the back of the book. But human beings differ so in the way they are made and function, in how they feel about each other from time to time, in what various types of behavior mean to them, and in what they are trying to do in a given situation, that a dogmatic answer is impossible.

How different the question—what's the harm in petting? —if the two persons know and love each other, or if they are male and female strangers; if the pair are about to be married, or if they are on the first date; if they are the same age, or if he is a grown man and she a young teen-ager; if they mutually seek each other, or if he aggressively forces himself upon her; if they have high standards of personal conduct, or see themselves as creatures of impulse. Not all teen-agers answer the question the same way at any given time—or should.

This is why the question has to be considered by every young person, in each succeeding generation. There always has been some kind of love-making between the sexes before marriage. Parents remember all too well their own courting behavior. This is one reason that they are concerned about yours. You may have seen the cartoon in a national

magazine showing Father pacing up and down in front of his bedroom window, which faced a car parked in front where his daughter and her date were profiled sitting close together by the light of the moon. Mother sitting up in her bed is saying, "Come on back to bed, Father. Can't you remember when you were young?" His reply is an explosive, "You bet I do. That's what I am all worked up about!"

CHAPERONES
in grandma's day

As long as a girl did her dating on the front porch or in the back parlor, she and her sweetheart were never far away from the eyes and ears of those who knew and loved her. On one pretext or another, members of her family drifted in and out of the room where yesterday's young woman was entertaining her young man. Without fail, when the porch swing stopped squeeking, Mother would appear with a pitcher of lemonade, or Dad would come smiling out to the young couple with a bowl of freshly popped corn or a dish of ice cream—providing without a word the supervision that kept young people's love-making from going too far.

When a young couple went out for the evening in most American communities two or three generations ago, they frequented places where friends of their families were sure to recognize them. All the way down the Old South Road the lace curtains would flutter as the young couple went by —indicating that the neighbors, led by Mrs. Grundy, were keeping an eye on the dating pairs in the neighborhood. Wherever the pair went they mingled with those who knew them and who were well acquainted with their families, and who expected them to behave as members of their families should.

In small towns and rural areas, where most people lived at the turn of the century (as you read in Chapter Eleven), young people met at the church socials and at the town halls and community centers, where whole families gathered for their good times. Young couples were expected to pair off at these affairs, but they were always close by the older and younger friends and family members, who did a pretty good job of seeing to it that love-making did not go too far.

DATING couples have less supervision now

You have more freedom and less supervision now than previous generations ever did. You may choose your dating partner from among those whom your parents do not know. A girl may date a boy who lives miles away from her home. Her parents may or may not know who his folks are, and the kind of life he leads. He suddenly appears for her with his car. Within a matter of minutes after they leave her home, they are far away from people who know them both and away from supervision and watchful interest. What they do is their responsibility in a way that never before was true.

The automobile not only takes young couples out from under the interested concern of parents and neighbors but it provides a kind of intimate privacy that invites love-making.

When to this is added the stimulation that comes from having seen together an exciting movie, the urge to pet is apt to be insistent. Or, double-dating with a couple whose love-making practices are already well advanced may put added responsibility on the two who are not out for that kind of activity. Add the drinking that is not infrequently a part of a date among certain young people, and you have a setting in which almost anything can happen, unless somebody in the crowd has been educated to know when to stop and how, and has the skill for keeping love-making within bounds.

HOW
petting is defined

Petting is any combination of fondling, caressing, and kissing between members of opposite sexes which tends to be sexually exciting to one or both of the partners. Some young people make a distinction between necking and petting. Sometimes they put it this way: Necking is any love-making above the neck—kissing, sitting or standing cheek to cheek, the lighter expressions of affection. Petting involves the caressing of other more sensitive parts of the body in a crescendo of sexual stimulation. The "French kiss" or other stimulating kissing and fondling are in the latter category.

Petting actually is the love-making that precedes, and makes the couple ready for, full sex intercourse. In marriage this same thing is called the foreplay, because it comes before and prepares the couple for coitus. Thus in marriage, petting has a very real role in getting the woman ready to receive her sex partner in the fullest sense. Before marriage, petting stimulates both male and female in the same way, without offering them the final step in consummation. What to do about petting, therefore, is a challenge to all young unmarried people today. They must answer for themselves: (1) how far they mean to go; (2) how they can tell where to stop; (3) how to stop; and (4) what petting means to them.

THE
urge to pet

It is normal to want to be near the person you like. This is true even in the most casual gathering. You enter a room, your eyes scan the people already there for a friendly face, an inviting glance. You go at once to be near the people you like and in whose friendliness you feel secure. When you are free to choose whom you will sit by, you seek out the one you like to be with. As significant things are said or common experiences recalled, you look at each other in a personal way, you touch the other's hand, you seek contact with the person who means something to you. When you like a person, you want to be close to him or her. You enjoy physical contact with those you like. This is true not only between members of opposite sexes but also of persons in the same sex group.

Sam was talking with a bunch of fellows after school one day when he felt an arm thrown over his shoulder from behind. He turned and recognized his pal Jeff. Without halting the story he was telling, he grinned at Jeff and pulled him into the circle. It was all so natural that neither of them realized how differently Sam might have responded if that arm over his shoulder had belonged to some person he did not like! We take it for granted that friends will seek and enjoy contact with each other.

When those friends are of different sexes, a peculiarly pleasant quality is added. A girl thrills to just being close to a boy she likes very much. A boy goes out of his way to walk with, talk with, look at, listen to, touch, and be touched by the girl who especially appeals to him. Little gestures that indicate that the other is enjoying being near can be exquisitely enjoyable. Such a couple soon find their hands seeking each other as they sit together in a movie, or walk down a path. Hand holding brings both a warm sense of response that tends to continue. From then on the friendly kiss, the deeper lovers' kiss, the urge to hold the other close, to fondle and caress, come as normally as breathing. The attraction of members of one sex to the other is strangely compelling, strongly demanding, urgently insistent, and all too little understood in these days when so much freedom of expression is possible.

PETTING
as a game

Some irresponsible young people play at love-making as a kind of game. There are boys and men who deliberately get girls into petting situations just to see how far they can go. Such males take advantage of the unwary and are always a challenge to any woman, however sophisticated. Adolph bragged around school about the number of girls he had "had." He rarely went back to the same girl twice, but rather played a game of seeing how many girls he could seduce with his love act.

Some unscrupulous girls will lead boys and men on in much the same way. Such girls do not and cannot really love the men they go out with. They are exploiting men for the sense of power they may gain over them. Such love-pirates only play a kind of risky game, with none of love's richness, none of its real satisfaction, none of its beauty and permanence. Being seduced by such a person is no compliment, and should be no temptation to the young person who knows the difference between expressing deep affection and using sex for temporary gratification.

THE
process of petting

Whether in an exploitative situation, as just described, or between mutually devoted couples who express in their love-making their deepest concerns for each other's welfare, petting is a process of physical involvement between members of the opposite sex which follows patterns that can be predicted. One step leads to the next in a way that can be reliably anticipated. The various steps in the process can be identified as they move toward goals that are recognizable. Let us analyze these characteristics of petting.

LOVE-MAKING tends to be habit forming

The ways of expressing affection that a person has learned in the past tend to become habitual. In a real sense, we learn to make love in our earliest relationships within our families. The little girl who has always adored her daddy, who has snuggled close to him and enjoyed his squeezes as a child, will take this expectation of being held close in warm lovable ways into her more adult contacts with boys later on. The boy who has learned to enjoy the giving and receiving of love pats and kisses and various caresses within his family will quite naturally use these same love expressions as he finds himself in love with girls in his teens.

We learn to love and be loved first of all in our families. These earliest learnings are elaborated and developed as we mature and have warm contacts with beloved friends. Here, too, the habit-forming elements continue. The boy who has learned to hold his girl's hand as he walks down the street with her will tend to do so habitually. The girl and boy who say goodnight with a kiss tend to expect it, to feel deprived if they do not have it, and to come together in that kiss spontaneously, almost without thinking.

In much the same way, persons who have learned to pet when with an attractive person of the other sex soon develop the habit of petting to the point where it is extremely difficult not to. They tend to expect and to demand the level of expression to which they are accustomed, and only with will power and conscious control are they able to stop short of that point.

Fred and Nan had developed the habit of petting to the place where they could enjoy little else. All through the early part of the evening, each was preoccupied with thoughts of what would happen when they finally got off alone. Everything else faded out, and only their petting seemed important. Finally their relationship became so focused on petting, and petting alone, that they decided to break up and not see each other so much. The first girls that Fred dated after he and Nan stopped going steady had quite a time with him, for he tried to fondle them in the same way that he had Nan over the months. It wasn't because he cared specially for them, but rather that he had developed the petting habit to the place where any girl was a stimulus to the routine.

The sex urge is universal. Its satisfaction is learned. We learn to satisfy our feelings of attraction and response to others in many different ways, depending upon who we are, where we live, and what we expect of ourselves. It is something like our satisfaction of hunger. We all feel hungry at times. But the way we eat, and what, and with whom, and how often, and how we feel about it, differ enormously from one person to the next, as well as from one culture to another. So it is with sex satisfaction. The sex urge is native and universal. Sex satisfaction is learned and highly individualized.

SEX tends to focus on the person

Just as Fred and Nan found that each brought forth in the other the urge to pet, so sex expression tends to focus on the individual with whom there has been some previous experience. C. K. always kissed Caroline when he saw her, not because Caroline wanted him to, or even because he found her particularly kissable. The simple reason was that soon after they had met, they were together at the wedding of a mutual friend where everyone was kissing everyone else. He kissed her then, and continued the habit.

When a boy has been out on a petting party with a girl, he tends to think of her ever after as a petting partner. She will have much more difficulty keeping their relationship on a platonic level after she has once permitted love-making than if it had never been a part of their relationship. This seems to be something of what boys mean when they speak of a girl's being "that kind of woman," or "not that kind of woman." She is, in their eyes, one who allows petting or one who does not. And she finds that her relationships with boys tend to follow the patterns she has already established.

When we realize that the relationship between the sexes finds its greatest meanings and satisfactions when it is based upon mutual affection, mutual respect, and a real love for each other as whole personalities, then we can see that becoming just a sex object in the other's eyes can warp the whole relationship. Sex is always there. It lies close to the surface in all male-female relationships. It can always be called forth to intensify a relationship between the sexes. But as soon as sex is given free expression, the relationship tends to fixate on a sexual level, except of course after marriage when all life is encompassed in the fullness of the relationship.

SEX play builds to climax

Any physical intimacy between the members of opposite sexes tends to lead to the next step in the sequence of love-making that leads to the climax of complete release. Left uncontrolled, the urgencies of stimulation rush a couple through stage after stage of their involvement until nature has satisfied herself in intercourse.

These forces are often very strong and insistent. Once released they tend to press for completion. One step leads to the next in the crescendo of sexual excitement that builds to climax, as normally happens in marriage. When going all the way is their purpose, then the two partners give themselves without restraint to the satisfaction of their sexual urges, then and there. But there are times, and places, and persons that call for sex controls to keep the relationship within suitable bounds.

SEX
controls are necessary

Sex controls are necessary to keep an individual from being exploited. There are predatory boys and men who make a game of seeing how far they can go with their female companions. Some girls demand more response than a fellow may feel is appropriate. To protect oneself from "the wolf" of either sex, a boy or girl or a man or woman finds sex controls necessary in many a potentially exploitive situation.

Sex controls are necessary to maintain one's standards

of moral conduct. Each individual grows up with a sense of what is right in all sorts of situations. There are wide variations in the moral codes held by individuals of different cultural groups and religious backgrounds. At the same time, there is general agreement on what is clearly wrong—incest, child molestation, adultery, and flagrant promiscuity, for instance, in our society. Even in these generally disapproved types of sexual contact there are some individuals who do not conform, just as there are those who break other laws of the land. But since most of us have built-in standards that are a part of us, we must restrain our behavior to fit our sense of what is right as we have learned it, in order to live at peace with ourselves.

Sex and love belong together. This is why a boy's relationship with a prostitute or a pick-up, and a girl's giving in to the demands of a casual date, are so unrewarding. Sex without love satisfies only the animal passions and violates the essentially human qualities of a person—the ability to feel with and to care for another human being. The habitually promiscuous individual is usually a lonely soul, deprived of the lasting affections that give meaning to life. The more he chases the more lost he feels in an aloneness that no physical intercourse can assuage.

But what if the two persons love each other? If the boy and girl feel that they belong to each other, is there any reason why they should not express their love for one another intimately? If they are sure that they can prevent having a baby until they have a home in which to care for it, is their sex conduct their own business? If they avoid being part of the rising number of cases of venereal disease among young people, is there any danger of going all the way? If they can face their friends and families comfortably in case their conduct becomes known, are they safe in taking the chance? If in good conscience their behavior seems "right" to them, why not? These questions are being asked by many young people today and call for far more helpful answers than are usually available.

One sobering fact is that feelings of love for another person cannot be counted upon to last indefinitely. Especially during the second decade of life, the girl or boy is maturing emotionally through a process of changing feelings toward self and others. Normally through the teen years a girl loves a series of boys, each in a special way, for awhile. A boy too may love a girl, perhaps deeply, devotedly, but not necessarily permanently. It is not until one has developed the capacity to love and be loved over the years that one is ready for a mature continuing love—enough for marriage. The big question then is, which of the loves experienced before marriage warrants sexual expression? Until a person is very sure of his or her answer, sex controls are helpful even with—especially with—a much beloved partner.

Another fact in this connection is that your life is all of a piece. What you are now is the result of what you have been in the past. What you will become will be the natural culmination of your experiences and reactions to life as you have lived it all along. Your own personal way of life is being developed now in the way you respond to others, in the way you feel about yourself, and in the paths of conduct you choose to follow. How you behave on a date reflects your own sense of who you are and what you aspire to, as Chapter Twenty reviews for you.

Sex controls are necessary to secure the larger goals you have for your life. Your sex standards are part of your other relationships with people. Your sex conduct and controls determine your associates, your friends, and your prospects for marriage. Those who are free in their sex conduct attract others of the same type. Those whose goals are secure and enduring relationships do what is necessary to gain and protect them. This is the basis of the policy calling for restriction of sex relations to the one with whom one joins in the establishment of a family—in which the interests of both the couple and their children are protected by marriage. When a couple marry they publicly assume responsibility for living together as man and wife in an ongoing relationship. Their sex life then is controlled by their mutual responsibility for the children they have, and by the mutual love that forms the heart of their home.

Every man, woman, and teen-ager must learn to control his sexual behavior. No matter what one's standards may be, or how permissive or strict one is before or within marriage, some controls upon one's conduct are necessary. So it is a wise couple, an intelligent young person, who knows when to stop and how.

PHYSICAL signs

When the expression of affection begins to be sexually exciting, certain physical signs appear which can be detected by one or both of the couple. Because of the differences between boys and girls in the way they are made and the ways in which they have been brought up, the boy usually experiences the first symptoms of sexual expression. His face may become flushed. Usually his breathing becomes rapid, his pulse is fast, and his heart starts to pound. Changes in his sex organs are obvious. The girl as well as the boy may find that hands perspire freely under sexual stimulation. Girls tend to experience an all-over relaxation. The alert couple can detect other physical signs of arousal of sex feelings that should operate as caution signals.

COMPULSION to continue

When either or both feel urgently impelled to continue, it is a sign that sexual stimulation is already present. Nature causes us to respond in a spiraling crescendo of feeling that is easier to stop in its early stages than it is near the peak of excitability. The couple who really love each other enough to protect themselves and their relationships from ill-advised behavior guard against getting so involved that there is a compulsion to continue. Likewise the individual girl or boy, caught in a petting situation with a person who wants only that, can recognize the first hint of urgency as a stop sign.

YOUR own feeling of rightness and wrongness

You can gauge where to stop by how you feel after various kinds of dates. If you feel embarrassed about what you did on last night's date when you wake up in the morning, you probably overstepped your own sense of what is right. If you find it hard to look in each other's eyes when you next meet, then apparently you both feel that what you have done was not quite as it should have been. But if you awaken after a date with a feeling of happiness and joy of living, if you find yourself eagerly looking forward to seeing your date again, if you like being together, working together, sharing all sorts of things with each other, it probably means your physical love-making is appropriate.

HOW
to stop

THE girl's responsibility

Down through the ages it has been considered the female's responsibility to keep relationships between the sexes under control. The big reason apparently is that women are less easily excited by sex stimulation and more slowly moved to demand sexual contact. It is true that on the whole girls are more slowly aroused and can stop love-making more easily than the average male can. The female's response is an all-over one, generalized rather than localized, and more gradual in its build-up than that of the typical male.

Coupled with this physiologic difference is the fact that girls and boys alike, as well as almost everyone else, consider it the girl's responsibility "to keep the boys in line." If two lovers are swept off their feet, it is the girl that is blamed. She is held responsible. She should have known better.

Getting a boy to stop his love-making is hard for some girls. They are so hungry for loving that they cling to any expression of affection that they can evoke. Girls may be so afraid of losing the boy's attention that they dare not refuse him intimacies that he seems to enjoy. Some girls just do not know how to say no to a boy without hurting his feelings or offending something in their relationship. Yet a girl can keep the expressions of affection between herself and her boy friends on a comfortable basis without losing his love, or his friendship, or the sense of everything's being all right between them.

Alyce was telling her younger sister how to say goodnight to an amorous boy friend who seemed all set for a more intimate expression than she felt was wise. Alyce said, "Just take the situation in both your hands, squeeze warmly, and skip in through the door." What she meant was that the girl could anticipate the "hold" that seemed imminent and, taking the boy's hands in both of hers, she could give them such a meaningful little squeeze that he would have a sense of having been loved without anything too intense having happened.

Coming across the campus of a coeducational institution one evening were a couple very much in love. As they neared the girl's dormitory at closing time, they saw that every available spot on the porch steps was already occupied. Yet, even then, that couple did not find it necessary to add their too-obvious goodnight to all the others. She turned as they approached the stairs, looked up into his face with hers beaming, put her finger on his chin in a sweetly personal way as she said, "It's been wonderful. You're swell." As she ran up the steps, he turned back toward his dorm with such a satisfied look on his face that one knew he did not realize what he had missed! In fact, it was evident that he had not missed anything really important. She had told him everything a boy wants to hear from a girl he cares about. She had told him that she enjoyed being with him, that she had had a wonderful time, and that she liked him very much and in a very special way.

The language of love has many forms beside those which play upon the most elemental senses. As young people learn the variety and the fullness of deep love feelings, they develop many ways of expressing affection. That girl in the paragraph above, of course, did not go around touching men on the chin all the time! But she was learning, as you can, to show love in a multitude of little gestures and acts that are a delight to the beloved because they are warmly personal, uniquely his, and prompted by the kind of love that all men need.

Stopping love-making that is already advancing at a rapid rate is not easy. But it can be done. Cora was snuggling close to her boy friend in the car late one night. They were both relaxed and happy. They were very fond of each other. He began to kiss her, and she responded eagerly. Then something new came into their love-making as his hand slipped down between her breasts and his kiss took on an intensity that was frightening. Cora struggled free of his embrace, shook her curls with a jerky little laugh saying, "Ooooh, please, you are too much for me."

Hazel takes a different tack. When a date's hands begin to wander into the no man's land which she considers untouchable, she firmly removes the hand as she says with surprise, "Why, this isn't Tuesday, is it?" The humor, "corny" as it is, is usually enough to stop all but the most exploitative of boys.

One girl reports that when she is parked with a boy who insists on going faster in his petting than either of them has brakes for, she turns the key in the ignition and sweetly says, "Will you drive, or shall I?" The particular technique a girl uses in assuming her responsibility does not matter so long as it works. If she can do it without making either of them feel shabby, she should by all means. She does not need to preach or to use words at all. Anything she can do which will tell him that she likes him, at the same time that she cannot permit certain behavior, will usually work. Some boys are so insistent, that a girl has to know her own mind and be able to back it up with effective methods if she is to hold to her standards.

It comes down, in the last analysis, to how sure a girl is of herself. If she knows who she is in her own heart, if she cares about building toward a rich and full future as a woman, she will be able to put off some of the blind-alley activities that lead nowhere except into crack-ups. Petting is neither good nor bad in itself. It is what it means and what it stands for in a long lifetime of relations with men that gives the perspective a girl needs.

THE boy's responsibility

Boys too have a responsibility for controls in their relationships with girls. A boy who takes a girl out without the supervision and the chaperonage that once prevailed is duty bound to see to it that he returns her to her home unharmed. Furthermore, he is jointly responsible with her for the quality and the nature of their relationship. It is as much his duty as hers to keep their friendship on a basis that both can continue to enjoy without endangering themselves or those they hold dear.

Boys are usually aware of sexually stimulating situations before the average girl senses what is happening. Boys sometimes are baffled by the things nice girls do that are sexually exciting, without realizing that oftentimes the girl has no idea of how provocative her behavior may be. The boy in such a situation gently eases them both into a more comfortable position without taking advantage of her innocent seduction. Sometimes it becomes necessary for a boy to instruct his girl friend on some of the facts of life.

Fritz and Jane were very fond of each other. They had been going together steadily for some time, when Fritz found it necessary to talk things over with her. He said something like this: "I love you very much, so much that I want you close to me always. But when you sit on my lap like this, my feelings become almost more than I can cope with. So slide over on your own side of the seat and let's go get a hamburger." Fritz was taking his share of the responsibility for their relationship.

LOVING
the person versus "loving, period"

There is a vast difference between loving another person and going through the motions of loving for its own sake. The boy or girl who goes in for "loving, period" is one who is always on the prowl, always after more sexual excitement, always ready to be stimulated by anyone anywhere. The way young people use the word "period" to denote the end very well describes the blind-alley, end-in-itself kind of thing that "loving, period" becomes.

Loving another person is a deeply satisfying experience. It is a feeling that calls for expression in many ways. Of course, there will be appropriate physical expression of that love. And it will have meaning and be very beautiful to the extent to which it expresses the depth and loveliness of the feelings each has for the other. Such loving that wells up as an expression of the best and finest that a person can feel for another is fine, and it is fun too. Love-making in its best sense is highly pleasurable, not only for the excitation that each calls forth in the other, but also because it draws on the magnetism of the human spirit as well as the attraction of the body. True love is compounded of both elements. The kind of love-making that builds toward marriage unites the two persons in a unity of devotion because it expresses their growing love, in a rich and meaningful sense.

When should

CHAPTER 14

you say No –
and how?

ONE OF THE HARDEST THINGS most of us have to
learn is how to say no. It is a little word, and one of the
first that we use as children, but as we grow older, knowing
when and how to say it is not easy.

How do you refuse an invitation without hurting the
other's feelings? How can you say no when your date
wants to go somewhere you do not feel you should? Should
you say no when drinks are served? Can you refuse a cigarette when everyone else is smoking? How do you let a
boy know that you do not want to be kissed? How do you
go about turning down a date, refusing to go steady or get
pinned or become engaged or even married?

WHEN
you have to refuse a date

Girls need to know how to refuse dates comfortably and
pleasantly. Many circumstances arise in the life of every
girl when she must know how to say no to a date. She may
have other plans for that particular time. She may not
want to date the particular boy. She may not be allowed
to date at all for a period of time.

The girl who has another engagement can say so simply
and easily. It sounds something like this: "Oh, I'm so sorry
but I'm already tied up for then." If she would like to date
that particular boy, she may add a few words that will

tell him that she will welcome another invitation. She may thank him for thinking of her and tell him that she hopes that she can go out with him another time.

Sometimes a girl would like to accept a date, but she cannot do what is being proposed at that time. One common illustration is that of a girl's being invited to go swimming at a time when she will be menstruating. Many a girl is embarrassed in refusing such a date. She could go with the boy to something else or she could go swimming with him at some other time. She feels she cannot come right out and give the real reason. If she is too indefinite in her refusal, the boy may misunderstand and feel that she is not interested.

Girls should know that most boys old enough to date know about menstruation. If a girl says, "I'm sorry, I can't go swimming Saturday; how about a picnic instead?" the average boy will understand that she is refusing the swimming and not the date. Or, she may say, "Sorry, not this week; how about next Saturday at the pool?" This lets him know that it is the timing that she is concerned about and not him or the swimming itself.

It is discourteous for a boy to ask why when a girl tells him that she cannot do something that he asks. When a boy pushes for explanation of a girl's refusal, she is justified in kidding him about his persistence, or in simply changing the subject.

If a girl does not ever want to date a particular boy, she does him a kindness when she gives him no encouragement whatsoever. To lead a boy on, when she never intends to go out with him, does him an injustice and unnecessarily prolongs the refusals. There are many reasons that a girl may refuse to consider dating a particular boy. He may drink, or run around with a fast set, or have a bad reputation, or be the kind of person whom for other reasons she does not feel she can associate with. If he is not datable from her point of view, she will be wise to refuse his attentions courteously but with firmness and finality.

HOW
to handle unwelcome advances

How does a girl refuse a boy a kiss without hurting his feelings? How can a young man go easy in his lovemaking and still have his girl feel that he likes her? Sometimes we feel deeply about these questions. A girl wants to feel that she is kissable even when she does not want to be kissed. A boy wants to feel that he is not repulsive even when he is put off. And a boy does not want to be considered slow if he is a bit restrained in his kissing. A great deal is involved in these expressions of affection. Our need for loving and being loved by others, our desire for real response, our feeling that we are desirable, and our sense of making progress, all are intertwined.

The kindest refusal is firm and yet considerate of the other's feelings. A girl who refuses to kiss a boy should be careful that she does not reject him even when she very definitely rejects his caress. She can say simply, "Sorry, Bill, not just now." Or she can use any of the subtle looks or words or gestures that tell the boy that she likes him even when she must refuse his kiss.

A boy may find himself in a situation where the girl obviously expects him to display his affection in a way that he feels would not be wise. His responsibility is to slip out from under her demands without letting her down too rudely. Paying her some little compliment at the same time that he makes a quiet retreat is a time-honored means out of such a situation.

REFUSING
to go to questionable spots

You have not been dating long before someone is sure to suggest going to a place about which you have a question. Your parents may have put it "out of bounds." You may have heard that a rather fast crowd goes there. Whether it be a tavern, a roadhouse, a public dance hall, a skating rink, bowling alley, or whatever is not important. The very fact that you have a question about whether you should go may at times make that particular spot unduly attractive to you. Sometimes, just when you are trying to appear grown up and free to do what you please with the rest of the crowd, you are torn between two decisions you could make. One side of yourself begs to joins the crowd just to prove that you can go if you want to. Another side of yourself reminds you that refusing to go where you know you shouldn't proves still more strongly your freedom of choice and your grownupness. Which wins out?

When you are in your teens, these moments come more often than at any other time in your life. It is then that you are emancipating yourself from your old childish dependencies upon your parents, and testing their rules and authority in general. As you get a little older the desire to do the forbidden, to show that you can, will pass, and you will be able to say no more easily. But now you are in your teens, so let's face it and see what can be done.

"Is it worth it?" you can ask yourself. Stop for a moment and think over what may happen. Think of how your parents will feel when they learn you have gone. Consider what your best friends will say. Ask yourself how you yourself will feel about it after it is all over. Is an hour or two of excursion into forbidden places worth the pain you will cause those who care about you? Is it worth your own feelings of uneasiness and guilt when it is over? Feeling as you do, will you be really able to have much fun there? For a good many young people the answer will be, "No, I won't go. It just isn't worth it." For others it will still be hard to say no to the tempting lure of the adventure into the unknown.

Better be pretty sure, too, that you are not doing something questionable just to hurt someone you love. That is a common trap that catches the unwary. You have just been hurt by a friend or a member of the family for whom you care very deeply. You find yourself wanting to hurt back, to get even, to show the other that you don't care. You get in deeper than ever as you try to show how little you care by cutting yourself off from those you love, doing things you do not really enjoy, and fooling nobody, not even yourself!

WILL it take you where you want to go in life?

One may ask oneself quite seriously, "Who do you think you are?" What do you want out of life? Would going to this particular spot help you along the road to the kind of life you visualize for yourself? Or is it off in another direction?

The person who thinks of himself as a creature of appetites may seek momentary satisfaction to gratify a whim. A boy or girl with faith in the future will hesitate to do anything that will jeopardize the goals toward which he is striving. Such a person can say rather easily, "Sorry, that is not for me," because he is fairly sure of where he is going in life and what roads lead to his goals. When you become sure of yourself, such decisions are increasingly easy.

HOW can you say no?

Let us say you have decided that you really do not want to go to the questionable spot at all. You have settled the question in your own mind. How do you convey your decision to the others involved without being an unpleasant wet blanket, spoiling their fun, and getting yourself labeled a goody-goody?

The easiest way to say no is the simplest: "I am sorry, but I am not coming." It usually is not necessary to go into long explanations or to preach to the others about how bad such a jaunt would be. You do not even have to tell a white lie. If it makes you feel any more comfortable to add a word to your refusal, you can tell the other(s) what you are going to do instead. It can sound something like this: "No, I think I will go get something to eat (or whatever) instead." If you are sure of your decision in your own mind, your voice will relay your decisiveness. You will not have an argument on your hands about it so long as you stand firm and sure yourself.

IF
you do not want to drink

Drinking, at best, is a social crutch. Drinkers report that they take a drink to give them courage for a difficult situation or to loosen their tongues when they may find it hard to talk. It is when young people feel insecure and inadequate that they are most likely to resort to the support they hope to get from alcohol.

At worst, drinking is a serious illness brought on by the bad habit of propping oneself up too often and too long with alcoholic stimulation. Everybody knows that drinking and driving do not mix; nor do drinking and dates;

nor drinking and family life; nor drinking and most of the other worthwhile things of life.

Yet alcoholic beverages are so often served that almost all young people must learn how to handle social drinking situations without being left out of good times with pleasant companions.

If you do not want to drink, the best way to avoid it is to go around with other people who feel as you do about it. It is when you find yourself with a drinking set that you will find it hardest to refuse. If you choose your friends among the many interesting people who do not drink, then the matter of refusing to drink becomes relatively easy.

But suppose you are out with a crowd who order drinks, what do you do then? When the gaze turns on you with the what-will-you-have query, you must be ready with an answer. That is not the time to stammer with indecision, or to mutter that you had better not, or to mention that your folks disapprove. Any of these responses is apt to make you conspicuous. The direct answer to the question, "What will you have?" is something like, "Make mine a root beer (or name your flavor), please."

One popular girl goes with several different groups in which occasionally there is a little drinking. When it comes her turn to order, she smiles and says, "I'll have a large ginger ale *straight*, please." This usually brings a laugh, and the crowd respects her choice. One of her boy friends followed her lead and made a flourish of ordering "One Seven-Up, with lime *and* ice, please." While the others had their cocktails, he had great fun mixing his lime, Seven-Up, and ice, complete with swizzle stick!

Refusing a drink is not too hard once you have made up your own mind that you really do not want it and that you can have a good time without it. Any crowd that makes it uncomfortable for you to refuse cannot care too much for you as a person and very possibly is not the kind of gang with whom you can have the most interesting companionship.

CAN you ask your date to stop drinking?

Many a girl has been embarrassed to find herself out with a boy who drinks beyond the point where he is a good escort. He can no longer give her the kind of attention she wishes when he is under the influence of alcohol. He is not a safe driver of an automobile. And he quite possibly becomes ill when he has had too much. How can the girl get him to stop drinking?

A boy sometimes finds that the girl with him begins to drink too much. She acts silly, giggles too much, raises her voice to a pitch that attracts attention, and otherwise embarrasses him. He does not want to be responsible for her behavior. He is concerned about what her family will say when he brings her home. In such a situation, what is one to do?

It is sometimes harder to say no to another's behavior than it is to one's own. Yet in situations such as these, it is certainly necessary. What you do depends to a considerable extent on how well you know the other person, and how much influence you have over him or her. If this is a first date (as it often is), you may simply say, "Shall we call this the last drink now and then go on home?" If he has already had more than is safe for driving, the girl has the right, even the responsibility, to ask him for the keys and drive the car herself. If for some reason that is not possible, she may make some other arrangement.

Emily went to the interfraternity ball with a man she had known only casually before he asked her to the affair. It was still early when he began to drink. By the time couples began to leave, he could not be trusted to drive. Emily did not know how to drive the car herself. Fortunately, one of the fraternity brothers sensed the situation and invited Emily and her escort to ride home with his girl and him. It was good that they did, for on the way home Emily's escort was sick and had to be assisted into the fraternity house even before the girls could be taken home. Before the evening was over, Emily realized that dating a boy who would get into that condition at a dance was not much fun, and a considerable responsibility.

Before accepting an invitation to a party where drinks may be served, a girl may tell her date that she does not drink, and does not enjoy being with a boy who does. If he cannot have a good time without drinking, then telling him frankly of her standards will make it possible for him to back out and for her to be spared the painful necessity of a scene at the social occasion itself. It often happens that a boy would rather not get into the drinking habit. He may appreciate his girl's taking a firm stand that he is glad to follow.

Ted came from a family where no drinking was done. In high school he got in with a set in which it was difficult to refuse when drinks were served. Then Ted began dating Ann, who came from the same kind of family and felt strongly that she could have a better time without drinking. She let Ted know that she liked him but that she would not go out with him if he had to drink. Ted liked her all the more for her stand and preferred dating Ann to going along with the gang. It was not long before Ann and Ted found a congenial group of friends who had good times together on a non-drinking basis.

There are all kinds of people in the world. Some feel that they have to drink to have a good time. There are those who just as honestly think that they can have a better time without drinking. The individual young person can find others who feel the same way, if he tries.

THE
question of smoking

Refusing to smoke may be even harder than turning down a drink. Smoking is so very common that not smoking may make one feel odd or peculiar.

It is easier not to get started in the smoking habit than it is to break it off. Many young people find that if they can make up their own minds not to smoke, refusing a cigarette is not too difficult. When a cigarette is offered, a girl may simply smile and say, "No, thank you." No elaborate explanation is necessary. She does not have to say that she does not smoke, or that she feels that smoking is an unpleasant habit. In fact, the less said about it the better. She can turn the conversation in another direction at the same time that she refuses the smoke, for the cigarette itself is something not very important.

Jerry carries a roll of candy mints in his pocket. Whenever he is with a group in which cigarettes are passed, he refuses the smoke at the same time that he offers his mints to the members of the group. He finds that he can be just as sociable with his little lifesavers as the other fellows are with their smokes. In fact, he has been pleasantly surprised to find that other boys and girls often seem grateful for the mint in such a situation.

WHY do people smoke?

People begin to smoke for a variety of reasons. It may start as a little adventure in acting grown up. Adults smoke, the young person says to himself. I am growing up. I am no longer a child, therefore it is time that I began to smoke. This is understandable. It leads to the secret tryouts behind the garage, or in the privacy of one's own room, or even more often with a crowd of one's friends who feel the same urge to prove their grownupness.

A second reason for beginning to smoke is to prove to yourself that you can. If parents have opposed smoking among young people, their children who are growing up may be tempted to defy them at times and to smoke just to resist them. This rebelling against parental controls is part of the breaking away from childish dependence on parents' authority. It is regrettable when young people feel they have to do something just because their parents object. It is childish and it can lead to difficulties.

Another reason that young people begin to smoke is that the rest of the crowd does and it is easier to go along than to hold back and be different. Many of the boys in the armed services say they started to smoke simply because everyone else in uniform did it. The shrewdness with which tobacco and cigarette companies advertise and distribute their products makes smoking seem so general that it is hard to avoid concluding that, after all, everyone does smoke.

Smoking is said to reduce tension. When you feel uneasy, when you are facing a difficult assignment, when you have come through a grueling experience, when you do not know quite what to do, a cigarette is supposed to be the answer. Smoking may be a smoke screen for feelings of insecurity. During a moment of felt inadequacy, as a cover-up for feelings of self-consciousness, the smoke offers something to do that makes one feel more at ease and self-assured.

Tobacco is habit forming. Once one has begun to smoke,

he finds that he has to continue. Without a cigarette, one feels restless, his head aches, he "just can't wait for a smoke." This is what led one young man to observe wryly:

> Tobacco is a nasty weed, I love it;
> Tobacco is an expensive habit, I love it;
> Tobacco is a messy practice, I love it;
> Tobacco is a social crutch, I love it;
> Tobacco is my master, I love it!

ARE cigarettes coffin nails?

Boys often jokingly refer to their cigarettes as "cancer sticks," or "coffin nails," the idea being that every cigarette you smoke brings you that much closer to the Grim Reaper. Actually it would take a long time to kill yourself smoking. Yet tobacco is not good for you. Boys who really want to keep themselves in good condition, as athletes do, voluntarily refrain from smoking. Heart, lungs, muscles, and especially the capillaries in the circulatory system are adversely affected by smoking.

HOW do you stop smoking?

Some people who have been smoking decide that for reasons of health or money or neatness or pleasing someone they care for, or because of their own feeling of not wishing to be a slave to anything, they will stop smoking. Some do stop completely all at once. Others try tapering off by smoking a little less every day. Either method is hard. It takes real determination and strength of character to stop the habit. Yet it can be done. Talk with anyone who has broken himself of the smoking habit and you will find a sense of self-satisfaction and personal mastery in the accomplishment.

REFUSING
to be prematurely committed

When a boy urges a girl to go steady with him, or to accept his fraternity pin, or to commit herself to him in any way at a time when she does not want to be "signed up," how can she refuse his offer without hurting his feelings? This question baffles many girls. They feel that it is a compliment to a girl to be asked to save herself for one boy only, and that the boy is committing himself to be exclusively hers in his request. Yet they may not be ready to be tied down to that extent, or they may not be sure that theirs is the kind of steady friendship that would do well. Theirs is the task of stalling the proposal and letting time settle whether or not they will ever want to be more definitely committed to the particular boy.

Many girls find that if they come right out with the truth about how they feel, boys are able to understand and to accept a negative answer. Ruth had been going with Al for some time. They enjoyed each other's company, and Ruth was not too surprised one evening to hear Al asking her to wear his pin and go with him exclusively. Because she had already thought about it, she was able to tell Al that she was not yet ready to settle down to any one boy, that she liked him and enjoyed being with him, but that she felt it was too soon for them to fence themselves off from all other friendships. To her amazement, Al seemed a little relieved and confessed that he felt the same way. They had gone together so much, however, that he felt she probably expected him to offer his pin, and he didn't want to disappoint her!

It makes good sense, too, to postpone an engagement until both of the partners are really sure that they want to undertake all that being engaged to be married means. When so many engagements break up rather than lead into marriage, it looks as though many young people need a little practice in saying no all along the line.

All through life there will be many opportunities to use the skill of saying no. A man or woman cannot do all the things they are asked to do. There will always be dates to refuse, temptations to avoid, burdensome responsibilities to escape, and lesser values to deny. Life is full of choices. If you choose to do one thing, you must necessarily refuse to do something else. Learning how to say no easily, comfortably, courteously, and definitely is important. It involves much more than the pronouncing of a single syllable. It means making up your own mind as to what you want to have happen, and then taking your stand.

What makes for successful entertaining?

YOU DO NOT HAVE TO BE "the hostess with the mostest" to entertain successfully. Your hospitality is one of the nicest things that you can offer to those you like. When you open your home to your friends, you give them something of yourself as well as a good time. The way you go about giving a party is important. There are certain tried and true principles that make for successful entertaining.

GIVING
parties

A popular way for girls to get boys started in dating is to invite them to parties. Girls' clubs, such as the Y-Teens, the Tri-Hi-Y, the Girl Scouts, or church clubs and school

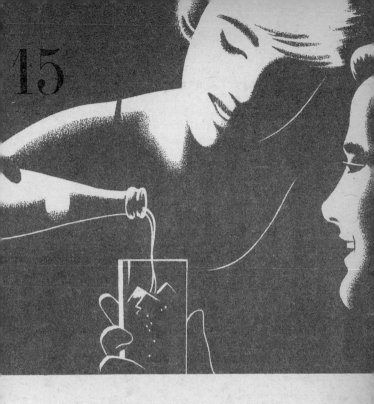

organizations, often plan social functions with the idea that the girls may invite boys to come as their escorts. A girl may invite any boy she wishes to come to such a party. She usually invites some boy whom she knows at least slightly. It might be a boy who has shown interest in her in some way, perhaps by smiling at her or walking to class with her or talking with her or even walking her home from some event.

Parties that girls give should be planned for the participation of all the guests. Activities like square dances and folk games, with a good caller, are well suited to mixed parties in which the girls invite the boys, for they encourage a great deal of mixed activity without demanding that the boy be responsible for a girl for a long period of time, as is true of social dancing. One of the complaints girls have about boys at dances is that they hang around in a corner or in a stag line and let the girls dance either with each other or not at all. This is usually because a boy hates to be responsible for a girl in as much dancing and conversation and social know-how as a dance involves. He is afraid he will not know what to say or what to do. Rather than be embarrassed, he stands back with his pals and just watches.

Mixers of various kinds should be planned at intervals in parties for boys and girls just beginning to go together. This makes it possible for a good many persons to meet others, and prevents one person's getting "stuck" with some other for uncomfortable intervals. Asking a good group leader to come in and keep things moving is usually a safeguard against a party's going stale or breaking up because nothing clicks.

CONGENIAL
people enjoy each other

Whether you have two or two hundred guests, do what you can to make sure that they will be congenial. As their host or hostess your responsibility is to provide opportunities for persons to enjoy one another. The first step in this direction is to choose people who share enough of the same interests and are basically similar enough to have a good time together.

Congenial people are usually of about the same age. Some parties can be planned to include great differences in age, as picnics and barn dances have proved. Usually, however, the more nearly the same general age group, the more the persons will enjoy being together.

People who go together well have enough tastes in common so that they like to do the same things. Inviting a girl who does not play cards to a bridge party would be a thoughtless thing to do. Trying to mix a drinking and smoking set with those who do not indulge might be difficult for members of both groups. When you are giving a party where dancing will be the main entertainment and some guests are known not to dance, you will want to provide other forms of fun, like games or cards, where the non-dancers may have a good time together.

Personal factors, like who is going with whom and who

has just broken up, should be taken into account if you want to make sure that everyone has a good time. Freda found herself with two hostile camps on her hands at a party she gave. She made the mistake of inviting Randy and his current girl friend as well as Harriet, with whom he had recently stopped going steady. The two girls were so jealous of each other that the whole party soon revolved around the hostilities they generated. None of Freda's plans was powerful enough to overcome the unfortunate effects of the two rival girls. Thoughtful hosts and hostesses do what they can to make sure that those they invite to their homes will like to be together.

KEEPING
hospitality simple

A party does not have to be elaborate in order to be good. The most successful parties are usually simple ones. The hostess who wears herself out doing a complete house-cleaning job before her guests arrive may find it hard to give her guests the relaxed and pleasant attention that will make for a good time. Food that is too elaborate or difficult to serve may absorb so much time that the hostess' primary concern goes to it rather than to the people who are to enjoy it. Decorations should set a mood. The general rule is to plan everything carefully so that during the party you may enjoy your guests.

LETTING your guests help

Some of the best parties are those in which everyone pitches in and helps. The considerate host does not try to do everything himself. He shares the participation with the others. If guests can help, they often feel much more at home than if they are left in the front room to be waited on.

Sharing in the fullest sense may begin even before the party itself starts. Bonnie consulted three of her closest friends about a party she was planning. Together the four of them thought it through and shared in planning for it down to the last detail. When the night of the party finally arrived, Bonnie felt that she had three responsible allies with her. Not only was she freer to have a good time, but her three girl friends felt that they belonged there in a special sort of way that would not have happened if Bonnie had not shared the planning with them.

During the party itself, guests can be enlisted for all sorts of functions. Planning to use the talents of the various guests is an art. This goes far beyond just asking the boys to move chairs. It includes calling upon the boy who tells a good yarn to tell his latest to the group. It may include asking an especially gracious girl to supervise the serving of refreshments. It even may go so far as to ask for volunteers to be the clean-up squad and help you to settle the place after the other guests have gone. As guests have opportunities to function as they best can, they will feel that they are "in" as well as "at" your party. When everybody feels that he or she belongs, everyone has a good time.

MAKE
your guests feel at home

There is a neat balance between keeping things natural and entertaining in too extravagant a way. It is better to err in the direction of having things just the way they usually are than to try to have everything too elaborate. In the take-us-as-we-are atmosphere, both the hosts and the guest may feel comfortable and at home. When too much effort is being made to entertain a guest, the strain is apt to show.

Nothing is quite so much fun as visiting a friend's home for a meal or overnight or for longer. Young people who enjoy being together get particular pleasure out of sharing their homes with each other. This is especially so when both host and guest do things that make for the other's easy enjoyment of the situation.

When you have a friend in, you will want to do something special to express your pleasure in being a host. If the guest comes for overnight, for instance, you will probably see to it that your dresser is cleared of some of its accumulated stuff, so that your guest's things will have a place. Having a guest in for a meal sometimes call for more than just setting an extra plate at the table. Most families have practices that differ somewhat if there are guests present. The big point is to keep these differences down to a comfortable minimum. If your mother has to launder all the curtains before you can ask a friend in, your entertaining will be restricted considerably!

HAVE
your parents at your parties

When you entertain in your home, your parents should be there. They do not have to be in everything that goes on; it is better if they are not. But they should help to greet the guests when they arrive. They may be provided with some comfortable role to play sometime during the party itself. Dad may be especially good at popping corn, a nice job for him to do that will be appreciated.

Your mother need not be a drudge, waiting upon everyone as mothers sometimes do, nor does she need to be relegated to her bedroom. She may read a book or sew in a comfortable spot out of the main traffic of the party, and come forth to help with the refreshments or to chat with the guests as they ready themselves for departure. If some of your friends enjoy her as a person, they may seek her out during the party for a little chat. You may want to consult her about something or get her assistance in an emergency that arises. This makes her feel that she belongs in her own home.

Young people can see many reasons for the necessity of having their parents at home when they entertain. If the party gets noisy, some nervous neighbor may complain. The whole neighborhood will feel better about that complaint if your parents are there than if you are "just a rowdy bunch of teen-agers" without responsible adults present. The same is true in situations when an accident occurs. Other parents usually feel better about having their sons and daughters come to your house if they know that your parents will be in evidence. Too many unfortunate things can happen to risk going without the protection that adults lend by their presence.

BEING
a good guest

Some people are always welcome wherever they go because they know how to be good guests. Other persons find that they are not so frequently invited out and that even when they are guests, they do not enjoy it as much as they might. These two things go together. If you are a good guest, you are invited out and you do have a good time.

ENTER into the spirit of enjoyment

A good guest goes all ready to enjoy himself. He lets himself anticipate some of the pleasure he is to share, and by the time the occasion comes his appetite is whetted for it. He arrives with enthusiasm and opens himself to the opportunities provided for his pleasure.

An attitude of pseudosophistication is unfortunate both for the person himself and for those with whom he associates. When a boy or girl acts as though nothing that can be done will possibly interest him or her, the whole atmosphere is dampened. Such attitudes frequently stem from feelings of uneasiness and can be outgrown and overcome as the person matures.

Complainers and comparers are rarely welcome guests. The person who finds fault is not only being discourteous: he is spoiling his own and others' fun. The individual who compares the present party with one he has attended elsewhere is indulging in a dangerous sport.

If for some reason you cannot visualize yourself enjoying a particular party, it is better not to accept the invitation than to go prepared not to have a good time. As a guest you have the responsibility of being ready to share a good time with others.

When you go as a guest, you are expected to enter with good grace into whatever activities are provided. You enter the place with easy friendliness that puts the others at their ease, too. One definition of a good guest is "one who makes the host feel at home." This means that you are able to relax with him and to enjoy fun together without tension or embarrassment.

There will probably be some things that you feel you cannot do or share. This is all right. You do not need to do those things which you do not like. You need only refuse graciously and unobtrusively. When some food or drink is offered that you do not take, you either accept it without comment and lay it aside, or you say "'No, thank you" and go on enjoying those that you can take. Similarly with things to do, you have fun in the activities that you can enjoy and let the others do the things in which you are not interested. The spoil-sport is the person who makes a scene about the things he cannot enjoy with others. The welcome guest has fun with the others when they are doing the things he likes, and slips into the background quietly when he cannot participate fully with them.

THANKING your host in sincerity

A thoughtful guest always thanks his host for the hospitality he has enjoyed. This may take one or more of several forms that should be mastered early in one's social experience. Such courtesies take little effort, yet they are extremely important. Once recognized clearly, they are easy to learn and simple to practice.

Upon leaving a party, the guests always thank their hosts. If for some reason the host is not at the door, the guest looks him up and expresses his appreciation for being invited. If it is necessary to leave early, the guest does it as inconspicuously as possible and is careful not to take his host away from other guests in expressing his thanks. The thank-you need not be effusive. A simple expression, such as "I have had such a good time. Thank you for inviting me," is far better than insincere gushing. If you honestly have not had a very good time, you can still be sincere and gracious by telling your host that you appreciate being invited, that it has been nice to be included, or something of the sort.

Young people being entertained in each other's homes should thank not only their friends of their own age but also the parents. If the parents are not on hand as the guests depart, you may relay your appreciation through the host or hostess of your own age by saying something like this, "Tell your folks 'thank you' for me, too." When one or both of the parents are nearby as you leave, make a point of expressing your thanks to them. This can be done very simply, especially if there are several of you in the group leaving at the same time. If you are alone with your adult host or hostess for a moment or so, some little additional comment is usually appreciated. You may want to relay to them greetings from your parents, or comment upon how much you enjoy the son or daughter of the house, or upon the pleasure you get from visiting in their home.

ACCIDENTS
will happen

When a guest has an accident in another's home, who is responsible for the damage? If a guest spills something at the table, he merely expresses his regret and quietly helps to clean up the mess. The host and his parents usually do what they can to minimize the accident. The spilled milk is wiped up, the pieces of dish are picked up, a napkin is thrown over the unseemly spot, and the meal proceeds without undue comment. Some little jest may ease such an uncomfortable moment, but it should not be exaggerated or prolonged. The less said about such things, the better.

If some household equipment is broken or damaged by a guest, there is some question as to the extent of his responsibility for repairing or replacing it. If the damage was entirely his fault, he faces more responsibility than if the accident was a joint affair. If he can afford it, he should replace the damaged article as soon as possible. If the damage done is beyond his ability to care for, the guest can express his sorrow at causing it and perhaps offer to do what he can to make it up to his host.

Gwen broke a platter at the home of her friend. Fortunately it was from open stock, so Gwen bought another just like it and sent it with a little note to her hostess the next Saturday afternoon. Verne was not so fortunate. He was fooling around and knocked a chair through the television screen at Rob's house. He could not afford to replace such an expensive item. All he could do was to seek out Rob's parents, tell them of his sincere regret, and offer to help pay for the damage. Rob's parents were understanding and excused what had happened as an accident, but they appreciated Verne's taking responsibility for telling them about the accident and acknowledging that the fault was his. Even though he could not repay the damage, his responsible attitude of offering to help was appreciated by them.

When you enter a home as a guest, you have a responsibility for being nice to the various members of the family. Teen-age guests who are courteous to the older adults, the grandmas, and the aunts and uncles who may be around, are guests of whom the family usually approves. It does not take much effort to ask the grandmother what she is knitting, or to reply pleasantly to the uncle's question about the school team.

The very fact that you are a guest means that you have added something out of the ordinary to the lives of the children in the house. If you notice the youngsters and do some little thing that lets them know you are interested in them, you fare better than if you ignore them completely. Children like to feel that they are accepted. They respond to being noticed. They may be annoying if they have to get attention by kicking up a fuss.

Slightly older brothers and sisters who may appear attractive are a different kind of problem. Iris loves to visit Barbara's home, not so much because she is fond of Barbara as because she finds the older brother attractive. When Iris comes to visit, the whole family is aware of her interest in the older brother. It has become so embarrassing to him that he tries to duck out the back door whenever Iris comes in the front. By her too obvious interest in this brother of her friend, Iris has not only made herself an object of amusement in the family, but at the same time she has lost the favor of the very person in whom she is so interested.

Sometimes teen-age girls become overly interested in the fathers of their friends. This, too, can be difficult and embarrassing unless the girl keeps her interest pretty much to herself. When Father teases his daughter's friends or otherwise gives them especial attention, they have the task of accepting him graciously without letting their behavior with him get out of bounds. The goal is friendly interaction without the too intense interest in either direction that may cause someone to become uneasy about the guest's presence. You succeed by being pleasant and courteous to all the members of the family, without playing favorites with anyone.

KEEP
family confidences to yourself

As a guest in another's home, you are exposed to family intimacies that should not be shared outside. It is inexcusable to repeat a confidence. It is not good taste to tell others about the way your host lives or arranges household affairs or settles family disputes. Such things can cause a great deal of damage. They are rarely pleasant.

Bunny overheard Cora's father speaking harshly to her mother the last time she visited Cora's house. She foolishly repeated what she had heard and caused a rumor to be circulated that Cora's parents were considering a divorce. Bunny had not realized the dangerous power of gossip, and out of her ignorant thoughtlessness she became responsible for a great injustice. It is far better to act as though you have heard nothing than to consider such things seriously or to repeat them.

Guests do not enter into family squabbles or take sides on issues when they visit other's homes. If you are asked for an opinion on some point that is being argued, you can avoid committing yourself with some twist of humor or indication that you know your opinion would not be pertinent to the discussion. Alan was put on such a spot by Ben's father one time. Ben was arguing with his dad about polishing the family car. Ben's father turned to Alan in search of support for his position. By that time the discussion was so heated that Alan knew he could not afford to put himself between father and son. So he dodged the position by saying, "I'm hardly an expert on cars, with only a jalopy to practice on."

Accepting another's hospitality means that you accept responsibility for not violating the privacy of the family. You do not poke into things that are obviously for the family alone. You keep out of family business that may be discussed in your presence. You do not repeat outside the things you have heard or compare one family with another. All these things violate the trust the family put in you by having you in their home.

As you become adult, you realize the importance of keeping to yourself the things you have seen or heard, or been told in confidence. Just as you do not want your personal life to become common gossip, so you respect others' privacy.

THE
art of entertaining

As long as you live you will be exchanging hospitality with your friends. The arts and skills involved in being a gracious giver, a hospitable host, a welcome guest, and a comfortable recipient are important. Such know-how makes the difference between friendly, easy interaction among friends and forced, uncomfortable relations that may become strained to the breaking point.

Your deepening friendships, your loved ones, your future as well as your present relationships are dependent upon your learning and practicing the skills of comfortable courtesy. Crude clumsiness is no more "natural" than courteous thoughtfulness. Both are learned in the way you move among people in everyday interaction. It is up to you to develop the arts of social interaction to the point where they lubricate your contacts with others and make you welcome wherever you go.

Caught between your parents

ARE THERE TIMES WHEN YOUR parents and your dating do not mix at all well? Is there sometimes trouble at home about the friends you choose? Do disagreements come up around the proper hour for getting in at night? If so, yours are the problems that concern many teen-age young people and their parents.

You are fortunate if you and your parents have worked out your dating policies by now, for dating is much more satisfactory when it has their approval. You enjoy home life more, too, when there is basic agreement in the family about such important things as your dates.

PARENTS
are interested

No question about it, most parents are very much interested in their teen-agers' dating. Too much interested, you may

CHAPTER 16

*your
and
dates?*

say. And it may seem so at times. But there are good reasons why they should be.

PARENTS have an investment in you

Did you ever stop to think of how much your parents have invested in you? By the time you reach high school age, your parents have already spent thousands of dollars for your care and upkeep in food, clothing, shelter, and services you have needed through the years. In the average American family, the children represent the most substantial investment the family has yet made, or possibly ever will make.

Beyond the money invested in you are the time and attention and affection that have already been expended upon you by your parents. Such things tend to become habitual. By the time you are in your teens, your parents have grown used to caring for you, being interested in you, investing themselves in you.

PARENTS are responsible for you

Here is a sober thought that may not have occurred to you. If anything happened to you, if you got into trouble, your parents would be called to account for it. If you have an accident, your parents are legally responsible for any damages incurred. This will be true until you reach legal age. As long as you are in your teens, your parents are legally as well as morally responsible for you.

It is this responsibility for children that so often puts parents on the spot in the community. If you start going around with a questionable set, the neighbors may start talking about what your parents should do about it. If you smash up the car, your father's friends will probably offer advice to him on how they would handle it—and you! As long as things go smoothly for you, your parents are relatively free to supervise you and your dating as they see fit. When trouble comes along, then your parents, as well as you, are involved, whether you like it or not.

PARENTS want you to be a credit to the family

When parents are asked what they expect of their children, many of them say, "Children should be a credit to the family." What does this mean? It indicates that parents want their children to express in their conduct the standards in which the family believes.

Parents are usually experienced enough to know how important reputation is. A man or a woman with a good reputation moves easily and freely among others in his community. When the slightest question arises about him or her, doors close as he approaches, backs are turned, tongues wag. Many young people have learned to their sorrow that a bad reputation is much easier to get than to get rid of. One impetuous friend, one impulsive moment, may break the social standing of years.

Therefore, parents are generally interested in seeing that you date the kind of persons who will be acceptable to the rest of the community. They want you to do the things that are generally approved and to conduct yourself in ways that will be a credit to them as well as to yourself.

PARENTS are concerned for your welfare

More than you may know, your parents are concerned for you as a person. They are interested in your welfare. They love you and want you to have the advantages of the good things of life. They want you to be happy, well-liked, and successful.

Your parents realize that the people you go around with and the friends you make play a great part in your happiness and well-being. If you get in with the right people, things are easy for you. You have friends almost without effort and are invited to social affairs as a matter of course.

Your development as a person depends upon your dates too. You grow through interaction with others. Your personality is formed through friendships and responses to others. Throughout your childhood, your parents were the most important people in your life. Now that you are teenagers, other young people become increasingly important influences in your personality development. Sensing this, your parents may be especially eager that you go around with those who will be "good for you."

SHOULD parents choose your friends?

One of the most frequent points of disagreement between parents and their teen-age youth is that of the choice of friends. The tendency is for youth to seek more variety in their friends than most parents feel is wise. Another problem arises when youth are not as socially active as their parents wish they would be.

PARENTS prefer that you date your own kind

Probably most parents, if they could choose their children's friends, would select them from among the families of their own set. They would prefer that their young people date those with the same general background—national, religious, and social—as their own.

Gordon, who had always been active in the Methodist church, began dating a girl from a completely different faith when he went to high school. His parents did not make a scene about it, but his father was plainly disturbed when he asked Gordon, "Can't you find some nice little Methodist girl to get interested in?"

Some young people feel that the tendency of parents to limit the friendships of their sons and daughters is "narrow-minded," "prejudiced." They may wish to be more demo-cratic than their parents desire. The issue, as they see it, is the choice between doing what the parents prefer and run-ning the risk of being narrow-minded, or making friends with whom they will at the risk of their parents' disfavor. Considerate boys and girls try to be kind, and not thought-lessly cause their parents anxiety. Indeed, some parents are pleased to see their children cross the barriers of race, reli-gion, and class in their choice of friends.

YOU choose your friends—but

In the last analysis, you must choose your own friends. Your parents cannot do it for you. But you are usually wise when you listen to your parents' preferences and take their points into consideration as you make your own decisions.

You should try to avoid the impulse to rush into affairs *just because* your parents disapprove. Some young people do this as a way of showing how independent they are. Sensible young people realize that doing something just to "show" someone else that they can, often leads straight to trouble.

On the other hand, you may find it necessary at some time or other to take a stand for some principle on which you feel strongly. Issues of tolerance, democracy, brother-hood, and fair play may seem more important to you than conforming to some tradition. If we are ever to have One World, you may argue, it must begin in the hearts of men, and in the day-to-day contacts we have with real people.

When parents seriously object to a certain friend, it is wise to try to find out why. Parents oftentimes know things that young people can learn to their advantage. If, in spite of a real effort, you still cannot see your parents' position, it may be wise to consult some trusted counselor about the situation.

PARENTS
meet your date

Parents gain confidence in your friends if they have a chance to meet them. The boy whom they have referred to as "that young fellow" becomes a specific person when they get to know him themselves. The girl who may have been just a name and a giggle over the telephone becomes a flesh-and-blood individual when the boy's parents have met and talked with her. Seeing to it that both sets of parents know you is just good sense, especially when you are dating each other rather frequently.

BOY calls for girl

As was illustrated in the pattern for the first date in Chapter Twelve, it is customary for the boy to call for the girl at her home. This serves several purposes. It is safer, simpler, more comfortable, and more hospitable than meeting her on the corner or in some public spot, where the family's interest is not represented. It further gives the boy a chance to get acquainted with her in her own family setting; and it gives the girl an opportunity to see her boy friend in her own home. This is especially true of new friends. After you have been dating the same person for some time, there may be occasions when it is more convenient to meet at some central place. But the first time or so it is very important that the boy call for the girl at her own home.

NO apologies are needed

It is not necessary that the family and the home be put into top-notch order to impress a calling boy friend. Most of the time the boy is nervous enough not to notice such things. He may be put at ease by informality, which makes some normal disorder a positive asset. Girls often fuss far more than is necessary to have their parents and their home appear to great advantage when some boy comes to call.

Anita was so embarrassed by the shabbiness of the dining room rug that she ran to close the dining room door every time the front doorbell rang. She discovered to her surprise one night that a boy she had been dating for weeks had never noticed the rug, even though he had been through the dining room on numerous occasions.

Another girl fussed in vain with her father to try to get him to put on a tie when she was expecting a boy to call for her. She could hardly believe her ears one evening when she overheard one of her boy friends confiding in her father that he always felt at home there because everything was so informal.

Being embarrassed about the boy friend makes just as little sense as being embarrassed about the family. No apologies are needed for friends or family when one meets the other. If you like them both, they can be expected to like each other. The best way to assure this result is to have their meeting simple and friendly.

INTRODUCE *your date to your parents*

Introductions should always be kept simple. Keep in mind that you address first the more important of the two (more important in the matter of age, social position, and the like), introducing the other person to him or her. To introduce a boy of her own age to her parents, a girl always mentions her parent's name first, and her friend's name second. She says, "Mother, this is Jim Clark. Jim—my mother"; or "Dad, this is Jerry McConnell," and turning to Jerry—"my father."

When the boy takes the girl to his home he is eager to introduce her to his mother and father in the proper way. He may use the same formula as the girl uses to introduce him to her parents. If his parents are together, he says: "Mother and Dad, this is Barbara Holmes," and turning to Barbara—"my mother and father." If his mother is alone he says, "Mother, this is Barbara Holmes. Babs—my mother." The same form of introduction is proper in the case of his father. However, out of courtesy to the girl, he may introduce his father to her, "Barbara, this is my dad. Dad—Barbara Holmes."

When introducing a boy or girl or a child to an elderly person it is courteous to address the older person first; for example, "Grandfather, may I present Barbara Holmes? Barbara—my grandfather, Mr. Wright."

THE
rest of the family want to know your date, too

Others in the family beside your parents may be interested. Grandmothers have been known to be around when young men call, with much the same interest in their grandchildren's dating as they took in their own children's affairs. Brothers and sisters may be much in evidence.

GRANDPARENTS and dating

There are all kinds of grandparents, just as there are all kinds of people. Some grandparents are still living in the past when things were done quite differently. They may be worried about the hours that young people keep, and they may do a lot of talking about how times have changed since they were young. Of course, they are right. Times have changed. The automobile and the drive-in movie, to mention just two inventions, have made great differences in the nature of dating. Grandparents who feel unhappy about these changes are apt to do a lot of fussing. You may have the real task of helping them to feel easier about it, by interpreting the new ways to them and at the same time letting them know that you love and respect them. A touch of good-natured kidding and affectionate humor is a great help in situations like this.

Other grandparents are great allies. Grandmothers and grandfathers who have remained flexible through the years and who have attained a warm, happy outlook on life may serve from time to time as comfortable buffers between their grandchildren and their children-now-grown-to-parents. Mrs. Jones is a precious person. At least she seems so to her granddaughter, who tells her everything because she is so understanding. Whenever something comes up that the parents may be a little hasty about, it is Grandmother Jones who smooths it over and works it out. Her experience in three generations of dating gives her a perspective that both other generations respect and find helpful.

Brothers and sisters can be a help or a handicap in dating. They help when they assist us to get started, when they take us with them to social affairs, when they introduce us to congenial persons, when they really understand and do what they can to help.

Brothers and sisters are a nuisance when they tease and bother and provoke us. The kid brother who hangs around when his sister has a date may be a pest. He may be doing it to annoy his sister, or he may be there to see what happens. Whatever his reason, it tends to annoy his sister. She manages the situation well when she takes his feelings into account as well as her own.

Shirley found that her little brother was especially obnoxious whenever she had been ignoring him or belittling his efforts. She finally tried asking him to tell her some of his new jokes before her date arrived. Even this little consideration was sufficient to make her brother feel secure enough in her attention so that he did not have to be a nuisance to command it. Brothers and sisters cannot be ignored. The more you make them a part of your lives, with the attention all persons need, the more pleasant your relations with them will be.

HOW
do you dress for your date?

Dressing for a date may become a family affair. When the facilities of the home are taxed to the utmost, when things that belong to others are appropriated, when there is stress and strain upon the parents, getting dressed may be a whole family enterprise.

WHAT to wear

The most important principle in dressing is to wear something that is appropriate to the occasion. Alexander embarrassed his date considerably by escorting her to a dance in a plaid jacket instead of his suit coat. As she put it, she would not have minded if he had not had a suit coat. But since he did, she was provoked with him for appearing so informally when she had gone to such pains to look her very nicest for the dance with him. Such things mean a great deal to some people, especially when they feel strongly about how they look.

Variety is nice, but it is not essential. Girls have been known to refuse to wear a dress because they have already worn it once with the same group. If it is an attractive dress, becoming and appropriate, there is no reason why it should not be worn to many similar occasions. Insisting on always wearing something different sometimes makes a girl wail that she simply has "nothing to wear."

On the whole it is wiser to dress *down* than it is to dress *up* for an occasion that allows various modes of dress. At the party where anything from sweaters to formals may be in evidence, it usually is more appropriate to appear in a costume that is neither one extreme nor the other. If some choice must be made, the simpler, less elaborate clothes are usually preferred.

The boy and girl may find it wise to consult with each other about what to wear. If he wears a sport jacket, she should not appear in a long gown. If each of them wears clothes appropriate to the other's costume, they both feel more suitably attired. Some girls ask their dates when the invitation is accepted what kind of clothing will be worn: stockings or socks, long dress or short, dress or skirt and sweater, and so on. Girls having friends in their homes may specify the costume expected. The range may be anything from "come-as-you-are" to "formal."

TAXING home facilities

A frequent complaint of parents of teen-agers is that they monopolize the bathroom whenever they dress for a date. Some thoughtless young people spend so much time in bathing and grooming that the rest of the family must often remain locked out of the bathroom for uncomfortable periods of time. This usually is not necessary. A girl with a big date coming up can take her bath early enough to be out of the way when the family is around. Nails and hair can usually be done as well in her room as in the family bathroom.

It is wise to equip one's own room with whatever is

needed for personal grooming. Elliot's mother used to complain that he wanted to shave in the kitchen just when she had to do up the supper work. The congestion there was relieved when an extra electric plug and a mirror were installed in Elliot's room where he could shave with dad's electric razor without interfering with others in the family. Sometimes just the addition of a good light and mirror will make a room adequate for dressing and grooming. A simple dressing table can be made of two orange crates topped by a board of the desired length and covered with some bright fabric. Toilet articles, hairbrush and comb, and personal clothing are better kept in one's own room than in the family bathroom. Such planning makes the difference between strained congestion and pleasant independence within the family.

BORROWING clothing from the family

Families have different ideas about wearing each other's clothes. Some families operate almost on a community basis. This may be especially true in the clothes shared by the girls, and perhaps by a girl and her mother, when they are of about the same size. Other families have the strict rule that no one ever wears anything belonging to another. Between the two extremes are many families in which an article of clothing may be loaned for special occasions.

There are both advantages and disadvantages in sharing clothing with others. Sharing gives each family member more of a variety in clothing for less money than would be required to supply the same quantity and quality of clothing for each. This applies especially to those items which are soon outdated. Two teen-age sisters who can wear each other's party dresses find that each has more choice and greater variety when they share their clothes.

The big disadvantage of freely using each other's things is that you may be without something you had counted on wearing just when you want it most. Ella found her best blouse too soiled to use. Her sister had worn it the night before and had not yet laundered it. You may accidentally spill something on your mother's coat that will tie it up at the cleaner's for more time than your mother can conveniently spare it.

When members of the family do share each other's clothing, it is important that they ask permission to do so. Red has always been very careful about this. Because his coloring is so much like his father's, he looks well in his father's ties. From time to time on occasions when Red wants to look particularly nice, he asks his dad to lend him a favorite tie. There never has been any difficulty about it because Red asks for the loan of the tie, returns it when he has finished with it, and thanks his dad for the use of it.

Dressing becomes a comfortable procedure for both the family and the dater when grooming routines are established, personal facilities are available for each member of the family, and each respects the other's property rights.

HOW
late should a date last?

Numerous questions about the hour and the method of concluding a date merit the consideration of every thoughtful young person. There is so much variation in what is considered proper, and so much difference in methods used, that we take up the questions one by one.

The hour at which a date is over depends upon many factors. The following are a few of the more common ones:

1. The age and experience of the daters
   (Younger people usually must be in earlier than will be necessary when they are older.)
2. The confidence the parents (especially the girl's) have in the young people
   (The more trust, the more leeway, generally)
3. The customs of the community
   (Some communities frown upon late dating; others are more lenient.)
4. The nature of the date
   (A movie date will be over much earlier than a prom.)
5. The responsibility and sensibleness of the boy and the girl
   (Irresponsible couples may impulsively stay out later than necessary.)
6. Unexpected and unforeseen occurrences
   (Accidents do happen; sometimes the motor really won't start.)

WHO decides?

With all the preceding factors in mind, who decides what time a girl should arrive home? Should her parents tell her the zero hour? May the girl use her own judgment entirely? Or is the question one for which the boy is responsible? The best answer seems to be a mixture of all these. Surely the parents are interested. The girl faces real responsibility, and so does the boy. So the question is, who takes the initiative and how is it most easily worked out?

One of the more usual methods is for the girl to tell her parents ahead of time something of the nature of the plans for the evening, where she is to go, and about the time she expects to be home. This gives her parents enough understanding of the engagement so that they can more easily tolerate an unexpected late arrival home.

Most girls find, if they are to be much later getting home than they had told their parents, that it is wise to telephone and tell what has happened, where they are, and by what hour they should be coming home. This indicates that the girl is taking responsibility for herself, and lessens the parents' concern. It also lets the boy know that the girl's parents are interested and to be reckoned with if he keeps her out too late.

The boy too has a stake in the question of the hour of homecoming. Some boys groan about girls who expect them to be out all night when they have to work the next day and should be getting some sleep. Others complain that sometimes they must rush their dates home when a party has barely begun. Even more frequent is the uncertainty a boy faces in not knowing what time a girl feels she should be home. This confusion can be avoided by either the girl or the boy taking the initiative for discussing the matter before they leave the girl's house.

Some young people get into the habit of doing two or three things in a single evening. They seem never to have had enough. One girl reports that in her set they go to the early movie, then to the skating rink and skate until that closes, then move on to the bowling alley and bowl until it closes, and then usually top it off by driving to a hamburger place ten miles down the road for something to eat. This particular girl does not enjoy so extensive an evening. She would prefer doing just one thing and getting home early to make cocoa and pop corn in the kitchen; but she does not want to be a wet blanket, so she goes along without comment. One wonders if others may not feel the same way.

SHOULD
the girl ask her date in?

In some places it is customary for the girl to ask the boy into her home when they return from a date. In others, the practice is rare. The big advantage of having the date in for a little while upon returning home is to get something to eat, talk over the evening in privacy, and have a leisurely goodnight in the comfort of the girl's home.

A girl does not invite a boy into her home if the hour is late, or if she knows that her parents have already retired. If it is still fairly early, and if someone is still around, then she may if she wishes. A boy should not insist that she do so. Her hospitality is hers to offer. There may be reasons that it would not be wise to ask her date in on a given evening. These are her business, which she need not share with her date unless she wants to. If she would really like to have him in, and perhaps has before, but cannot this time, she may say something like this, "I'd like to ask you in, but Mother hasn't been feeling well so I'd better not tonight." Even this is not necessary. A thoughtful boy will assume that he is to come in only when he is invited.

DATES
on school nights?

Most young people agree that dates should be limited to week ends when there will not be school the next day. Homework, sleep, and the routines of the week keep most teen-agers busy from Monday through Thursday evenings. Even so, there are occasional exceptions to this general rule.

STUDY dates

The date to study together may be an exception to the no-dates-on-school-nights rule. Occasionally a girl and boy taking the same classes together may find that they can study well together. Then she may invite him over to her home, where they study at the dining room table or in some other convenient spot, munch on something, and stop work long enough to have a cool drink and listen to the radio for a few minutes before he leaves for home.

Study dates can be fun. The meeting of minds of a boy and a girl as they work on some common problem together is often very gratifying and companionable. On the other hand, it can be a wasted evening for both of them. If they do much clowning about, each may keep the other from getting his work done. The success of the study date depends on the ability of the two to get down to work.

WALKING her home

Another way in which young people see each other during the week in almost-dating situations occurs when he walks her home from a school or community affair. Perhaps they have been at band practice, or at a meeting of one of their clubs, or at a play rehearsal or some church function. As the affair lets out, it may be easy for the boy to fall into step with a girl he likes and walk her to her home. He may even have requested the privilege ahead of time. Or it may have become the mutually expected thing. In any case, it usually is a simple walkie-talkie date. The boy may or may not invite the girl to stop at a soda fountain for refreshment. She may or may not invite him in for something to eat when they get to her house. Neither needs to feel any particular responsibility for entertaining the other. Such dates are fun partly because they are so spontaneous.

SHOULD
a girl entertain when her folks are away?

Some girls wonder if they should have their friends in when the other members of the family are away. Sometimes when parents must be away overnight, they give their daughter permission to have a girl friend in to spend the night with her so that she will not be lonely. That is usually considered to be all right. But should the girl have a boy friend in for the evening? Or, may the two girls have a couple of boys in for a while during the evening when no one else is at home?

In general, girls do not have boys in their homes unless their parents are present. There are many good reasons for this: unforeseen accidents, the neighbors' talk, the boy's attitude toward the girl who entertains him alone, and other reasons. The same holds true of boys entertaining girls in their homes. It is not wise unless one or more adults are to be present.

SOME other don'ts

There are other things to keep in mind when entertaining boy friends at home. Don't turn out all the lights. It is not necessary, nor very smart, and it may be greatly misunderstood. Do not close the door to the room in which one or more couples are seated. Keep it ajar, and there will be no question raised, usually. Do not allow mixed groups in the bathroom at the same time. Anita found herself in hot water over this one. She offered to get a splinter out of Jay's finger, and they went into the bathroom for some merthiolate for the open wound. Somebody played a prank on them and slammed the door while they were inside, just as Anita's father came by. He was so shocked that he ordered the young guests to leave the house at once and kept Anita in from dates for the rest of the month. Such things are just not worth risking, are they?

Two other things to avoid if you would have your parents approve of your having dates at home are (1) raiding the icebox of tomorrow's food supply and (2) making home impossible for others in the family. The first can be prevented readily by clearing ahead of time as to what may be eaten. The second unpleasantness can be avoided by keeping the radio down below the screeching level, the party within bounds where it will not annoy family members in the house, and rowdiness out of the picture entirely.

"HERE'S your hat"

It sometimes is necessary to know what to do when a guest stays on and on beyond a suitable time for his departure.

Girls often ask how to get a boy to go home before too late an hour. This does not need to be a difficult problem. The hostess herself may take the initiative for his leave taking if he doesn't. She may casually say, "My, it's getting late. It was good of you to come. Come again, won't you?" Having thus dismissed him, she may get his coat and bid him goodbye.

Some boys feel that they should wait until the girl dismisses them. A boy will say, "What do you do if she doesn't let you know that it is time to leave?" Here, too, the situation can be met quite easily. When the time comes that a boy feels he should be leaving, he stands and bids his hostess a courteous goodbye. He may say something like, "It's been fun being here. Thank you for asking me," or anything of the sort that comes easily for him. The important rule for the guest to remember is to leave when he says he must, and not ooze out with prolonged goodbyes.

USING
the family car

The family automobile has been a boon to civilization, but it certainly has become a problem in the lives of many teen-agers and their parents. The questions of who may use the car, and for what, and under what circumstances, and at what age, tend to be baffling at times.

HOW old should you be?

The question of the age at which you are allowed to use the family car depends upon the state law for drivers' licenses, and partly upon your parents and whether they consider you to be a reliable person.

Most parents allow their teen-age young people to use the car when they can trust them with it. This confidence depends on other things beside age. It depends a great deal on how well the young person can drive, and his skill in handling the automobile in all sorts of situations. It depends to some extent upon what other families in the neighborhood allow. It depends upon the general trustworthiness of the young person, and his ability to assume responsibility and to handle himself wisely in an emergency.

Your responsibility begins as soon as you have permission to use the car. You should find out if there is an adequate supply of gas and oil in it and, if not, what arrangement should be made to fuel it for your use. You should have some definite agreement as to whose responsibility it is to pay for the gas and oil you consume while using the car.

You have responsibility for keeping the tires inflated to the proper pressure, the oil up to the recommended level, and other routine matters checked as often as needed. You also have responsibility for bringing the car back in condition ready for the next person's use. Leaving the automobile in the garage with a gas tank nearly empty is not taking full responsibility. You may hear about it if Dad runs out of gas on his way to work next morning!

When you are responsible for the car, you do not drive it "like crazy," giving a further boost to the reputation that teen-age drivers have earned. You must obey all the rules, regulations, and traffic signs if you drive safely. Perhaps you know that many insurance policies on automobiles carry an extra fee if a teen-age youth drives the car. This is not a matter of prejudice, but of cold figures showing a higher accident rate for teen-agers than for adults.

The family car in your care should not be lent to others. You are responsible for it and should not let it out of your control until it is safely home. Others may mean well, but if anything happens when they have the car, there will be trouble for them, for you, and both sets of parents.

Filling the car full of people beyond its normal capacitiy is one way of bringing disfavor upon yourself and further endangering your reputation as a trustworthy young person. Some places have legal restrictions on the number of persons to be carried. The danger is not only in the hampering of the driver's vision and movement, but in diverting his attention from the driving of the car.

HOW
much should you tell your parents about your date?

Young people who find it easy to confide in their parents are fortunate. It is fun to share things with the folks at home when you feel that they will understand. Experiences on dates often improve with the telling and are enjoyed all over again when you can relate them to some sympathetic ear at home.

You will feel better if you can share confidences with your parents. If you keep yourself too completely from your folks, you will be lonely, terribly lonely at times. You may try to convince yourself that you cannot tell them anything because they do not understand you. But by putting all the blame upon others, you will not satisfy the deep longings within yourself to be understood. Interaction in the family is a two-way process. Your parents will understand only what you can share with them. They can be in your life only as you let them in.

Even in the most understanding family there will be some things that you will not want to talk about. It is not that your parents would misunderstand or be shocked necessarily. It is just that some things are too personal to be shared. It is particularly true of young people growing up, learning to think and feel and be persons on their own.

As you grow up, yours is the task of maintaining a satisfying and mutually comfortable relationship with your parents at the same time that you wean yourself from them and seek your more mature self in relationships with others of your own age. In the words of the vernacular, "That ain't easy." Granted, but it is worthwhile. Upon your success in this task hangs your future happiness as a man or woman, a husband or wife, with all that is involved in growing up and falling in love and making a home of your own some day.

part FOUR

YOUR
LIFE
AND
LOVES

CHAPTER 17

Is going steady a good idea?

GOING STEADY IS THE PRACTICE of dating one person exclusively. It is distinguished from *going steadily* in which two persons go together on dates often but do not restrict their dating to each other.

There are actually two forms of going steady nowadays. The earlier type is seen in a pair of young teen-agers, starting to date by clinging to each other for mutual support. There has been an increase in this type of going steady in recent years, related to the younger age at which dating begins, the larger consolidated schools, and the more complex modern communities. As Beulah puts it, "Sure I go steady—it's just a lot safer that way." There are other fellows whom Beulah might date, but she does not know them or their standards so well, and she fears that she might not be able to manage the situations that they could introduce. So she goes steady with a boy like herself, with whom she feels safe and secure in dating situations.

The other form of going steady is found among more mature young people, further along in their relationship with each other, who may "have an understanding." This in many ways is similar to what used to be known as "keeping steady company" preliminary to being engaged to be married. In either case, there is a tendency to focus one's time, attention, and interest upon the steady dating partner.

You are not unusual if you feel some special attraction for one particular person. At any time you may be drawn in a very special way to one person of the other sex, even when you still are dating others. It becomes more and more true as you center your attention on your "one and only."

THAT
feeling of belonging

Have you noticed how the one special person in your life tends to haunt you even when you are apart? Your first waking in the morning may be marked with the feeling of belonging that the "one and only" gives you. Your last thoughts at bedtime are possibly of her (him) too. He or she is even in your dreams. Thoughts turn often to *the one* all through the day. You wonder what the other is doing now, how he feels, and where he is. You find yourself planning things to say to him (her) when next you meet. At intervals between your meetings you store up special little things to share with each other. You find yourself wanting to know how the other feels about something that has just occurred to you. Even when you are separated by many miles or months your "special person" is often present in spirit and seems closer than the people in the same room.

FIRST in time and attention

No question about it, the one and only comes first. He, or she, has a definite priority on your time and attention. Given a choice of several companions, it is *the one* whom you choose. In fact it is hard sometimes to give a fair share of your attention to others when your own special one is present, his or her companionship is so all-absorbing.

Even in letter writing, it is your special one who hears from you regularly, and often. Other friends may be quite as interesting, and equally good correspondents, but you do not feel like writing them nearly as often. When you sit down to write a letter, your thoughts flow freely out to your particular person, while letters to others limp along without quite the same ease or friendly give-and-take.

BEING faithful

When you feel that you "belong" to someone of the other sex, you want to be faithful to him or her. There are certain evidences of affection that you allow only each other. A certain exclusiveness keeps you from wanting to let others into the activities and feelings you reserve for each other. In many cases, dating is restricted to just the one person. This usually is true of couples who have an "understanding." It often holds, too, for those who are "going steady." Being faithful means being true to the other in whatever sense you have mutually agreed upon.

REASONS
for going steady

There must be good reasons for going steady, because so many people do it! As a matter of fact, there are many reasons that young people restrict their dates to one person to the exclusion of others.

DATING the person you prefer

One of the reasons mentioned most frequently by young people is that they like that one person better than anyone else. This is understandable. In any given community there will be congenial and not-so-congenial people; there will be attractive and not-so-attractive persons; there will be those who are mutually interested and those who do not interest each other.

When two persons discover in each other a genuine congeniality, a mutual admiration, and a strong attraction, they may prefer each other's company to that of anyone else. Hetty puts it this way: "Why should I date any other boy when Jay and I suit each other so perfectly?" Hetty and Jay prefer each other to any other person either of them might date.

This is often thought to be the only reason that young people go steady. But there are several other reasons that should be understood.

SAVING time and money

Warren made this point very neatly at a meeting of teen-agers when he said, "Sure, I go steady, and why not? It's cheaper that way." After the laughter died down, he went on to explain that when he dated a new girl she expected him to take her to interesting places and to spend money on her entertainment. But his steady girl knew that his finances were limited and that she would see him more often if they did things together that did not cost much. She frequently had him over at her house for the evening. Even when he took her out, she was quite satisfied with a simple, inexpensive kind of date.

Boys and girls often find, too, that going steady saves time as well as money. They can have fun just getting together over a job to be done. Norman goes over to Ava's house and helps her to wash the car on Saturday afternoons. This done, they both get to work on their assignments for the next week. Both jobs are fun when done together. A Saturday afternoon that might have been either a waste of time or sheer work becomes fun and accomplishment at the same time. Some couples stimulate each other so that they actually study and work better when together. Others, however, find it almost impossible to do anything but concentrate on each other when together. For the couples who are not distracted in this way, going steady may be a great saving of time and money.

SOCIAL security

In some communities a young person who does not go steady is socially handicapped. Some high schools and colleges are so tightly organized on a steady-couples basis that a solitary boy or girl feels left out of most of the social activities. In such places going steady protects one from being an outsider and gives one a certain social standing.

It is unfortunate that this pattern of almost compulsory going steady has become so widely accepted among teen-agers, because it means that many young people have been forced into it in order to enjoy any social life at all.

A girl may go steady because then she is sure of a date. If she plays the field, she may not be invited to some social affair that she would have enjoyed. If she has a steady boy friend, she is more sure of being asked.

Boys say that this reason holds for them, too. It takes a good deal of courage to ask a new girl out for the first time. If he must worry over whom to invite, screw up the courage to ask her, and then run the chance of being refused, it may be that he will let it all go by default. If he has a steady girl, however, the process is simple. She sees to it that he gets out to things. Her expectation of being escorted takes him to many affairs that he might have missed otherwise.

COMPANIONSHIP in a special sense

As you go steady with someone who especially appeals to you, you are enabled to become acquainted in a way that would be difficult otherwise. You see each other in many settings. You do all sorts of things together. Your acquaintance becomes full and interesting when you see each other in all sorts of garb, doing many types of things, in a variety of moods and feelings. This sharing of interests is to your mutual advantage.

Clint had never cared much for music until he began going with Babs, who sang in the chorus. Calling for her after rehearsals, Clint met other members of the chorus and heard a great deal of the plans and music-talk that went on in the group. When the school asked for volunteers to go Christmas caroling, Clint was right on hand. Now he sings in the chorus and likes it—all because Bab's interest became his, too.

Two persons who see a lot of each other not only share their old interests but quite probably cultivate new ones. Carol and Herb had not been going together long when try-outs for the school play were announced. Neither of them had participated in anything dramatic before, but both of them got parts, and had great fun through the Spring Term going to rehearsals and talking about their production. It was such a satisfying experience that drama became a central interest for them both.

EXCHANGING confidences

Two congenial persons get to know each other so well that they find it easy to communicate with each other. After they have shared many common experiences and have gone to many places together, they often find that they have developed a kind of special language. One word will stand for a whole situation; one phrase or gesture will indicate an entire mood when it has grown out of a mutually shared experience.

When such a communication system is established between them, they find it easy to share all sorts of confidences. Each comes to know how the other feels about things and what he or she means by certain phrases and expressions. They become so well acquainted with all the things that are important to each other that they do not have to back up and lay the foundation for any new development. Because they already know what is important, either one can come right out with the news of the moment without going into minute detail about its past history. For this reason it is easier to write to and talk to a person with whom you have maintained a close contact than it is to communicate with someone whom you see or write to only infrequently. You can start right where you are and be understood. Thus you are able to share more confidences with each other.

You often find that the more you know about another person, the more interested in him or her you become. You begin to care deeply about what happens to each other. You feel that you are understanding and being understood at the same time. A mutual sympathy develops that makes you sure of the other's interest in whatever interests you, certain of his concern in anything that affects you. By the same token, you are deeply interested in him (or her) and want to hear about anything that he or she cares to share with you.

As couples exchange confidences, they often find that they mutually encourage and stimulate each other. As soon as someone else really cares about what happens to you and listens to your troubles and trials, your hopes and fears, your ambitions and dreams, you are often encouraged to improve and to work out your problems better than before.

Ross was doing only average work in school, although he had superior ability. Then he began going steady with Karen, who enjoyed being a good student. She was sympathetic with Ross's difficulties and encouraged him to discuss them with her. Calmly she helped him to gain the self-confidence he needed. They both made the honor roll —and stayed there. They had motivated and encouraged each other to work at a high level of accomplishment.

This is not to say that all couples who go steady become

better students. Not at all! Sometimes just the opposite is true, and steady couples find that their work falls off to a dangerous degree. It is well for any couple to ask themselves this question: Is going steady good for each of us and for our particular tasks? There is something not quite right about a relationship that results in a lowering of achievement and sense of responsibility.

WHEN
going steady is not wise

Granted that there are real advantages in going steady under certain circumstances and among certain people, there are situations when going steady may not be wise for a given person at a particular time. Here are a few of them:

IF you start too young

When you start going steady at too young an age, you cut yourself off from other friendships that might mean a great deal to you. All the others of the opposite sex whom you might have become acquainted with through dating are cut out as possibilities if you start going steady with one person too soon.

Playing the field is an experience all its own. Being able to date members of the other sex without undue restriction is an experience that comes only once during the entire lifetime of the average person, that is, during the teen years. As soon as you begin to narrow your time and attention to one person, you reduce your opportunities for knowing other congenial people whom you might enjoy.

Some persons who start at an early age later regret that they have not had more contact with others. Marrying a childhood sweetheart whom one had dated exclusively all through the teen years may find one or both wishing that more time had been given to other possible partners before settling down.

When you start too soon, you may find yourself paired off with a person who is only moderately interesting to you. In order to protect yourself from such a lukewarm relationship, it is wise to know each other fairly well before you allow yourselves to become committed to going steady.

Parents, too, may become disturbed when their children start at an early age. They realize that dating with a steady takes on a quality quite different from that in casual dating. They therefore frequently prefer that their sons and daughters do a good deal of general dating before getting into the habit of going steady.

IF you are maneuvered into it

In some schools if a girl accepts a date three times in a row with the same boy, she is considered to be going steady with him. This happened to Leah and Keith. Keith took Leah out on Friday night where several of their classmates saw them together. On Saturday Leah went to the game in the school gym with Keith. By Sunday evening when Keith walked her home from the church young people's meeting, the rest of their friends assumed that they were going together. On Monday, it was evident that the other boys in school considered her Keith's girl. They did not ask her out again. Although Leah and Keith had not decided to go steady together, they were maneuvered into it by the attitude of their friends. Friends seem to enjoy pairing off couples who begin to show an interest in each other. The fact that it is premature and not the doing of the couple itself is unfortunate.

IF you are separated

It may not be wise to try to go steady while you are widely separated. To promise to go steady with a friend whom you cannot see often may mean a serious curtailing of his activities as well as yours. When you cannot date another person because of the distance that lies between you, it is often selfishly possessive to insist that he or she not go with anybody else. The fact that you cannot be with the one you like best is no reason that you should not carry on normal social living during the intervals between your seeing each other. Even when it seems wise to restrict your dating to "the one," you will be less lonely if you participate in some outside interests while you are separated.

When Irma went away to school, she and Alex vowed

that they would remain faithful to each other and not date others while they were separated. Before Thanksgiving they both saw how foolish their agreement was. It meant that Irma was missing out on most of the fun at her school. She could not go to any of the dances or even have a Saturday night date. Alex had to confess that he could not keep up his end of the agreement and had been dating other girls off and on for several weeks. They sensibly decided not to go steady while they were separated. They continued to see each other whenever Irma came home and wrote each other regularly, but both went out with others.

IF you get too involved

It may not be wise to continue going steady if you reach the point when you are so involved with each other that nothing else matters much any more. Some couples find themselves too entangled emotionally when they date each other exclusively. They fall so hopelessly in love that they cannot eat or sleep or study or keep up any of the normal activities that once were such fun. When this state of affairs develops, it is time to try to get back on an even keel.

This condition frequently occurs when one person is more seriously interested than the other. He or she clings to the relationship frantically. Sensing that the feelings are not returned, the frustration of unrequited love may make him (it is sometimes her) become extremely possessive, and preoccupied with holding the other's attention. This sense of frustration continues until one or both decide it is best to break up.

Going steady is not wise when it results in physical stimulation and excitation that is too frequent or too intense. When two persons who are fond of each other spend a great deal of time together in privacy, they may begin habits of necking and petting that bring them to a high point of sexual excitement. Occasionally couples get to a place where they can enjoy each other only in their solitary love-making. Then they are apt to work each other up to such a pitch of excitation that they are helpless to control it wisely. When such a situation arises, it is time to call a halt before it gets out of bounds.

There is an important difference between enjoying another fine person in a full, rich companionship and getting so involved with him or her that you are unable to keep your attention on a variety of activities and moods. Before you get so involved that the balance is gone from your life, it is time to regain your perspective.

IF you outgrow each other

Some steadies may go together too long. When one of the couple outgrows the other, the friendship has lost its foundation. Sometimes each outgrows the other and realizes it. Frequently one outgrows the other but remains going steady rather than hurt the friend's feelings.

Simon and Brenda had been steadies for some time. Gradually Simon began to find Brenda not so interesting as other girls in his classes. With them, he could talk intelligently and with animation and get a ready response. With Brenda, there was a noticeable cooling off every time he tried to discuss with her the things in which he was becoming increasingly interested. He felt trapped. Brenda had allowed so much love-making that Simon felt honor bound to go with her, even though he realized she was not so congenial a companion as some of the other girls. The fact was that Simon had outgrown Brenda intellectually. Continuing to go with her after the companionship basis for their friendship had gone led to distress for them both. If he had had the courage, or had known how, he would have broken off with her long ago.

HOW
to break off without hurting

Continuing with someone whom it is no longer wise to see so regularly is no kindness to either person. There are many other good reasons for breaking up beyond those mentioned in the section above. Yet the problem often becomes a difficult one because you do not know how to break off without hurting the other's feelings.

The steps in breaking off with someone without hurting too much look somewhat like this: First, let the other know how you are feeling. Share your first questions about staying together or breaking up with the other person. Try to think it through together. Talk it over calmly. Encourage the other person to tell you how he or she feels about it. Do everything possible to understand how each of you is interpreting your relationship. Then discuss as openly as you can what next steps might be taken. You may find that the other person has been having some of the same thoughts and fears that you have hesitated to share.

A second point to keep in mind is to do everything possible to help the other person save face. If the girl feels that she has been jilted, she will be doubly hurt. Her pride suffers as well as her love. If the boy senses that his girl is running out on him, he too is hurt. Whatever is done, each should feel that the other is still an attractive person and that it was just the relationship that did not work out.

Young people often make this step hard for themselves by trying to extract from their retreating lovers "the reasons why you do not love me anymore." This so often leads to a list of characteristics that are unpleasant, or a counting up of shortcomings, that the discarded lover feels unworthy as well as unloved.

It is better to recognize that friendships change and shift with time. During the teen years, when growth is rapid and interests change quickly, it is to be expected that friends will change, too. If two persons who have found each other's company pleasant come to the place where it is not wise to continue seeing each other, they should face the fact without hurting each other's pride. They may blame the relationship, they may blame their youthfulness, but every effort should be made not to blame each other.

Another thing that helps to make a break painless is gradually to let others into your confidence. As your friends begin to realize that you are no longer so close as you once were, they will quite possibly stop throwing you together so much. They will need to know eventually. Telling them soon after you have discussed it between yourselves will make it possible for them to help.

GETTING
over a broken heart

Mary Martin shampooed her hair on the stage of *South Pacific* as she sang, "I'm Gonna Wash That Man Right

Outa My Hair." In one of her inimitable poems, Edna St. Vincent Millay recommended putting a red ribbon in one's hair and going out for a new love. Through song and story, poetry and drama come many suggestions for recovering from a broken love affair. We all know that it is not easy to get back to normal again. The anguish of a disappointment in love is about as acute as any torture can be. Some become so torn by it that they never recover, but go on year after year nursing a broken heart. Normally we want to recover. Even when they are not easy, even when they hurt, we do things that are necessary to get over a lost love. Here are ten practical suggestions.

TEN ways to forget him or her

1. Take the picture out of the frame and either burn it or bury it deep down under things you rarely use. Seeing it will only open the old wound again.
2. Destroy all letters. If you cannot get yourself to tear them up, then at least put them away where you will not be tempted to reread them.
3. Dispose of the gifts exchanged. Return the things that are valuable. Give the others away, or at least lock them up where you won't see them for a long time.
4. Start a new diary. The old one is so full of him or her that every time you write a new entry you will be reminded of something you did together. It is just not worth it.
5. Get rid of the music to your special song. Break the record of it, or send it to a worthy charity. Don't sing it yourself any more unless you can jazz it up with a new twist. The more you let yourself melt into sentimental moments, the longer it will take to forget.
6. Erase the name and number from your address book, so that you will not be reminded every time you use the book.
7. Make some definite plan with other friends for any special anniversary that might leave you with nothing to do for the evening.
8. Get into a new set of people where your friends will not always be looking as though they feel sorry for you, or thoughtlessly inquiring for your lost steady.

You can start on your new status with a new crowd.

9. Develop a new interest that you have not had time for before. Take up something entirely new that you would enjoy, and throw yourself wholeheartedly into it.

10. Whenever you find yourself thinking about him or her, change the subject! Get busy at something you like to do. Put on your hat and visit someone you enjoy. Throw yourself into your work. Brooding will not help, and it will make you miserable if you let it.

DATING
once more

Getting back into circulation after having broken up with a steady can be difficult. It may take some time to get into the right mood again. While you are still a little heartsick, it may be that you will not want to see a date. That is understandable. The interlude will give you a chance to do other things for a change.

TAKE a breather

Having a little time to yourself after having gone steady may be like taking a long, deep breath. You have your evenings free. You are not tied up every week end. You have time to get your clothes in order, to reorganize your room, to make progress on your favorite hobby, to get caught up on your practicing, perhaps even to get some extra homework done.

Girls and boys both report that such an interval of leisure after having dated steadily can be something of a relief emotionally, too. You may feel free and unfettered. You may rediscover your family and find yourself able to enjoy doing things at home that you haven't had time for in ages. Your mother and father may sigh with relief that at last you have "come to your senses." Deep down inside, you may silently agree, as you take the opportunity to delve into your personal philosophy, religion, and goals in life.

Breaking up after going steady does not need to be all pain. If you can take the new tempo and mood of things as they come, you may find yourself actually enjoying part of your convalescence.

LET your friends know that you are available

As soon as you begin to want some social life again, let your friends know that you are interested. Tell your close friends what has happened, and be available for any double dates or other invitations that they may offer you. Go stag to some of the affairs when you can. Get yourself into the crowd that does not go steady and enjoy these more casual mixed groups for a while. The important thing is to let yourself have a good time on a new basis, without pining for the days that are no more.

TAKE up some new interests

When the time comes to close a chapter in your life, nothing will be quite so effective as taking up new interests. Get out into new circles and you will find yourself stretching up to new challenges. You may discover that these new friends are quite as interesting and appealing as the old set to which you clung for so long. You may find that you enjoy doing certain things that have been neglected in your life. As you develop new skills and make new friends, the old ones fade into proper perspective.

AVOID going steady again on the rebound

While you are still somewhat emotionally sore from the last break-up, be unusually careful not to go steady again too soon. It is easy to get caught in the trap of your own feelings at a time like this. You may find yourself hurrying things with some new-found friend, just to prove to yourself that you can win and hold a person of the other sex. This is your pride crying for a little support. You have felt rejected by your old love, so you let yourself in for anything that will comfort your deflated ego.

You have heard about people who marry for spite. When something happens to break up an old affair, one or the other of the pair rushes into a new union just to show the other that "it did not matter after all." An effort to show your lost lover that you don't care lies back of these lunges into a new affair. What your actions really say is that you *did* care very much, or you wouldn't be rushing off to prove otherwise. Unfortunately, such hasty unions on the rebound rarely work out. They tend to be grossly unfair to the new partner, and they certainly are no help to either of the persons who have recently stopped going together.

If you want to return to the dating routines normally, take it easy. Do not attempt to re-establish yourself all at once. Enjoy the interlude that comes restfully at the conclusion of the smash-up, and then gradually, as you feel ready, start out again. Time is wonderful medicine. Let it work for you. You may live to thank your lucky stars that that particular romance did not work out well after all.

GETTING
pinned

There is a practice common in many schools and colleges of a boy's giving his fraternity pin to the girl of his choice. The girls popularly call this "getting pinned." Its meaning differs from place to place and from couple to couple. At what point in the courtship should the boy offer his pin to the girl? What does her acceptance of it commit her to? These are good questions that will bear some discussion.

WHAT accepting a pin means

Because pinning is so differently interpreted, it is rather important to know what each of the partners means by the step. Is it the same as an engagement? Or is it just cementing the fact of going steady? Does being pinned mean that neither of you will date anyone else? not even old friends of the family? not even when you are separated for a long while? not even for coke dates between classes? Just how much leeway is each of you to have now that you are to be "pinned" to each other? Does accepting a boy's pin mean that he is entitled to intimacies that have been denied before? If so, how much more familiarity is to be allowed? These are just a few of the questions that two young persons may well consider before she accepts his pin. Their answers will depend in part upon the customs of the community in which they live and in part upon their own standards, ideals, and ideas. What they decide is not so important as the fact that together they have arrived at a mutually satisfactory agreement as to just what is involved in their being pinned.

INTERPRETING *the pinning to both families*

An important step like being pinned is news that should be broken to both families in a way that will help them to understand what is involved. This may be simple or it may be rather difficult. Some mothers take a girl's acceptance of a pin as their cue to give a big engagement party, to announce their daughter's betrothal, and to publicize the occasion too handsomely. This may prove exceedingly embarrassing, especially if the couple do not consider the pinning an engagement.

Families sometimes minimize pinning and make light of what their young people consider a very serious step. June's father refused to take her acceptance of Marvin's pin seriously. He joked about her "bauble," as he called it. He made it obvious that he considered the whole affair just "kid stuff." Marvin was hurt by this flippant attitude and felt that June should have discussed with her father just how much being pinned really meant to them both.

Between these two extremes of parents' acceptance of pinning is the middle road of understanding. Most parents do try to understand their children. It is not always easy, especially when there are so many different ways of interpreting behavior. In so far as they can, it is the responsibility of youth themselves to help their families understand what they are doing and what it means to them.

HAVING
an understanding

Some couples say that they are "engaged to be engaged." They have an understanding that if all goes well when they have finished school and are ready to take such a step, they will be engaged to be married at some later date. They consider each other as their "one and only." They probably date steadily. They feel that they love each other, and they anticipate that their love will last. Yet having this kind of understanding is not the same as an engagement.

The fundamental difference between having an understanding and becoming engaged is one of formal commitment. When you become engaged, your parents are consulted. Some public announcement is often made in the newspapers. Everyone knows that you have promised to marry each other. When you have an "understanding," you have a personal, private agreement, just between yourselves and perhaps your closest friends and family, that *if* you still love each other and *if* you still want to, *when* you are ready, you *may* become engaged. When you become engaged, it is definite and public. When you have an understanding, it is private and tentative, or "iffy" as the late President Franklin D. Roosevelt used to say.

SOMETIMES lasting, sometimes not

Going steady or having an understanding does not mean that you eventually will marry. Oftentimes the relationship does not last long enough to go on into engagement and marriage. This is not a cause for sorrow. Perhaps the relationship should not continue. While you are young and susceptible, you will be attracted to all sorts of people who are interesting at one stage of your growing up but may not wear well enough to be interesting to you at your next level of development. You grow rapidly through the entire second decade of your life, and as you grow your interests and ideals grow, too. Some changes and shifts in your affections are inevitable.

If the relationship becomes increasingly satisfying with time, your understanding may mature into a full-fledged engagement. But only time will tell. You cannot safely rush your love life. It must mature and blossom at its own rate.

What does it mean to be engaged?

A COUPLE MAY HAVE LOOKED forward to becoming engaged for so long that when the day finally comes, their happiness is unbounded. The girl shows her ring to her friends with pride and pleasure. Their good wishes are sweet to her ears. She has a feeling that she has arrived and that her ring gives her a new status.

The young man may get some good-natured ribbing from his men friends, but beneath it he senses their congratulations. Now that he is engaged, they regard him more seriously. He has stopped playing around and is ready to settle down.

This special relationship to the one you love brings its peculiar satisfactions. A deep sense of belonging comes with getting engaged that going steady or having an understanding does not give so completely. Others now recognize

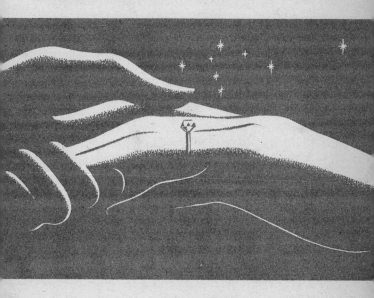

and openly accept the fact that you belong to each other.

Becoming engaged clears the field of other suitors, and the affianced pair may devote themselves to each other without the threat of competition or interruption. It is recognized that they want to be alone together from time to time. As engaged persons, they are expected to prefer each other's company to others and consequently are left to develop their relationship as they will.

Getting engaged is so satisfying and so thrilling in itself that some young people do not pay enough attention to what it really stands for in relation to their future lives. It is a serious step. It anticipates a life together as man and wife. One of the most important functions of an engagement is to make sure that you belong together in a sense that will last through the years.

MAKE
sure you are sure

As you become engaged, you are wise to do everything possible to make sure you are sure. You will want your engagement and the marriage that may follow to be successful. Not all engagements lead to marriage. They break up before the wedding bells ring. Sometimes this is wise, for not all people who get engaged are suitable marriage partners. Engagement should be a testing time for both of you.

IS this the one for you?

Research now tells us what to look for in a mate to insure a successful marriage. The findings tell us in general the most important qualities and factors. A particular marriage may succeed even though some factors differ from the average; nevertheless, it is wise to look seriously at the points that tend to be most significant. Here are five important questions to ask yourself:

1. Is this person going your way? Ask yourself this question early. Does he (or she) look forward to the same sort of life that you do? Is there a similarity of hopes and dreams and ambitions for the future? Are you reasonably sure that you both are working toward the same life goals? If you are to be a good team, pulling together through the years, you had best be headed in the same direction. Marriages in which the partners are pulling at cross purposes do not get very far.

2. Is this your kind of person? Does he or she like the same things you do? Do you come from the same general background? Are your families somewhat similar? Do you share a common religious faith? Did you grow up in the same sort of community? Are you accustomed to approximately the same standard of living? Do you agree upon most of the important issues of life? You may be able to work out a mixed marriage that is "mixed" in the sense that the partners come from different races, religions, or other backgrounds. Some people do. But it is usually more difficult to bridge wide differences than to span a narrow gulf between two people in marriage. You will do well to try to make sure that you are basically the same kind of

persons before you attempt to live out a lifetime together.

3. Do both sets of parents approve? Does your family think that the engagement is a good idea? Are they happy for you? Does his (her) family like you? Do you like them? Do you have the blessing of your parents in this important step? Your parents' approval is not compulsory for a good relationship, but it will be a powerful asset. You may think that you are not marrying the other's family, that just the two of you are all that matters. Do not fool yourself on this. When you marry, both families are involved. You become members of each other's families. They become part of yours. If yours is to be a marriage that leads into harmonious family living, your parents' approval of your match will be a decided asset.

4. Do you respect and admire, as well as love, one another? Love is not all that matters. When you begin a lifetime together, it is imperative that you admire and respect one another completely. In marriage you will share everything that is important to each: your belongings, your money, your thoughts, your time, your dreams, your most intimate moments, and your most precious values. Only if you fully trust each other will you feel completely safe and secure. You may think that when you marry, some of the things that worry you about the other will disappear, that you will be able to change qualities that you cannot admire now, or that some deep psychological disturbance will automatically be cleared up and forgotten. This rarely happens. It is wiser by far to make sure before you marry that your union is based upon mutual trust and respect.

5. Are you good companions? All the other questions may be answered favorably, and still you may not be sure of the success of your marriage unless you can answer this one affirmatively. Most of us want companionship in our marriages. We need the kind of relationship that allows us to be ourselves completely, without having to play a part or put on an act. We need to feel that we are understood. We need to be able to communicate with each other and to share all sorts of things without embarrassment or restraint. Good companions sense their compatibility in the things they have to say to each other, in their enjoyment of being together, and in the strong current of belongingness that flows between the two of them.

This is the time to be certain that you are ready to take such an important step as linking your life to another's. Are you ready to stop playing around? Do you really want to settle down?

When you are ready, you will be mature enough to enjoy the responsibilities as well as the opportunities of engagement, marriage, and family life. Statistics on divorce show that the teen years are the riskiest period for marriage. Young people who wait until they are in their twenties before they marry greatly increase their chance of success. By that time they are more likely to be mature enough to take such an important step.

Sensible young people face the fact that marriages between persons not yet fully grown up are very often failures. They see that immaturity often brews trouble, and so they give themselves time to mature before going into marriage.

When you are ready for marriage, you will have become able to find happiness wherever you go. Your ability to be happy lies within you. No one else can make you happy. Just being married will not bring happiness. If you find happiness in marriage, it will be because you have learned how to be happy. This explains, perhaps, why people who have grown up in happy families are apt to make happier marriages than those who were not so fortunate in their upbringing. If you had a happy childhood, you learned how to be a happy person even before you met your one and only. If you have been happy before marriage, the chances are that you will know how to be happy after marriage. So if you want to get married and live happily ever after, better first make sure that you have it in you to be a happy person.

WHAT
is the engagement period for?

The conversation of some young women would lead one to think that the chief reason for becoming engaged is to have the showers provided by their friends. There are far more important reasons for the engagement period than amassing things for the new home. Even the clothes for the wedding and honeymoon are not so important as the girl who wears them. Getting together a trousseau is fun, and collecting furnishings for the first little home is satisfying; but these are not the important reasons for the engagement period. *Things* can never be so important as *people* in a good marriage.

LEARNING about each other

The engagement period should be the time when the couple become fully acquainted with each other's whole personalities. They now have time to explore their many mutual interests together. They have the opportunity for discovering how each one feels and thinks about all sorts of things. They have the chance to see each other in various settings and in many moods. If they are fortunate, they observe each other's attitudes toward members of both family groups. This is the time when every effort should be made to visit in each other's homes, and to get to know the members of both families who are important to each of them.

Such mutual exploration of both personalities does not inevitably take place during the engagement. If the couple use their time together only for physical lovemaking, they will learn little new about each other, and they may get to the place where nothing else seems very important. Unless they purposely plan to share many different activities, they may find their relationship getting into a rut in which they keep on doing the same thing over and over again, with no chance to get acquainted in different moods and settings.

The engaged couple talk more intimately with each other than was possible before. Such topics of conversation as sex and babies and the kind of family life they want, subjects that were perhaps somewhat embarrassing before, now become not only peculiarly interesting but highly important. It is wise to learn how you both feel about life together as a married couple, before you marry. Just putting some of your emotions into words will be helpful in itself. Differences discovered beforehand are never quite so much of a shock as those that crop up as surprises after marriage. The effort should be made to become well enough acquainted during the engagement period that marriage will be a rediscovery rather than a disillusionment.

Just think of all the practical questions you face as you approach marriage. Decisions will have to be made on any number of matters. Where you will live is an urgent matter even when there is no housing shortage. How much does it cost to get married is another question that cannot easily be avoided. How much will it cost to live as a married couple? as a family when children come? Can two live as cheaply as one? or as two living separately? Should the wife work for a while after marriage to help out? How will the wife's working affect the marriage? Will the timing and number of children be planned or left to nature? How will they be raised? What will be your religious life? your social life? your in-law relationships? This is just a beginning of the roll call of urgent, practical questions that cry for answers as a couple face marriage together.

No one else can make decisions for you as well as you two together can make them. As you tackle each problem, you will find that almost anything can be worked out eventually. When you assume that things will get done without planning, you run into unpleasant surprises. When you let one person make all the decisions, you miss out on the democratic give-and-take that makes marriage fun.

ESTABLISHING yourselves as a pair

The engagement period accustoms friends and family to thinking of the girl and boy as a couple who belong to each other. Before they are definitely engaged, her grandmother, for instance, may talk about "that young man," and his dad may refer to "the girl friend." But with the reality of the engagement ring the families and friends must get used to recognizing the pair as very special persons who are about to become partners in marriage. This takes time and experience.

The engagement helps the members of the families to get used to including the two of them in invitations and to thinking of them as always being together. It is helpful for friends to get some practice in always inviting both rather than one of the two to affairs. As the two move about together and are everywhere recognized as a couple that belong together, they go far toward establishing themselves as a pair in the eyes of those who mean most to them.

FEELING your own oneness

When you are engaged you must become used to feeling and thinking as one, if you are to achieve real unity. For years you have thought of yourself and for yourself, with but occasional need to merge your thinking and feeling with another person. Now that you face marriage, you have the opportunity and the responsibility for learning to think and feel as a couple. You have to develop new habits of decision making. You find yourself asking, "How do *we* feel about this or that?" rather than in terms of yourself alone. You learn to discover the common values that both agree upon. You say to yourself, "We believe . . . we think . . . we plan . . . we wish . . . ," often "we" now that you are getting used to being one.

This kind of deep unity that brings meaning to the phrase "and the two shall be one" does not spring up full-blown from the engagement ring. It grows slowly through the months of being engaged, through the many joint decisions, through the countless plans that are made, through a great deal of actual experience in togetherness.

HOW long should the engagement be?

"Me, I don't believe in long engagements. I say, once you decide to get married you should not dillydally but go ahead and get it over with," says Hector. He is all for short engagements. He wants to rush into marriage. He takes a similar stand when he must visit the dentist. This kind of hasty entrance into marriage does not work out well in large numbers of marriages. It is good sense to ask yourself just how long an engagement should be to insure success in the marriage.

ENGAGEMENTS that are too long

Perhaps you know of a couple who have been engaged for eight or nine years and have not yet set a date for the wedding. This happens sometimes. It usually is a sign of indecision. He or she finds it's impossible to go through with the marriage. Of course, they often blame their long wait on a sick or needy parent, the housing shortage, a shift in his job, or some other "reason," but other couples marry in spite of these things. When an engagement drags on and on, it is probably because the man and the girl cannot bring themselves to take the final step. Under these circumstances, it is probably well that the marriage has not taken place.

Another thing to watch for in overlong engagements is the tension that builds up between the pair who "feel married" and yet cannot consummate their union. Engaged couples sometimes become so ardent in their love making that they overexcite each other. This is neither comfortable nor wise. They leave each other in a state of tension and both feel the strain of their relationship. They find themselves bickering over nothing. "Lovers' quarrels" crop up frequently. Little things begin to irritate and annoy simply because they live in a constant state of tension with each other.

Premarital sexual intercourse is not the solution; marrying as soon as they are ready for it is the answer. This point of "readiness" is important to ascertain. Just when are you ready for marriage? Just how long should an engagement be?

ENGAGEMENTS that are long enough

An engagement should be long enough to accomplish its purposes. It should be adequate for all the important engagement functions discussed earlier in this chapter. The engagement should be long enough to make sure you are sure, to learn about each other, to plan ahead for marriage, to get others used to your unity, and to feel your own oneness.

The actual time needed depends on how far along in these tasks you were when you became engaged, how much of yourselves you give to such progress after you are engaged, whether you are separated or not, how mature you both are, and a great many individual factors. The man and woman who must spend the engagement period many miles apart, depending chiefly upon letters as their means of communication, will need more time than the couple thrown together day after day. They will make better progress during prolonged separation, however, if they have the ability to put their thoughts and real feelings into their letters.

The engaged couple who grew up together, whose families have always been friends, whose interests and experiences have always been shared, have already accomplished many of the tasks of the engagement period. On the other hand, the two who have met recently, who know nothing of each other, or the families or friends or interests of the other, need considerable time during the engagement to fill in their backgrounds.

Two mature persons who know how to work and plan co-operatively, to understand other persons, to love and be loved at a stage far along on the ladder of love development that we discussed earlier, will not need so long a period of engagement to get ready for marriage as will the immature couple who need to grow up both as individuals and as a pair. Perhaps this is one reason for the success of some second marriages even after relatively short engagement periods.

How long should an engagement be? Long enough to get the couple ready for marriage, long enough to accomplish the purposes of the engagement period. When the job of mutual acquaintance, joint planning, and establishing of oneness is well under way, the couple may be considered ready for the next step—marriage.

STATISTICS give longer engagements the advantage

Studies of the length of the engagement as a factor in marital happiness show that the long engagement is much more frequently related to future marriage success than is the short engagement. The hasty marriage is usually a poor one. A man and girl who rush into marriage without an adequate acquaintance and a satisfactory engagement period start out with two strikes against them.

One series of studies indicates that engagements of two years or more work out better than those of less than six months. Most students of courtship and marriage agree that engagements measured in months rather than in weeks are definitely preferred. It takes that long for the average couple to complete the functions of engagement before they are ready to take on the challenge of marriage.

You may argue that you are not an average pair. Even so, it will be wise for you to heed the experience of other couples and avoid as many of the common pitfalls as possible. Of course, predictions do not always come true. Your engagement and marriage may run contrary to prediction. If it does, however, it proves nothing except your power to escape the law of averages. The wise person discovers the hazards as he goes along; and he chooses the best road available.

PROBLEMS
during the engagement

The engagement period is not one of unending bliss. Adjustments are to be expected between the best of lovers. The many areas of life to be shared will inevitably reveal many points of difference. Some of these will be pleasantly exhilarating; some will be frankly disturbing and perhaps frightening. All will call for understanding and mutual acceptance.

Because lovers do care for each other, they will at times hurt and annoy one another. So long as you are not personally wrapped up in another individual, what he (or she) does is not too important to you. But as soon as he becomes yours in a special sense, then you care tremendously about his behavior. Only your loved ones can hurt you deeply. The persons closest to you annoy you most often. As you increase your emotional investment in another person, you thereby increase the number of possible friction points between you.

This need not be a cause for alarm. The first lovers' quarrel is not necessarily a sign that your relationship is headed for a crack-up. It may be an indication of the growth and strength of the we-feeling. When one person always agrees with the other in order to avoid an argument, the two are not so close as when they both dare to be honest with each other. As they strengthen their relationship they will have increasing faith in it and will not have to spare each other the truth.

Real dangers, however, lurk in lovers' quarrels. It is not a question of disagreement. This is normal and to be expected. *How* you settle your differences is the important thing.

The first pitfall is personal pride. If one person's pride needs bolstering whenever any disagreement threatens him, the whole relationship is endangered. If the girl is too proud to admit that she was wrong, she will be unhappy as well as he. If the man has to show her who is boss by insisting on being right all the time, neither of them will feel right. As long as either one is preoccupied with his own hurt feelings, a constant threat hangs over both of them. Perhaps this is why maturity is important for the success of a relationship. When you are mature, you do not have to spend so much time bolstering up your ego feelings. Your maturity allows you to look out toward others rather than always nursing your own interests.

Turning a disagreement into a lashing is a second pitfall to avoid. When one or the other starts to blame, scold, nag, or complain, the point under discussion is lost and the belittled person suffers. The argument that develops into an enumeration of the other's faults and weaknesses is no dispute. It is a battle, with emphasis on hurting the other rather than solving a problem or answering a question.

Other people tend to widen the breach between arguing lovers. It is therefore not wise to call in friends or family to bolster your position. As people take sides and line up against each other, little is accomplished except a further separation of the couple. The quarrel between two lovers is usually resolved more easily when they work it out themselves.

One worthy exception is the wise use of counseling help. A good counselor can help you both to attain a better understanding of yourselves and your problems. You learn how to accept your own feelings and to know what they mean. As you talk with the counselor, you find yourself less inclined to take sides and more concerned with understanding both the problem and yourselves. Before any tangle becomes too difficult, it is good sense to get help in unraveling it.

A good relationship is not one without problems. Rather, it is one that is making progress in solving problems and bridging differences that tend to separate the two persons. Several definite steps may be taken in working out differences.

When a difference of opinion comes up, try to get the other person's point of view. Relax from a vigorous defense of your position and try to understand how the other person is feeling about the affair. What is he trying to accomplish? Why does he feel as strongly as he does about it? What previous experience has he had to make him react in this way? As you put yourself in his shoes, you will begin to sense what he is feeling, and why. You can see the matter from both points of view as you look at it together. Possibly you can find a better solution than either of you could have arrived at singly. Besides, understanding and being understood, even in a disagreement, is richly satisfying. You may not see eye to eye but if you can say, "I understand how you feel about it," your difference is less important than the sense of unity gained.

If you must quarrel, keep focused on the problem rather than on each other. This may not be easy. When a difference of opinion arises, a first impulse may be to label the other as "wrong," "stupid," or "thoughtless." A sober second thought may allow you to tackle the problem itself rather than jump to the conclusion that because someone differs he must be wrong. This quieter, problem-solving attitude works out better in the long run. If you can keep your energies focused upon getting the tangle unsnarled, you will not be so tempted to snap at each other and you'll be more likely to unwind the solution.

When you feel tense and under par, admit it and try not to take it out on others. When you are feeling particularly touchy and irritable, you should warn those with whom you are in close contact so that they will not be hurt by any crossness you may express. Couples sometimes use little personal storm signals that let each other know, even without talking, that something is wrong. A person who loves you will be sympathetic and helpful if he is assured that he is not the cause of your ill-humor.

A better prevention is to keep yourself in condition. The couple who get the rest they should and practice good mental and emotional habits are less inclined to fly off the handle than a couple that allow themselves to become over-fatigued or impulsively explosive. Recreation that will help you let off steam when you feel tense, like sports, a refreshing hobby, music, or even cleaning up your room, will do much to keep you on an even keel. If you let a lot of emotional dynamite pile up inside you, it may blow up right in the face of the one you love most. It is better by far to keep it to a minimum by practicing everyday mental hygiene.

WHEN
an engagement must be broken

Some engagements break up, rather than culminate in marriage. A few of these crack-ups were probably needless. Many were perhaps quite fortunate, for a broken engagement is far better than a broken marriage. The engagement period is a testing time. If the test works out successfully and the two parties seem well suited to each other and able to make their adjustments satisfactorily, they go on into marriage. But if for some reason the engagement does not succeed, the two have failed the test and should not take the chance of marrying.

YOU may be incompatible

During the engagement period you may find that you are not so much in agreement on important matters as you once thought you were. When you have the time and opportunity to become fully acquainted, you may discover characteristics in each other that are basically incompatible. If you both become increasingly sure that these differences cannot be resolved, you may decide that it is best to break the engagement.

If you find that your conflicts become increasingly frequent and difficult, you should at least consider postponing your wedding date until the prospect for working out a good marriage looks brighter. Unless you have achieved some success in making adjustments together while you are engaged, you are not ready for marriage. If eventually you feel that you are losing ground in your ability to adapt to one another, a break-up may be the best solution.

Another justification for breaking an engagement may be sheer boredom. If you find that your companionship is growing dull and neither of you can hold the other's interest, it may mean that you have outgrown one another or that the relationship has worn itself out. This happens at times. The two persons must form a growth-promoting and interest-stimulating combination or they become weary of each other. Such a state is a sign that neither is meeting the other's needs, and they are not likely to find happiness together in marriage. A broken engagement is better than a marriage of mutual boredom.

HOW does one break an engagement?

The process of breaking an engagement is similar to that of breaking off going steady, discussed in the preceding chapter. It may be complicated by the return of valuable presents, and especially giving back the engagement ring. But this is easy once the two have agreed upon the break itself.

Friends and family are more involved in a broken engagement than is usually true of a breaking up earlier in the involvement. They must be told of the shift of plans as soon as the couple themselves have come to their decision.

Gifts already received from well-wishing friends and family members may be returned according to the following rules of etiquette. The girl may return gifts of value which can be used by someone else with a simple note telling of the change in plans and thanking the giver for his thoughtfulness. In the case of such things as monogrammed linens or other articles that have been personalized for her alone, she need do nothing except inform the givers, as she does all other close friends and relatives, of her change in plans.

Sentimental individuals sometimes try to patch things up after the young couple have decided upon breaking off with each other. The couple can relieve the anxiety of such solicitous outsiders by having some objective counselor review their situation with them before making their final announcement. This step tends to satisfy those who feel that the break was hasty or ill-advised. It also may be of real help to the couple themselves in understanding what really happened to their relationship and how they each may avoid another crack-up later on.

WHAT
is a successful engagement?

A successful engagement is not measured by the size of the girl's ring. Indeed, that may be a very poor indication of the health of the relationship. Some young men mortgage their futures in order to buy an expensive engagement ring that is but a symbol and not a gauge of their love. Recently one couple decided that a diamond ring was a waste of money as far as they were concerned. They considered so many other things more essential that they dispensed with an engagement ring entirely and put their jewelry investment into a nice set of double wedding rings instead.

Another couple found a ring superfluous in their engagement. She was in nurses' training where rings were strictly forbidden while she was on duty. He was a struggling student preparing for the ministry. The symbol of their engagement was a lovely silver cross which she could wear on a chain around her neck, and which stood not only for their betrothal but also for the life of Christian service they looked forward to together.

The size of the engagement party is not a measure of the importance of the relationship. Some of the showiest parties launch the flimsiest marriages. The newspaper space given to the engagement announcement is no measure of its significance. A socially prominent family may command many lines of type to announce the approaching marriage of one of its young people, and the engagement of a modest young couple may appear in three lines on the back page of the home-town newspaper. Yet, the two marriages may hold equal promise of being successful.

The success of an engagement is measured by certain established criteria:

1. The extent to which the couple approach marriage with hope and confidence, ready for its challenges, opportunities, and responsibilities.

2. The extent to which the couple have prepared both friends and families for the marriage and are able to become part of the married community with ease and general approval.
3. The extent to which the couple have established skills of working out life situations together that give promise of their ability to meet marriage adjustments effectively.
4. The extent to which the man and the girl are ready and eager to continue to learn and to grow, both as individuals and as a team.

Successful engagements do not just happen. They occur most often among those who make them succeed. Couples who practice getting through to each other gradually develop the skills of communication that auger well for their relationship. They talk out their feelings and get to understand each other as they become more and more emotionally honest with one another. In time each becomes better able to predict the other's moods and wishes in the kind of *empathy* (the ability to sense the other's feelings) that goes with two-way understanding.

Planning together helps to build a strong relationship. As the engaged pair make more and more of their plans jointly, they establish the kind of mutuality that makes for success. As the engaged couple get more and more experience in laying joint plans they each find pleasure in postponing important decisions until the other can be a part of them. Such co-operative decision making protects both the fellow and the girl from becoming either chronically the boss or always the bossed in their life together.

SUCCESSFUL engagements predict successful marriages

Working together on projects that will carry over into marriage helps make an engagement succeed. Maria and Luis spend many happy hours refinishing old furniture for their home-to-be. Alexis and Andrew read aloud to each other from some of the many books on marriage they have found in the library and at nearby bookstores. Both these couples, and many others, enjoy the time they spend together partly because they are readying themselves for their life together as husband and wife. Marriage means working together toward common goals, and in a real sense a good engagement does too.

In the light of all this, it is not surprising that research studies clearly show successful engagements to be predictive of successful marriages. Couples who get along well during the time they are engaged tend to relate well in marriage. Conversely, the pair who fight like cat and dog in their engagement can hardly look forward to peace in their marriage. In a real sense, the engagement period is a testing time, as well as a building process, for the couple whose goal is a lifetime of happiness together.

These are the matters you should ponder when you become engaged and are approaching marriage. The important thing is not how pretty a bride you will be, but how fine a wife; not how rich a bridegroom, but how much of yourself you offer as a husband. Marriage today is neither a style show nor a business proposition. It is an adventure in living that calls for sturdy people with an understanding of what to expect in marriage.

*Do you know
what to expect*

of marriage?

DO YOU EXPECT THAT MARRIAGE will be years of unending bliss, with never a dull moment to relieve the excitement of being together? If so, you have much to learn about marriage, and about yourself. Do you expect that you will never be lonely once you are married? If so, you have yet to discover that loneliness is more a state of mind than of matrimony. Do you expect that your beloved will make you happy? If so, you can be assured that no one can MAKE you happy. Happiness in marriage is built by happy, loving persons who care enough about each other to prepare for their marriage and to develop their relationship in satisfying ways through the years.

Preparing for marriage calls for more than just collecting the clothes you both will wear. It involves finding out about what to expect of marriage, checking up on your readiness for the big step, and anticipating some of the adjustments you will have to make. Some adjustments in marriage are so universal that you may profitably explore them in anticipation and be ready for them when they come along.

SEX
adjustments in marriage

You probably are curious about the sex side of marriage—the one area of life that you are expected to postpone until after marriage. Naturally, there are many questions as to what it is all about.

WHAT happens in intercourse

The sexual union of man and woman is called intercourse, or coitus, or mating, or the sex act, or the marital relation, or popularly among youth, "going all the way." Physically it is a relatively simple procedure, as discussed in the chapters on sexual development. After an initial period of sexual excitation, the penis becomes erect and is thrust into the vagina. A series of in and out movements eventuates in the ejaculation of semen from the penis. The woman may or may not have a climax in which her sex tension is released. Following the sexual climax is a period of relaxation and usually sleep.

There is a wide variety of positions for and methods of intercourse. It may last for only a minute or two, or be prolonged with elaborate foreplay (petting and fondling) and afterplay (tender loving) to an hour or more. How long it takes or how it is performed is not important so long as both find it pleasant and satisfying.

Some people desire sex intercourse more frequently than others. The usual frequency in early marriage is every night or so. After a couple have been married for several years they may have intercourse on the average of twice a week. As people get older they have sex relationships less frequently. There is no prescription of what is right or best for every couple. The frequency of their sexual unions is theirs to determine. Should one of the couple want intercourse more often than the other, they will need to work out together a mutually satisfactory adjustment.

Either the husband or the wife may approach the other sexually. Couples work out their own signs and signals for communicating their sexual readiness. Women develop seductive little ways that arouse the interest of their husbands. Men are usually more direct in their love-making.

SEX response in men and women

The man's sex response tends to be rapid and definite. His excitation is readily recognized in the change in his sex organs. The woman's sex response is slower and less definite. She experiences an all-over excitement in which there may or may not be local sensations in her genitals. Usually it is only the more sexually experienced, mature woman who is aware of sexual excitation as soon as the average man is.

In the normal man sex excitement builds up rapidly to

ejaculation and then rapidly declines. Woman's response develops more slowly to climax and then more gradually tapers off. One of the usual adjustments to be made in marriage is that of slowing the man's response and hastening the woman's so that they may both reach a satisfying release of tension. This is not too difficult when the husband and wife love each other and want to work out the sex-love side of their marriage satisfactorily.

Still another difference between men and women is the way in which they look upon the sex act in relation to other areas of their adjustment. Men tend to feel that sex will solve any problem that arises. The man seems to say, "Sure, we do not see eye to eye, but if I can love her up, everything will be all right again." The woman, on the other hand, is likely to feel that sexual union should come as an expression of the larger harmonies of the marriage. She wants everything cleared up before the love-making. When there is some disagreement between the two, it is the woman who more often turns away from her husband's amorous approach with something like, "Do not come around me until you are willing to make things right in what we have been fussing about." This difference in the way man and woman view marriage relations must be worked out between the husband and wife if they are to live happily together.

LEARNING sex satisfaction

Ethel Merman made a hit with her singing of "Doin' What Comes Natcherly" in *Annie Get Your Gun*. Although the tune caught on, the words of the song repeated the most unfortunate of falsehoods. The lyrics of that number imply that any husband and wife can mate happily just by letting nature take its course. Dr. Judson T. Landis' study of happily married couples shows that only 52.7 per cent, or about one half, find sex satisfaction with each other from the first. Most couples need to work out mutually satisfying adjustments. Research findings indicate that this may take from a few months to many years. Some couples happily married for twenty years or more report that they still have not found complete mutual satisfaction. Professional counseling early in the relationship might have helped such marriages.

Sex relations are a kind of language that each couple must learn in marriage. At first the two are clumsy. As they become more expert and experienced with each other, the language of sex-love becomes more fluent and satisfying. They teach each other as they go along. The marriage that offers husband and wife periods of complete privacy, and a deep sense of basic security in their mutual love and devotion for each other, provides the atmosphere needed for learning the arts of love-making.

PREMARITAL
examinations and conferences

Getting ready for the sex adjustments in marriage involves making sure that both husband-to-be and wife-to-be are physically and psychologically ready. This cannot be discerned just by looking at a person. It calls for technical tests that only a doctor can perform, and some exploring that is best done with a well-trained counselor.

BLOOD tests

Most states now require the prospective bride and bridegroom to have tests for the presence of venereal disease. The most commonly used are the Wasserman or the Kahn tests, which detect the germs of syphilis in the blood when the person is actively infected. A small amount of blood is drawn from the person being tested, and this blood sample is sent to a laboratory. If the test is positive, the infected person must get adequate treatment before he is allowed to marry. If the test is negative, the person is declared free of syphilis and may marry at once. These tests are valuable in preventing the spread of venereal infections. They give a marriage a clean bill of health and thus avoid the risk of one of the pair infecting the other in marriage.

Even in states not requiring blood tests before marriage, a couple is wise to include them in premarital preparation. They care enough about their marriage to make sure that it starts off as it should, so they go to a doctor and have the necessary tests made at the same time that they explore still other physical factors in premarital examinations and conferences.

Couples desiring to plan for the arrival of their babies need expert medical assistance and a pelvic examination for the woman before marriage. A competent physician should check on the condition of her genital organs, to make sure that they are mature and normal. The woman with a severely immature genital development may be able neither to have sex relations nor to bear children. Certain other abnormalities may make intercourse difficult, if not impossible. Many of these conditions can be corrected before marriage. It is wise, therefore, to have the premarital examination some time prior to marriage so that any unexpected difficulties can be taken care of without disrupting the marriage plans.

The time of the pelvic examination gives a woman an excellent opportunity to talk over her menstrual cycle with the doctor and to get some advance information on what to expect during marriage, pregnancy, and childbirth.

GENERAL examination of both

Both the husband-to-be and the wife-to-be should consider getting a complete physical check-up before their marriage. They will want to make very sure that no disability will interfere with their marriage happiness. If either of them has some difficulty that may affect the marriage, both of them should face it frankly and openly before they marry.

Lola was surprised to discover during her premarital examination that one kidney was not functioning as it should. The doctor talked over with her what this might mean if she became pregnant. They discussed it with the prospective husband who agreed to see to it that she received the additional prenatal care her condition would require. Had they not discovered this difficulty, Lola might have run into serious problems in her first pregnancy. Knowing of her condition ahead of time made it possible for her and her husband to guard their marriage and parenthood from grave consequences.

Duncan's premarital examination uncovered latent tuberculosis, of which Duncan had had no previous warning. A brief period of treatment cleared up the condition and brought both Duncan and his bride to marriage without the shadow of illness over their marriage. Such a value was worth waiting for.

Usually the premarital examination reveals nothing of importance and the couple can go into marriage confident that they have no discoverable physical condition to mar the happiness of their life together.

GETTING *facts straight*

The premarital examination and conference is an excellent time to clear up any of the facts of sex and reproduction that may still be hazy. As the couple discuss with a competent guide their many unanswered questions, they get facts straight and feel better about it all.

Foolish fears that were caused by distorted ideas persisting from childhood can now be overcome. A clear understanding of the truth banishes many such haunting anxieties.

Straightening out halftruths and getting the facts takes time. And it requires close contact with a competent counselor. Some communities have excellent marriage counseling facilities to which young persons approaching marriage may go for premarital conferences. Other young people, far from such counseling services, must either make a special trip to the nearest city having a family service agency or a planned parenthood clinic, or get what help they can from their home-town pastors, doctors, and social workers.

PERSONALITY *exploration*

A sequence of personality tests of both parties before marriage often can reveal outstanding characteristics of which they should be aware. Not only do the two get objective information about each of themselves, but they often gain real insight as to how their two personalities will mesh into each other.

If both man and woman, for instance, tend to be dominant and to want their own way, they may anticipate some conflict as each one struggles for dominance. If one is outgoing and optimistic and the other is self-absorbed and pessimistic, they should not expect to view things in the same way. Having objective evidence about themselves beforehand often makes it easier to accept such differences when they crop up in the marriage. Personality exploration does not create such problems; it merely throws light upon them so that the two persons can better understand their own natures and how they fit together.

Exploring personality make-up before marriage is valuable in revealing attitudes that may affect the marriage. If the woman tends to have a feeling that all men will hurt her unless she is careful, her husband may find her on the defensive with him. If the man has attitudes of insecurity that came out of his earlier unhappiness as a boy, his happiness as a husband will be affected. Such feelings are not uncommon, and they need not be feared. They can be faced and accepted. Only as we understand our own attitudes can we make good adjustments in them. As each person entering marriage comes to terms with his or her own individual tendencies, the marriage itself is more solidly based.

The premarital conference in which the couple explore their individual and combined readiness for marriage is like the check-up for the automobile before a long trip. Unknown weaknesses are uncovered and some allowance made for them. Strengths and qualities of sturdiness are revealed. Conditions that may affect the coming adventure are brought to light. The couple leave the qualified counselor much as the family leaves the garage man's tune-up, with a feeling that they are ready for the journey.

THE
money side of marriage

A marriage adjustment that is sometimes difficult is that of spending the family income. It is not a question of whether there is much money or very little that makes or breaks a relationship. It is the way the husband and wife feel about what they have that is most important.

WHAT it costs to get married

The amount of money needed to get married on depends upon many things—what you both are used to, what you expect to have when you marry, what you have dreamed of through the years, and to what extent you can make your dreams match realities.

Fay had dreamed of getting married ever since she was a little girl, as many girls do. But Fay had accepted a sort of Cinderella fairy tale of marriage that does not jibe with what usually happens. She took the magazine advertisements personally and fully expected to have all the lovely things that the full-page ads of brides in the June issues of women's magazines portray. She expected to be married in a white satin gown in the traditional church wedding, to have a reception for all her friends and family, and to go away for a grand honeymoon. She dreamed of coming home with her bridegroom in their new-model automobile to a modern ranch-style house with its nice, fully equipped rooms, including a beautiful modern kitchen, an up-to-date television set, an heirloom chest of sterling silver, a closet full of monogrammed linens, and all the rest of the things the ads had promised her. It was a lovely dream. It made getting married something like hitting the jackpot. The trouble was that it did not materialize in real life. It usually does not. For Fay to have all she expected, her father would have had to be a wealthy man, and her bridegroom would have had to be among the few well-to-do young men who have inherited a lot of money to get started on. Most young couples start far more modestly.

Actually, getting married can be kept from becoming too expensive. Many couples have a simple little ceremony in the church following the morning service. They are married in clothes that will last them through a period of time as their "good clothes." They set up housekeeping in a little apartment or in a couple of rooms furnished with what friends and both sides of the family can spare them. They make a careful financial plan in terms of the money they actually have, and they keep within it. No one can say that such a marriage is any less secure than the one that starts with all the stuff of which dreams are made.

MAKING a money plan for marriage

Money matters can be worked harmoniously when both agree upon where the money is to come from and where it is to go. The sources of income for the newly married couple are few. Unless he is still a student, there are his earnings. If she is to work for a while after marriage, there will be her income. One or both of them may have some money saved up that may be used for getting established. One or both sets of parents may help out. When necessary, the couple may borrow money at first. Some of these sources of income are only temporary. You cannot indefinitely borrow money and keep your home solvent. Most couples do not want to take help from their parents over a long period of time. Most wives do not continue to work through the entire marriage. In the last analysis, it is usually the husband who is the wage-earner and breadwinner.

In considering any of the sources of income it is important that both are in agreement. Whether the wife is to work or not is his concern as husband as well as hers as wife. Taking help from parents is a matter of mutual interest. Borrowing money involves them both. Whatever is done to help establish the marriage, the planning should be done jointly and carefully. A money plan, to be a good one, should be selected together after a consideration of all the various possible alternatives.

Spending the family income involves many other decisions. It includes choices as to where and how the couple will live, what their standard of living will be, what things they consider essential and what they consider luxuries, whether they will pay cash for everything or buy on the installment plan, and most important of all, how they will divide their money among its many possible outlets—how they will budget it. One couple may be willing to sacrifice present pleasures for plenty of insurance. Another may choose to use up everything they both make so that they need not sacrifice their present satisfaction for an unknown future. Either way, a choice must be made. Choosing is itself the important step in the whole process of spending the family income. Whichever plan is selected, it should be *yours,* jointly arrived at and jointly lived up to.

THAT costly upkeep

It is not the initial cost but the upkeep that counts in getting married. It does not cost much to get married. Two dollars for a license is about all that is absolutely required. But after marriage, what then? Plans for the years, as well as money for the day, are important.

One way to get ready for the money adjustments in marriage is to live within individual personal budgets before marriage. When both the man and the woman know exactly what it has been costing them to live separately, they have some basic figures to start with. The girl who has been able to live within her personal budget before she marries has some realistic experience in handling money that is lacking in the girl who has "no idea where all the money goes." The fellow who has trained himself to save something out of every week's income is preparing himself for the realistic living within his income that will be called for in marriage. This couple will be able to put their personal expenditures together into a joint budget that will be based upon actual experience. Even then, it will need to be adapted to married living.

Two can live as cheaply as one, but only half as long. A married couple cannot live as cheaply as two when they were single. For when you marry, you develop new needs and appetites that you did not have before. You want to furnish your home nicely. You want to have babies and give your children the best. You want to have your friends in and entertain freely and easily. You want to look and act the part of successful, happily married people, and this takes money. And even more important, it takes careful planning.

The couple who are ready to assume the responsibilities of working out a sound financial plan for their marriage have already taken the first big step in meeting their money problems. As they gain experience in making decisions together and in keeping within the plans agreed upon, they find that the money side of marriage becomes a challenge rather than a burden.

YOU
may have children some day

Right now you may feel that your children are a long way off in the future. But if you are well into your teens, you can expect to be a parent within the next few years. Most couples have their first baby a year or two after they marry. That is a statistical average, and not a recommendation for you necessarily.

PLANNING for your children

You may want your children just as soon as you can have them. Or you may decide to wait until your adjustments as a couple are coming along nicely and you feel more ready for parenthood. Either way, the decision is yours to make. It should come as a result of your consideration of the factors that are important: the teachings of your religion, your financial condition, your age and health as a couple, and, of course, your own feelings about becoming parents.

Most young people today say that they want to have three or more children. You may want fewer than this, or more. You may have to be content with fewer children, or even none at all. Ten to fifteen per cent of all married couples cannot have babies when they want them. Doctors and special clinics can be of help to childless couples sometimes, and they certainly should be sought out as soon as the couple find that they cannot conceive.

Even after a baby is conceived, things sometimes go wrong. The woman may have a miscarriage and lose the baby before it is ready to be born. The baby may be born dead, or it may not live after it is born. These things happen rarely, but they do occur and should be taken as among the unfortunate disappointments of life.

The majority of couples today have as many children as they feel they can take care of. They can usually have them when they want them. Planning for a family can be one of the most challenging and creative experiences a couple can share. It involves becoming co-partners in the fulfillment of life itself. It is a responsibility not to be taken lightly nor unduly postponed.It is an obligation to posterity, and to the fulfillment of the parents themselves.

BRINGING up your children

Parents have a great responsibility today. There are many ways of bringing up children and every couple must choose its own philosophy and method of child rearing. You may decide to be strict and "old-fashioned." Or you may agree to be lenient and permissive. You may want to bring your children up according to the most modern scientific procedures. You are apt to be greatly influenced by the ways in which you were handled as a child, and especially by the ways in which you responded to your parents' rearing of you.

Father as well as mother is parent to the children. It is important that parents agree upon the methods of child rearing to be used. It does not seem to matter quite so much which procedure is used so long as the parents and children feel comfortable in it and agree upon it. Consistent discipline is better than discipline which vacillates between extreme leniency and severity. A child needs to know where he stands with his folks. You know how this is. Children's basic security is all wrapped up in the way in which their parents feel about them.

It is important, therefore, for people who are some day to become parents to begin to think about how children should be reared. Parent education best begins long before the children actually arrive. In some communities it is taught all through the schools. The more you have studied, talked, and planned about it beforehand, the better prepared for parenthood you will be.

YOU
will belong to each other's family

Getting ready for marriage involves becoming members of each other's family. In your romantic moments you may try to kid yourselves into believing that you are not marrying the family, you are marrying each other. That is only partly true. As soon as the first baby comes, or the first vacation visit rolls around, you discover each other's family as a very real part of your marriage.

This warning is not to scare you with in-law troubles. Most in-laws are very nice people. You will be one yourself as soon as you marry! Yet, achieving full membership in your spouse's family will take adjustments on both sides. Only by knowing you as you are can they understand you.

You can prepare for such two-family membership by a number of routes. First, even before you marry you can go out of your way to get acquainted with the other family. Visit them as often as you can. Do whatever will help you to know them as persons and to let them know you.

You will need to overcome some of your tendencies to try to hide facts of your family life from your one and only. When a person becomes especially yours, he or she needs to face with you whatever there is to share in the family situation. Only as two persons are honest with each other can they fully trust one another. Only as you know what you are dealing with can you become a full-fledged member of another family.

GROWING up and out to others

You become a good member of the other's family as you grow up and overcome your childish dependencies upon your own parents. When you can stand on your own feet and live your own life without having to defer constantly to your parents, you are ready to become a married person, able to share his or her family in mature ways. When you can enjoy your mother and father as persons and not just see them as parents-in-power, you probably can enjoy another set of older persons too.

As you mature, you may find that you have to give your parents a helping hand in growing up, too. Your mother may cling to you and find it hard to let you go. Then she will need your encouragement in securing interests and wider horizons to take the place of the attention she is accustomed to give you. Help her get out into community affairs. Encourage her to spruce up for the years of living she still has ahead after you have married. This may do a lot to help her and to untie the apron-strings that bind you to her.

Being a member of two families as you build still a third, will keep you busy. But it is one of the most rewarding of experiences and merits all the time and effort you can spend on it.

YOU
are never through learning

All your life long you can learn. This book began with the recognition that young people want to learn about themselves, and it ends with the conviction that they want to explore the complexities of family living. You will continue to learn and grow as long as you live. Here are some of the specific resources that may help.

BOOKS, *pamphlets, and films*

You are fortunate in living at a time when most of the things you want to know are written in ways that you can understand. There are many good books and pamphlets on boy-girl relationships, dating, love and lovemaking, preparation for marriage, baby care, child rearing, and all that goes into family living. The publisher of this book has lists of many of these for you. The library in your home community or those of your state department of education or state department of public health quite possibly have such materials. Your local bookstores and church bookshelf can help. Your minister may have books to share with you. Your school may have some things that will help you learn more about the facts of living together. There are films and charts and recordings and other aids to learning that you may be on the look-out for, since they are becoming available in most communities as young people like yourself ask for them.

COURSES *in schools, colleges, and community agencies*

Thousands of schools offer units and courses in family living. If you are not fortunate enough to live in a town with such a school program, perhaps you and your parents can start the ball rolling for the inclusion of such courses in your schools. It has been the insistence of people like you that has brought this kind of education into being. As you ask for it, school authorities are encouraged to consider it seriously.

Hundreds of colleges offer courses in marriage and family living to their students. Such courses are now accepted as important in the education of the college men and women. You may have a chance to take such a course in which you will explore even further some of the things discussed in this book.

Community agencies like the YMCA and YWCA, churches, social clubs, and other organizations for youth and young adults offer courses along these lines. In some communities you can take short courses in dating, in courtship, in preparation for marriage, in marriage adjustments, in expectant parenthood, in child development and guidance, in parent education, in adolescent behavior, and finish up with problems of the middle years and refresher courses for grandparents!

These intimate life adjustments are extremely important, and they are best made when they first arise. You need, therefore, to learn the new adjustments and the better ways of doing things at every stage of your life.

As a member of your school, your church, your club, your community, you can help to bring such educational opportunities into being. It may be your interest adding its weight to similar interests of others that will bring new services to your town. This was the way the schools themselves originally came into existence, and the churches, the hospitals, the libraries, and almost everything else of importance—by people caring enough to work for them in their home communities.

COUNSELORS and counseling services

As long as you live you will have new problems to face and new situations to work your way through. Some of these you will take in your stride. Some will be difficult. Some will all but defeat you completely. Any of them will be made more understandable and possible with the aid of competent counseling help. As you talk through a problem with an understanding counselor, you see it more clearly yourself, you get a more objective view of it, and you explore your own resources for meeting the new situation.

Just as you would not think of trying to fill your own tooth, so you may recognize that you cannot fix up all the emotional tangles in which you may find yourself. A competent specialist, trained to take care of the difficulty, is an aid not only to relief for the moment but also to future well-being. There may come a time when good counseling services are as accessible as good dentists, and for the same reason: to give expert attention when it is needed to get things in shape before they become too painful, and to prevent the loss of health by periodic check-up and general conditioning. If such care is important for our teeth, it is fully as important for our feelings, which are quite as vulnerable and just as painful when they ache.

You may have access to competent counselors in your school, your church, or your neighborhood. If so, do not hesitate to go to them with your questions. Even if they cannot help you to find the answers, you will feel better for having voiced the question and begun the search for an answer. If your community does not have such guidance facilities, you may get help in talking through your problems with an older person whom you can trust—your parents, one of your teachers, your religious leader, or perhaps your coach or club leader. Whoever it is, do not expect him to take over your problem and fix it all up for you. A good counselor cannot do this. His role is to hear you out and help you see how you feel, and why, and only then to encourage you to consider what you are going to do about your situation. Your life is yours to live. Only you can meet its challenges day by day. Therefore, a good counselor usually does not give advice. He or she helps you to work out your own solutions to your own problems.

YOUR eagerness to learn and to grow

Your life from now on will depend more upon your own willingness to keep on growing than upon any other factor. You can stop growing right now, as some people have. You may never open another book once you have stopped going to school. You may refuse to think or to plan or to try to understand yourself and others. Some people have become so defeated with life by the time they reach your age that they have lost all desire to try further. They are to be pitied, and helped if possible, for refusing to keep on growing is a real tragedy.

Others carry an open, inquiring mind into all situations of life. As long as they live they find life full and good.

They have the secret of learning and growing upon which all life is based. Such people do not need to keep on going to school, because they have the attitude for learning within themselves. They usually do continue in school, because learning is fun and there are always new things they want to understand. Whether they attend classes or not they find happiness and satisfaction wherever they go, because they are occupied in growth, and growth is the most satisfying thing we know.

As you learn, you grow; as you grow, you learn. The two go hand in hand. Keep on asking questions. Do not be satisfied with the answers you find. A good answer leads you to a host of still further questions. The more you understand, the more there will be to understand. The more clearly you see one truth, the larger will loom the unknowns beyond it. Such is life, ever expanding, ever widening its horizons, ever growing up and out in higher and wider circles. When you close this book after finishing the next chapter, do not close your mind to the questions that prompted you to open it. Take it as a simple introduction to a majestic question that will go on as you grow, becoming ever more wonderful with the years.

CHAPTER 20

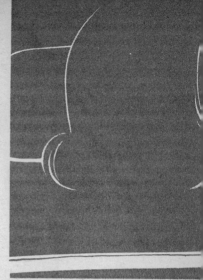

How involved is it

THE BIG QUESTION OF THE teen years is, how deeply involved does one get? Most people would agree that the teen-ager who stands off aloof from others, refusing to get involved with another person, not daring to love òr be loved, is losing a great deal of the most meaningful part of life.

There are quite as many adults and young people today who strongly feel that the teen-ager who rushes into an early marriage or gets involved in an intense affair before education is complete may soon regret such a premature involvement.

SENIOR
panic among girls

There is a disease so common among the seniors in some schools that it goes by the name of "senior panic." The

wise to get?

chief symptom is the anxiety the girls experience in their rush to get a man while the getting is good. Girls who have been doing all right in having interesting dates and worthwhile social activities suddenly begin to put pressure upon their dates to "get things settled." The girl who has been seeing a boy occasionally endeavors to get him to date her exclusively. The girl who has been going steady now pushes for a definite understanding with her boy friend. The girl who has been wearing a boy's ring now wants to set the date for the wedding.

All this might have made sense in an earlier day, when a woman's future depended upon her tying in early with the man of her choice. But now, when so many girls go on for further education and the ways are open for women to find themselves in all sorts of occupations, such precipitous lunging into premature commitments is unfortunate.

School-girl marriages more frequently break up in divorce, separation and annulment than do the unions of more mature couples. The reason is clear—marriage is not playing house. It requires a considerable amount of maturity to be ready to settle down and have a family. Most teen-agers are simply not ready for as much responsibility as marriage and family building require.

The girl who rushes too soon into marriage is cutting off her own chances for full development as a woman, and as a person. There are many things to learn, places to visit, and people to meet before a girl today is mature enough to find herself as a full-fledged woman. The school-girl bride struggles with roles too big for her. The more mature young woman finds fulfillment in her marriage because she is ready for both its responsibilities and its opportunities. Senior panic is unfortunate because it ensnares too many girls into precocious commitments for which they themselves are not ready.

ADOLESCENT
male sex aggression

There is among some teen-age boys a desire to prove themselves as males. These are the fellows who get in a car and drive to a neighborhood where they are not known in order to "pick up a couple of girls." Two or three or more of such boys may be found with a "bottle of courage" as they try to get the nerve to take advantage of whatever girls they can find. There is a lot of joking and risqué talk about sex among boys on the prowl.

Studies show that there are more situations in which the boys are sexually aggressive on first dates than with sweethearts whom they love. The reason is not hard to discern. With his sweetheart, a boy is tender and loving and considerate of her feelings as well as of their future. It is on the first date that a certain kind of boy is more apt to see how far a girl will go. Then he becomes offensive with his urgent pressures for more intimacy than the girl feels is appropriate.

Insistence upon sexual involvement before the two persons know each other puts the sex act on a sheer physical basis. Pressuring a girl for intimacy that is not based upon mutual affection is a crude type of exploitation. Getting sexually involved before the couple are ready to assume full responsibility for their behavior can blight their future as well as their present. Letting sex take the lead leaves heart and head and spirit sorry seconds in the living of a life.

A boy proves little of himself as man-in-the-making by demonstrating his sexual prowess. He shows himself much more the man as he controls his impulses and builds his relationships with others on a foundation of mutual respect and concern.

The idea that "everybody else is doing it" just is not true of sexual involvements before marriage. Dr. A. C. Kinsey found that among boys who go on to college fully half are still virgins when they marry. Even among those boys who have experienced sexual intercourse before marriage there are an uncounted number whose involvements have been limited to the girls who become their brides. Others have known only a single escapade, hardly enough to put them in the roué category. Still others brag beyond their experience, partly because other teen-age boys seem to expect it of them.

The boy who has never taken advantage of a girl has every reason to be proud of his restraint. The fellow who respects his girl or adores his sweetheart is not likely to pressure for more manifestations of her love than she is willing to give. Premature involvement sexually can be quite as hurtful as precocious marital involvements.

One of the saddest questions a high school boy can ask is that sent up at the close of a session on these matters, "My girl is pregnant; do I have to marry her?" This is an unhappy situation because there is no happy ending—for the boy, his girl friend, their families, or the baby-in-the-making. If he doesn't marry the girl, he may feel like a cad. If he does marry her just because he caused her pregnancy, what kind of start is this for marriage? If he marries her believing that he is the father of the baby and learns later that some other fellow could have been responsible for her pregnancy, what then? What about his chances now for continuing his education, and realizing his dreams for the future?

LOVE
is not to blame

A couple drop out of school and run away to get married. Their education is over, their parents are hurt, their future is shadowed. How do they explain their impulsive actions? The chances are that they blame it all on "love." Yet, how wrong they are. If their mutual feelings had been a mature kind of love, they would have encouraged each other to complete their schooling, they would have taken their parents into their confidence, and they would have prepared for their marriage responsibly instead of dashing into it.

A girl gets into trouble, a boy gets into a jam with a girl —how do they explain it? They say, "We couldn't help it, we were in love." Only sentimental children believe this kind of myth. Others know that such irresponsible actions are far more apt to be rebellious plunges taken to "prove" something than they are to be genuine feelings of love.

Of course teen-agers feel strongly about each other, all through the years. But those who impetuously give way to their feelings are acting, not out of love, but more often because of such negative feelings as fear, hatred, rebellion, jealousy, revenge, and insecurity.

The more you learn about your own ability to love and to be loved, the more you know that love comes in many guises and speaks in many tongues. The more mature you grow, the better able you are to distinguish immature, impetuous feelings for another person from the more permanent, fulfilling emotions that bind two persons together through the years.

Sex attraction, infatuation, and other intense feelings for others need not ruin teen-agers' lives or wreck their future development as persons. In fact, just because you feel strangely drawn toward another person is no indication that you have to rush into something foolish. You can enjoy the delicious feeling for what it is, without having to do anything at all about it. More often than not such emotions soon disappear, to be replaced by still other feelings about yourself and the special people in your life. In time you become capable of the mature loves upon which you can make lifelong plans. Until that time, you need not blame "love" for your behavior.

ACHIEVEMENT
and the ability to wait

There have been a number of studies that have found a relationship between a young person's achievement ability and his tendency to defer his gratifications. These findings suggest that the teen-age boy or girl who is accomplishing things academically, mechanically, musically, athletically, or otherwise, is apt to be the kind of person who does not have to follow every impulse with immediate gratification.

One way of interpreting such findings is to recognize that the person who is getting satisfaction in what he or she is accomplishing does not have to rush off and satisfy immediately every appetite that arises. The creature of impulse, on the other hand, dashes around catering to every whim so much that he has no energy left for the solid accomplishments that might satisfy his deeper hungers.

The ability to wait is related to one's maturity. The infantile person, like a baby, wants what he wants when he wants it. He cannot wait for satisfactions, but demands that his appetites be satiated at once. As an individual matures, he becomes increasingly able to handle his impulses and to wait for satisfactions until the time and conditions are appropriate.

Achievement comes with maturity, too. As one develops his skills through practice and patience, he is able to accomplish things that the impulsive baby is incapable of in his immature state. It is only as one assumes responsibility for himself that he is able to achieve, to produce, and to make a constructive contribution to his world.

LIFE
goals and aspirations

Young people with high aspirations are less likely to become involved than those who are adrift, with no life plans to keep them growing onward. The girl who sees herself as a teacher, a social worker, or a nurse is less apt to rush off on some path that leads nowhere than is the girl who has no plans for her life beyond the moment.

The boy whose life goals include college and graduate school, or as much night school as he can get, is not usually the one who gets prematurely involved with some girl. It is far more often some fellow who has lost confidence in himself who stops dreaming and planning for his own future, and so short-circuits his own chances of really getting anywhere.

The teen-ager who feels that no one cares what happens to him is one who may be discouraged in trying to make anything of himself. This is the kind of devil-may-care attitude that leads to trouble. Lose confidence in yourself, and you are ripe for any temptation that comes along. Take an honest look at your opportunities; put a sense of purpose into your plans for the future, no matter what the past has been—and you no longer will be so tempted to throw your life away.

The boy and girl who have long dreams for themselves pursue those paths that lead toward the fulfillment of their life plans. They are as interested ultimately in marriage as their classmates are, but they care enough about developing their potentials as persons, as well as marital partners, to postpone marriage until they are ready for it.

You get your goals for life from your sense of who you are and what you want to make out of your life. If your parents expect you to measure up to family standards, and if their standards continue to make sense to you, you probably try to as much as you can. If as a boy you admire your father or some other man, chances are you see yourself as following in his footsteps, at least up to a point. As a girl, you may plot your course along the lines that your mother, or a beloved aunt, or a much admired teacher followed. Your aspirations are the dreams you have of yourself as you might become.

Some of your aspirations will change as you mature, perhaps taking you in a somewhat different direction from the one you see now. However fine some dream or some other person may be, you grow toward your finest as you become ever more fully yourself.

THE
long look ahead

In simpler societies a teen-age boy and girl are capable of doing just about everything men and women do. Such skills as fishing, farming, making grass huts, and weaving fabrics from vegetable fibers are easily learned within a short period of time. In such a community, teen-agers marry, settle down, and have their families at quite young ages.

In our complex Western world, there is much to learn before a boy becomes mature, capable of doing everything that is expected of modern man. A girl in most American communities today is expected to get as much education as she is capable of, and to become a mature individual who knows enough to vote intelligently and be a constructive member of the society in and out of her home.

This means that modern young people face a period of ten to twelve years in preparing for complete adulthood, after they have emerged from childhood. It is not easy to wait. Time spent in preparation may be important, but it is often difficult. This is why some impatient young people tire of the process of preparation and rush into military service, work, or marriage before they have much to bring to their roles as men and women. All too often, they regret their hasty actions and wish that they had finished school and had a chance to find themselves before rushing into their adult roles.

It takes a long look at life to see yourself in perspective. You, as a modern young person, will spend ten to twelve years in your teens getting ready for fifty or more years as an adult. To a considerable extent these many years as a man or a woman will depend upon the way in which you spend your teen years.

The friends you are making now are helping you develop the social skills and interests that will shape your life in the years ahead. From your nearest and dearest companions you may eventually choose the one with whom you will spend the rest of your life. Even if your choice of a mate is delayed yet for some time, the image you have for what is desirable in members of the other sex is being shaped right now in your teen years.

The ways in which you relate yourself to members of the other sex now carry over into your life as a man or a woman. Patterns of mutual respect and appreciation between you now continue on into your marriage in the years ahead.

Express your affection in mutually thoughtful and considerate ways now and you are laying a foundation for tenderness, depth, and beauty in your sex relations throughout the rest of your life. Develop a wide repertoire of loving interaction through your teen years and you have a basis for the years of living together that you one day will enjoy in your own family.

Life is all of a piece. You can "live like crazy" now and go on into a "crazy mixed-up" life ahead. You can avoid the real issues now as a beatnik or a buffoon, but they are still there ahead of you yet to be faced. You can live every day as best you can, getting the thrill of developing, and the excitement of discovering yourself and others, in ways that you can continue as long as you live. What you do, you are. What you are, you tend to become even more as time goes on.

The big question of the teen years is not, how involved is it wise to get? But rather, involved with what? Too early involvement in irresponsible sexuality stunts growth as a complete human being. Getting involved too soon in going steady, falling in love, and getting married is all too often a dead-end street.

Becoming involved in life—your urgent business right now—means learning what your possibilities are and where your talents lie; it means starting to build the kind of personal and social world you want; it means discovering yourself intellectually, physically, emotionally, philosophically, and religiously. Become involved with these tasks now, and when the time comes for you to love and marry the one who will share the rest of your life, you will be ready. Then love and the facts of life will be working hand in hand to make your family the strong, happy one you would like it to be.

I*ndex*

E

F

G